HOLISTIC PERFORMANCE

THE SCIENCE-BACKED SYSTEM TO MAXIMIZE PRODUCTIVITY, MASTER FLOW, AND PREVENT BURNOUT

KEVIN AVENTURA

Published by Neo Press.
Created and Designed by Kevin Aventura.

This book is for educational purposes only and does not constitute medical, financial, or professional advice. While the information has been compiled from sources deemed reliable and is accurate to the best of the author's knowledge, no guarantee is made regarding its validity, completeness, or applicability. The author is not a licensed physician and makes no claims regarding diagnosis, treatment, or specific outcomes in performance, productivity, income, or lifestyle.

Risk & Responsibility: All lifestyle, health, and exercise recommendations carry inherent risks. Readers should assess their own experience, aptitude, and fitness level before applying any techniques. Consult a licensed physician before making significant changes to your health, training, or lifestyle. The author and publisher assume no responsibility for any liability, loss, or damage—direct or indirect—resulting from the use or interpretation of this material.

For permission requests, contact: Holistic Performance hello@holisticperformance.co

ISBN (e-Book): 978-1-957602-08-0
ISBN (Paperback): 978-1-957602-09-7
ISBN (Hardcover): 978-1-957602-10-3

First Edition

A BOOK THAT GIVES BACK

For every copy of *Holistic Performance* sold, $1 is donated to Pencils of Promise, helping to build schools, train teachers, and expand access to quality education in developing countries.

Thank you for being part of this journey.

By reading this book, you're not only investing in your own growth but also contributing to educational opportunities for children who need them most.

Together, we're creating ripples of positive change that extend far beyond these pages.

TABLE OF CONTENTS

THE HIDDEN COST OF HIGH PERFORMANCE

"If you want something you have never had, you must be willing to do something you have never done."

– Thomas Jefferson

If you're reading these words, chances are you're someone who thinks deeply about performance and potential – your own, and what's truly possible in a human life. Maybe you're already achieving goals that others admire, or perhaps you're working tirelessly toward them. Either way, you've got that fire inside you, that drive to maximize what you're capable of. Yet, something feels off, doesn't it?

You see, whether you're climbing the corporate ladder, building a business, pursuing academic excellence, or chasing any other meaningful goal, there's this persistent gap between where you are and where you want to be. Not just in terms of achievements but in how you feel along the way. Some days, it seems like no matter how much effort you put in, there's always more ground to cover, more skills to master, more milestones to reach – and never quite enough time or energy to get there.

I've spent years studying the science of human performance, and here's what fascinates me: the gap between achievement and fulfillment is rarely about capability. It's about sustainability. Think of your energy like the Earth's resources—we can extract them rapidly for short-term gain or create sustainable systems that generate power indefinitely. Right now, you might be running on the extractive model.

Let me paint a familiar picture: Your calendar is a masterpiece of efficiency. Every minute is optimized, every deadline is met, and every goal is methodically pursued. You've mastered the art of squeezing more into each day than most people manage in a week. From the outside, it looks like you're winning. But inside? Inside, there's an exhausting cognitive dissonance between your achievements and your experience of them.

I intimately understand this paradox because I lived it. For years, I was the poster child for traditional productivity. I collected morning routines like some people collect stamps. I turned time management into an extreme sport. My calendar was so precisely optimized that it would make a Swiss watchmaker proud. And yes, it worked – until it didn't.

The pattern was always the same: intense focus, remarkable progress, then – crash. Sometimes, it manifested as self-sabotage just as I neared my biggest goals. Other times, it was full-blown burnout that left me questioning everything. The higher I climbed, the harder I fell. It was like playing a game of achievement Jenga, pulling out pieces of my health and happiness to stack them on top of my career, knowing that eventually, something had to give.

What I discovered through years of research and personal experimentation is that this approach to high performance isn't just unsustainable – it's fundamentally misaligned with how our bodies and minds actually work. The contemporary productivity playbook treats humans like machines that just need better programming. Wake up earlier! Optimize harder! Push through the pain! But we're not machines. We're complex biological systems with rhythms, needs, and limitations that no amount of productivity hacks can override.

The real breakthrough came when I started looking at performance through the lens of systems thinking and neurobiology. High performance isn't about doing more – it's about doing better.

While the world is obsessed with 'productivity hacks' and rigid morning routines, the science of human performance tells a different story. Our bodies and minds don't operate on a one-size-fits-all schedule, and peak performance isn't about forcing yourself into someone else's template. It's about understanding your unique biological rhythms and creating systems that enhance your energy rather than deplete it. Most importantly, it's about achieving your goals while feeling alive, present, and genuinely well.

You don't need to wake up at 5 AM or try to squeeze in the latest atomic habit. You don't need to wage war against your body's need for rest or your mind's need for space. What you need is a fundamental shift in how you approach performance itself – a shift from the extractive to the regenerative, from the mechanical to the holistic.

This book is your guide to making that shift. It's about building a new operating system for achievement. One that's based on a scientific understanding of how humans actually function at their best. One that allows you to pursue excellence without sacrificing well-being. One that transforms "either/or" into "both/and" – both successful and healthy, both productive and present, both high-performing and happy.

Are you ready to reimagine what high performance could look like? Let's begin.

HOW TO USE THIS BOOK

Think of this book as your field guide to the science of sustainable excellence. Just as a biologist might map out an ecosystem, we're going to map out the interconnected systems that drive peak human performance. But unlike traditional academic texts that simply describe what they see, we're going to actively experiment with these systems – starting with your own life as our primary laboratory.

The journey ahead is structured in three distinct phases, each building upon the last like the layers of a biological system:

First, we'll decode the current reality of high performance. We'll examine why traditional approaches to productivity often backfire at a neurobiological level, and why even the most driven individuals find themselves caught in what I call the "allostatic loop" – where higher achievement leads to greater strain on our biological systems, eventually forcing a crash and reset.

Next, we'll dive deep into the Holistic Performance Framework – a system built on four fundamental pillars: Prioritization, Physiology, Psychology, and Performance Systems. Think of these pillars as the essential elements of peak performance, each one supporting and enhancing the others. Just as a cell needs all its organelles to function optimally, your performance requires all these elements to work in harmony.

Finally, we'll move from theory to practice, focusing on rapid implementation. Because understanding without action is like having a map but never taking the journey.

A NEW LENS ON PERFORMANCE

The difference lies in our foundation: instead of starting with productivity techniques and trying to force your biology to comply, we're starting with your biology and building systems that work in harmony with it.

This isn't about adding more to your plate – it's about optimizing the plate itself.

By the time you finish this book, you'll understand how to:

- Reclaim significant portions of your time without sacrificing results (we're talking 10+ hours per week).
- Turn your biology into your ally rather than fighting against it.
- Access flow states reliably, rather than waiting for them to happen by chance.
- Build systems that make peak performance your default state, not your stretch goal.

A NOTE ON IMPLEMENTATION

As we progress through this book, you'll notice something different about how it's structured. Rather than overwhelming you with theory before getting to practice, each chapter is designed to be immediately actionable. Think of it like a laboratory protocol – we'll examine the principle, then immediately test it in your own life.

I recommend keeping a journal as you read. Your brain operates differently when you're actively processing information versus passively consuming it. The neural networks involved in learning are strengthened through active engagement – that's not just theory; it's established neuroscience.

Let's start redesigning your approach to performance from the ground up.

WHY THIS BOOK HAD TO EXIST

You might be wondering why, in a world already saturated with productivity advice, I felt compelled to write this book. The answer lies in both personal experience and scientific necessity.

Picture a researcher who discovers something that fundamentally challenges the prevailing paradigm. That's how I felt when I finally understood why traditional productivity advice was failing so many of us. I had spent years in the trenches, essentially conducting an n=1 experiment on myself. Trying to force productivity, attempting to outwork every problem, and constantly teetering on the edge of burnout. If someone had shown me the neurobiological blueprint for sustainable high performance earlier, I could have saved years of unnecessary struggle.

But this book isn't about my journey. It exists because our current understanding of productivity is fundamentally incomplete – and that's not just my opinion; it's a biological fact. Think of it as trying to understand an ecosystem by studying only one species at a time. Traditional approaches to performance are like having separate experts who each understand one part of the forest: one studies the trees, another the soil, another the wildlife. But they never talk to each other.

That's exactly what's happening in the world of performance optimization. We have time management experts who don't consider energy cycles, productivity coaches who focus only on willpower while ignoring physiological foundations, and even flow state researchers who decode peak experiences but often miss how they connect to our daily biological rhythms. It's crazy – we can map the neurochemistry of flow states with incredible precision, understand how to trigger that cocktail of norepinephrine, dopamine, serotonin, and anandamide that Steven Kotler (one of the world's foremost flow researchers) describes so well, but then we completely ignore how our basic physiological state affects our ability to access these peak states in the first place.

This fragmented approach isn't just incomplete – it's potentially harmful. Managing time without understanding energy is like trying to run a marathon by only strengthening your legs and ignoring your cardiovascular system. Building habits without considering your neural wiring is like installing software without checking if it's compatible with your computer. And chasing flow states without optimizing your biological baseline? That's like trying to launch a rocket without checking the fuel quality – you might get lucky once or twice, but you'll never achieve reliable liftoff.

More critically, our modern work paradigm is broken at a systemic level. We're seeing an unprecedented epidemic of burnout among high achievers. We're producing more than ever, but at what biological cost? The metrics of productivity are up, but the markers of well-being are plummeting. It's time to shift from hustle-based productivity to a science-backed performance system that works with our biology, not against it.

This book represents years of research, testing, and refinement. It's the synthesis of countless experiments, both in my own life and in the lives of professionals, entrepreneurs, and executives who've used this framework to break free from the cycle of exhaustion and step into actual peak performance.

WHAT I WANT FOR YOU

By the time you finish this book, my goal isn't just for you to understand the science of peak performance – I want you to be living it. Think of it as the difference between reading about photosynthesis and actually watching a plant grow. Understanding is important, but experience is transformative.

I want you to reach the final page feeling a fundamental shift in your relationship with performance. Imagine having complete control over your time and energy, like a skilled scientist in a laboratory. Picture yourself accessing deep focus and creativity not by chance but by design. Envision being liberated from the stress and exhaustion that come with traditional productivity methods, operating instead from a place of biological alignment.

Most importantly, I want you to feel excited about what's possible when you work with your biology instead of against it. Because high performance isn't about pushing harder – it's about optimizing your entire system for sustainable success.

YOUR NEXT STEPS

Understanding these principles is one thing; implementing them is another entirely. It's like the difference between reading about how to swim and actually diving into the pool. You can study fluid dynamics all day, but until you feel the water against your skin and coordinate your movements, you won't really know how to swim.

If you've ever read a book and felt inspired but struggled to apply it in real life, you're not alone.

That's why I created the Holistic Performance Academy—to help people bridge the gap between knowledge and action. Inside, we take these principles and turn them into reality through structured guidance, real-time application, and the kind of accountability that ensures you don't just understand these concepts—you live them.

If you want to fast-track your journey from understanding to mastery, I invite you to explore how you can integrate the HPA framework into your life in a structured, supported way. To learn more about applying these strategies with personalized coaching and expert guidance, visit holisticperformance.co/hpa or scan the QR code at the end of this section.

This could be the bridge between where you are now and where you know you could be – the difference between knowing the path and walking it.

Now, let's begin our exploration of what's possible when cutting-edge science meets your untapped potential. Turn the page, and let's discover your new performance reality together.

Learn more about the Holistic Performance Academy:

PS. As a Holistic Performance reader, you can use the coupon code **HPREADER** for 50% off the DIY Course.

CHAPTER 1
A DAY IN THE NEW REALITY

"You can't go back and change the beginning, but you can start where you are and change the ending."

– C.S. Lewis

Imagine waking up feeling genuinely refreshed. Not because an alarm yanked you out of sleep, but because your body naturally completed its rest cycle. Your mind is clear, your energy is steady, and you're actually excited about the day ahead. When you sit down to work, something remarkable happens: you effortlessly slip into that coveted state of deep productivity—what scientists and artists call "flow." Hours pass like minutes as you accomplish more than you previously did in days of scattered effort.

But here's the real magic: when you step away from your desk, you're fully present with your family, your hobbies, your life. No mental residue from work, no racing thoughts about unfinished tasks. Just pure, focused engagement with the moments that matter most.

Sound like an impossible dream? That's exactly what Ashley, a startup founder, thought when she first heard about this approach.

"Let me guess," she said, eyes rolling during our first conversation, "another miracle morning routine? Another productivity system I need to force myself to follow?" Like most high achievers, she'd tried it all: the 5 AM club, time-blocking apps, motivation hacks. Her days were a blur of notifications, meetings, and that constant nagging feeling that she was missing something important. "I was doing everything the productivity gurus recommended," she admits, "but something still felt off. I was achieving my goals, but at what cost? I felt like I was constantly choosing between success and actually being present in my own life."

But here's what fascinated her: three months later, she wasn't just more productive—she was transformed. "It's not just about getting more done," she shares, a smile lighting up her face. "I haven't felt this good in ages. I'm waking up feeling great, my mind is clear, and I'm not just watching the day pass by... I'm actually present for it. The best part? Those flow states that used to feel rare and random? They're becoming my default way of working. Everything feels effortless."

You might be skeptical. Chris, who runs a thriving digital agency, certainly was. "Running an agency felt like trying to juggle while riding a unicycle through a hurricane," he jokes, shaking his head at the memory. "I thought I just needed better time management or more discipline." Instead, he discovered something far more powerful—a way to work with his natural rhythms rather than against them.

"The transformation was amazing," Chris reports. "My anxiety? Gone. Those constant digestive issues from stress? Gone. My racing mind that used to keep me from staying on task? Completely changed. I'm getting more done in less time, and even better, my team is naturally following suit. They see the difference in my leadership and energy."

But what about measurable results? Just ask Nicole, an executive who was drowning in responsibilities. "In just the first week of implementing these principles, I found twelve hours I was wasting without even realizing it," she says. "Twelve hours! And this wasn't about working faster or pushing harder. It was about working smarter in a way that felt natural."

Here's what captivates me about these transformations: none of them came from traditional productivity hacks. They didn't require superhuman discipline or complicated routines. Instead, they came from understanding and working with a simple truth: your body is already wired for peak performance. You just need to stop fighting against it.

Take Veronica, an executive assistant who used to rely on energy drinks to make it through the afternoon. "I thought midday crashes were just part of life," she admits. "But once I understood how to work with my body's natural patterns instead of against them, everything changed. I haven't needed artificial stimulants since, and my focus is sharper than ever."

Or consider Andreia, who spent years postponing her dream of starting her own business because she couldn't imagine handling it all. "I was waiting to magically develop superhuman productivity powers," she laughs. "Instead, I learned something far more valuable—how to create sustainable success without sacrificing my well-being."

The pattern is clear: when high achievers stop trying to force productivity and start working with their natural rhythms, something remarkable happens. They don't just perform better—they feel better. They don't just get more done—they get the right things done, with energy left over for what matters most.

But here's what really gets me excited: this isn't about following some guru's perfect morning routine or adopting a one-size-fits-all productivity system. It's about understanding the fundamental principles that govern human performance and applying them in a way that works for you.

In the chapters ahead, we'll dive deep into exactly how these transformations happen. You'll discover why traditional productivity advice often backfires, and more importantly, you'll learn how to create your own sustainable path to peak performance.

Ready to see what's possible when you stop fighting your biology and start working with it instead? Let's begin.

CHAPTER 2
THE SCIENCE OF STRUGGLE

"It's not the load that breaks you down, it's the way you carry it."

– Lou Holtz

Remember that scene where Chris described running his agency like "juggling while riding a unicycle through a hurricane"? There's fascinating science behind why so many high performers feel this way—and it's not what most productivity experts would have you believe.

Imagine you're looking at an electric sports car that's not reaching its full potential speed. What would most people do? They'd probably start by upgrading the tires, maybe adding some fancy aerodynamic features, hiring the best driver in town, or even installing a nitrous system for that extra boost (you know, like in The Fast and the Furious). They'll try everything to make it go faster, except checking if the battery is properly charging and delivering power to the system.

That's exactly what's happening in the world of high performance. We're all trying to upgrade our 'performance features'—downloading the latest productivity apps, fine-tuning our morning routines, optimizing our calendars down to the minute. But we're completely ignoring our biological battery— the fundamental energy system that powers everything we do.

For decades, we've been taught that high performance follows a simple chain reaction: Thoughts influence feelings, which drive actions, which create results. It's why traditional coaching focuses so heavily on mindset work, motivation techniques, and habit formation. And they're not entirely wrong—these elements matter.

But they're missing something crucial. Something that happens before that first domino even falls.

Think of it like this: Your brain, incredible as it is, isn't floating in space. It's powered by your biology. Before you can have that empowering thought, before you can feel that motivation, before you can take that decisive action— your physiology is already setting the stage. It's determining which neurotransmitters are available, how efficiently your brain can use energy, and whether your body is in a state of thriving or merely surviving.

This isn't just theory. When we look at neurochemistry, we see something remarkable: your physiology isn't just influencing your thoughts—it's actively shaping them through a complex dance of hormones and neurotransmitters. Serotonin impacts your sense of well-being. Dopamine drives your motivation. Cortisol affects your stress response. And that's just scratching the surface.

THE NEW PARADIGM:

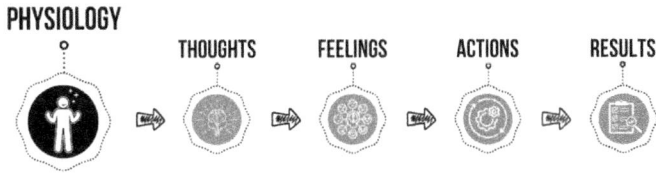

The Energy Paradox: When More Becomes Less

Here's something that might shock you: According to a groundbreaking Stanford University study, productivity per hour drops so sharply after 50 hours of work per week that putting in any more hours becomes pointless. After 55 hours, you're literally getting the same amount of work done as someone who stopped at 55, even if you're grinding away for 70 hours. Think about that for a second—those extra 15 hours? They're not just useless; they're actively damaging your performance battery.

But most of us aren't listening to this science. Instead, we're caught in the "Magic Pill Mentality." When our energy crashes, what do we do? We reach for stimulants. There's an epidemic of entrepreneurs and executives hooked on Adderall and other brain drugs, desperately trying to keep up with the competition. Wall Street traders, software engineers, dentists, nurses— professionals across every industry are literally "cracking out of their minds" trying to maintain their edge. Some have even lost their lives mixing these drugs with alcohol.

The data is staggering. In a 2018 research project with thousands of business leaders and entrepreneurs:

- 75% experienced regular brain fog
- 82% battled constant procrastination
- 71% dealt with high levels of stress

- 58% couldn't wake up feeling refreshed
- 62% struggled with inconsistent energy throughout the day

We're not just tired—we're systematically burning out our biological batteries. And here's what's really fascinating: this isn't just about being exhausted. When you consistently override your body's natural rhythms, you trigger a cascade of biological changes that actively work against high performance.

The Focus Fallacy: The Hidden Cost of Mental Multitasking

Here's a mind-bending statistic that might make you rethink your entire workday: it is estimated that the average office worker is only truly productive for 2 hours and 53 minutes per day. Not because they're lazy or unmotivated, but because they're trapped in what philosopher Josef Pieper called 'Total Work' – a state where work fills every waking moment, yet much of it is not focused or meaningful.

It's like trying to stream Netflix, Prime, and Disney+ simultaneously on a dial-up internet connection. Sure, technically, you're "watching" all three, but you're not really experiencing any of them. Your brain works the same way. Every time you switch tasks—whether it's checking email during a meeting, responding to emails while writing a report, or even just thinking about your to-do list while talking to a colleague—you're not actually multitasking. You're forcing your brain to do an entire system reboot over and over again.

The numbers tell a shocking story:
- 6 average disruptions daily
- 44% of distractions are self-imposed
- Only 11 minutes of uninterrupted focus at a time

But here's where it gets really interesting: each of these interruptions doesn't just waste time—it triggers what neuroscientists call "attention residue." Imagine leaving a browser tab open in the background of your computer. Even if you're not actively using it, it's still consuming RAM and slowing down your system. Your brain works the same way. Every task switch leaves a little piece of your mental processing power stuck on the previous task, gradually degrading your ability to focus deeply on anything.

The Recovery Deficit: Why Rest Isn't Just a Luxury

You know that old saying about being "slowly boiled like a frog"? It's a perfect metaphor for how we've normalized chronic stress and sleep deprivation. If you dropped a frog into boiling water, it would jump right out. But put it in comfortable water and slowly turn up the heat. It won't notice the danger until it's too late.

That's exactly what's happening to high performers today. We've gradually accepted a state of constant activation as normal. Can't sleep? There's an app for that. Feeling foggy? Here's another coffee. Afternoon crash? Time for an energy drink. We're masking the warning signals our bodies are desperately trying to send us.

The science is clear: your body isn't designed for constant output. It operates in cycles—what scientists call ultradian rhythms. Think of it like interval training for your brain. Just as athletes know they can't maintain sprint speed indefinitely, your brain needs regular periods of recovery to maintain peak performance.

But here's what nobody talks about: rest isn't passive. When you're "doing nothing," your brain is actually hard at work:

- Consolidating memories and learning
- Replenishing neurotransmitters
- Clearing out cellular debris
- Rebalancing hormones
- Preparing for the next period of focused work

The Flow Block: Unlocking Your Ultimate Leverage

Here's a mind-bending question: What if I told you there's a way to get a week's worth of work done in a single day? Not through some productivity hack or fancy app, but by tapping into your brain's natural capacity for extraordinary performance.

We live in an exponential world with linear brains. Our neural hardware wasn't designed for the pace and complexity of modern life. It's like trying to run Chrome with Windows 95. Most of us are barely keeping up, let alone getting ahead. But here's where it gets interesting: flow states might be nature's solution to this evolutionary mismatch.

Think of flow as the ultimate performance hack. But instead of being external, like all the other leverage tools we typically rely on, flow is internal leverage. It's like discovering you've had a hidden supercomputer inside your brain all along.

The data is nothing short of extraordinary:

- McKinsey's 10-year study found top executives experienced 500% productivity increases in flow
- DARPA research showed flow states accelerated learning by 490%
- The University of Sydney demonstrated a 430% increase in problem-solving capability
- Google's internal research revealed a 70% boost in focus
- Harvard researchers discovered these cognitive enhancements can persist for up to three days after a flow state

But here's what makes flow genuinely unique among all our leverage opportunities: while time is finite and external resources have limits, your capacity for flow is infinitely developable. Achieving flow is akin to unlocking the ultimate leverage within yourself, allowing productivity and creativity to soar. You're not just working faster—you're literally upgrading your brain's operating system.

The tragedy is that most of us are inadvertently blocking our access to these states. Every notification, every context switch, every stress response triggered by our overloaded schedules—they're all flow blockers. We're literally neurobiologically preventing ourselves from accessing our peak performance states.

The Performance Gap: The True Cost of Fragmented Focus

The more we learn about human potential, the further we seem to fall from achieving it. It's like climbing a mountain only to discover it's actually part of a much larger mountain range—each peak of knowledge revealing three more peaks of possibility behind it.

I call this the Performance Gap, and it's one of the most interesting psychological torments of our time. With every book you read, every success story you encounter, every breakthrough you learn about, your awareness of what's possible expands. Social media amplifies this effect, constantly showing us highlight reels of peak performance and extraordinary achievement. But here's the twist: while our understanding of what's possible grows exponentially, our actual performance often inches forward linearly—if at all.

Think of it as having an ever-expanding map but walking at the same speed. Each day, you discover new territories of potential, new peaks of possibility, but your ability to traverse that territory isn't keeping pace with your growing awareness of it. The result? A widening chasm between where you are and where you know you could be.

Most high achievers who implement real performance optimization strategies encounter a paradoxical challenge that defies conventional wisdom—things frequently become more difficult before improving. Similar to an athlete refining their technique, you might temporarily experience a performance dip while rewiring your muscle memory. But once that new pattern clicks into place, you'll break through to entirely new levels of achievement that weren't previously accessible.

Think about it: Installing a new productivity system initially makes you feel less productive. Starting a proper recovery routine first makes you feel like you're falling behind. However, that's just the Leverage Gap—that uncomfortable space between implementing better strategies and seeing the results.

When we study high performers who successfully bridge this gap, we see that the initial dip in productivity typically lasts 2-4 weeks. But here's the kicker—once they push through this adaptation period, their performance doesn't just return to baseline; it shoots past it exponentially. It's like upgrading your operating system: there's that annoying installation period where everything runs slower, but once it's complete, you're operating at a whole new level. Unless, of course, you're using a Mac or an iPhone, like I do. Then, every upgrade seems to slow things down. Allegedly, of course. (My lawyers insisted on that disclaimer.) But seriously, the real challenge comes when most people try to implement new systems while maintaining their current output. They attempt to:

- Build better workflows while keeping up with their existing workload
- Learn new skills while maintaining full productivity
- Establish recovery routines without letting anything slip
- Master flow states while staying constantly available

It's like trying to change the wheels on a moving car. Technically possible, but incredibly stressful and likely to fail.

The key insight? This gap isn't a bug in the system—it's a feature. Just like a caterpillar has to enter its chrysalis phase (where it literally turns to goo!)

before emerging as a butterfly, you have to get comfortable with this temporary period of apparent regression to achieve true transformation.

The most successful performers I've worked with don't just accept this gap—they plan for it. They create "transformation buffers"—strategic periods where they intentionally decrease their output to implement better systems. They understand that sometimes you need to slow down to speed up.

So there you have it—five fundamental challenges that keep even the most driven high performers caught in cycles of diminishing returns. Like a complex biological system, each challenge amplifies the others: The Energy Paradox drains our batteries, the Focus Fallacy scatters our attention, the Recovery Deficit keeps us running on empty, the Flow Block prevents access to our peak states, and the Performance Gap keeps widening as our awareness outpaces our execution.

Think of it as a neural network of obstacles, each one strengthening the others' signals. When your energy drops, your focus fragments. When your focus scatters, flow becomes impossible. When you can't access flow, performance suffers. When performance drops, you push harder, further depleting your energy... and the cycle spins on.

But here's the thing about complex systems—once you understand how they work, you can begin to reprogram them.

Before we dive into solutions, though, we need to do something that might make us feel uncomfortable: We need to get precise about your current coordinates in this performance landscape. Just like a scientist wouldn't start an experiment without baseline measurements, we need to understand exactly where you're starting from.

In the next chapter, we'll explore some eye-opening metrics and assessment tools that will help you map your current state. Not to judge, but to establish clear markers for your transformation. Because let's be real: you can't navigate to your destination if you don't know your starting point.

Ready to discover where you really stand in the performance spectrum? Turn the page, and let's get scientific about your potential.

RESEARCH & RESOURCES

Throughout our journey together in this book, I make various claims, reference scientific studies, and recommend specific tools that can transform your performance. Rather than cluttering these pages with footnotes and citations that might interrupt our flow, I've created something more valuable.

The Holistic Performance Resource Hub is an online companion to this book—a digital library where you can explore the research behind the concepts we're discussing, access recommended tools, and download additional resources to implement what you're learning.

Think of it as the engine room behind everything we're exploring together. While the book focuses on practical applications and clear explanations, the Resource Hub provides the scientific foundation and implementation tools that support your journey.

This Resource Hub is exclusively available to you as a reader of this book. To access it, simply scan the QR code below or visit hplink.org/resourcehub

The hub is organized by chapter, allowing you to easily find the specific resources relevant to what you're currently reading. I'll include a reminder at the end of key sections where additional resources are particularly valuable, but you can access the complete hub at any time.

CHAPTER 3
MAPPING YOUR PERFORMANCE LANDSCAPE

"You cannot get to where you are going until you have learned all
there is to learn about where you are."

– Iyanla Vanzant

When Iyanla Vanzant wrote these words, she probably wasn't thinking about neurochemistry and performance metrics—but she might as well have been. Think about it: even the most sophisticated GPS can't plot your route without knowing your current coordinates. Your biological GPS works the same way.

Remember our electric car analogy from before? Before making any upgrades or optimizations, a good mechanic runs diagnostics—checking battery health, system efficiency, and performance metrics. They don't just guess what might be wrong or jump straight to solutions. They measure. They analyze. They establish a baseline.

That's precisely what we're going to do with your performance system.

But here's where it gets interesting: measuring human performance is infinitely more complex than running car diagnostics. We're not just checking a single battery—we're analyzing an intricate web of biological, psychological, and behavioral systems that all influence each other.

That's why we need to look at three fundamental dimensions of performance: Cognitive function, Energy management, and Productivity output—what I call the CEP Framework. Think of these as your performance blood work. They tell us exactly where your system needs attention before we define the treatment plan.

THE THREE DIMENSIONS OF PERFORMANCE
Your Cognitive Score, Energy Score, and Productivity Score work together to give us a baseline understanding of your current performance state. But measuring human performance isn't like checking the temperature or stepping on a scale. Our biological systems are far more complex, and many crucial aspects of performance can't be captured by objective measurements alone.

Think about focus, for instance. While we can measure time spent on tasks or track how often you switch between applications, these metrics don't tell us about the quality of your attention or how meaningful your work feels. That's why we need both subjective and objective data points—like using both a compass and a map to navigate unfamiliar terrain.

Let's explore what each dimension reveals:

Your **Cognitive Score** measures how well your brain is operating right now. Not how well you think it's working or how well you want it to work—but its real, current operational state. Just as a computer's processing power affects everything from calculation speed to graphics rendering, your cognitive function influences your information processing, decision-making quality, analytical depth, focus maintenance, and creative problem-solving abilities.

What sets the **Energy Score** apart is its role as your biological battery monitor. Remember how we talked about most high performers being stuck in energy debt? This score helps us understand not just your current energy levels but your entire energy management system—from how efficiently you recharge to how well you handle stress and maintain sustainable output.

Finally, your **Productivity Score** moves beyond simple input metrics like hours worked or tasks completed. Instead, it reveals your effectiveness at converting time and energy into meaningful results. Think of it as your performance ROI—how efficiently you turn effort into impact, align tasks with goals, and optimize your resources for maximum effect.

When you think about your peak performance moments—those times when everything just clicked—what was happening in your body and brain? Most people can describe how it felt, but very few can tell you why it happened or how to recreate it. That's where these measurements become game-changers.

Here's what makes the CEP Framework so powerful: these three dimensions don't exist in isolation. They form a dynamic triangle of performance, each affecting and being affected by the others. It's like a biological symphony where every instrument needs to be in tune. When your cognitive function dips, it drags down your productivity. When your energy tanks, your mental clarity suffers. When your productivity feels off, you often compensate by working longer hours, which further depletes your energy... and around we go.

But understanding these relationships gives us a map. Think of it like solving one of those complex escape room puzzles. Once you learn how all the pieces connect, what seemed like random obstacles suddenly become clear stepping stones to the solution.

THE POWER OF OBJECTIVE DATA

Remember that eye-opening statistic about the average office worker being truly productive for only 2 hours and 53 minutes per day? Most people immediately think, "Not me—I'm different." Here's the thing: we're all remarkably good at overestimating our productive time and underestimating our distractions. It's not because we're lying to ourselves; it's just how our brains are wired.

That's why we need hard data. Think of your device activity tracker as a truth serum for productivity. It doesn't care about your good intentions or carefully crafted schedule. It shows you exactly where your time and attention are going. Those "quick" social media checks? That "brief" email check that turned into an hour-long response spree? Your screen time data reveals all.

But here's where it gets interesting: even your devices don't tell the whole story. They can't track offline activities, personal interactions, or those moments of deep thinking that look like "doing nothing" to an outside observer. That's why we need to go old-school.

YOUR PERFORMANCE AUDIT

Let's get practical about gathering your baseline data. Think of this as creating a high-resolution map of your current performance landscape. Here's exactly what you need to do:

Step 1: Assess Your CEP Scores.

Take these three quick assessments (about 3 minutes each) to establish your baseline:

| FUNCTIONAL COGNITIVE SCORE | FUNCTIONAL ENERGY SCORE | FUNCTIONAL PRODUCTIVITY SCORE |
| hplink.org/fcs | hplink.org/fes | hplink.org/fps |

Write down your scores in a notebook. We'll revisit these later to measure your progress. And remember: these aren't grades; they're coordinates on your performance map.

Step 2: Track Your Digital Reality.

Time to get real about how you're spending your screen time:

- Pull up your phone's data (Screen Time for iPhone, Digital Wellbeing for Android)
- Check your computer usage (Screen Time on Mac, or RescueTime/similar on PC)
- Document the key metrics:
  - o Total daily screen time.
  - o Most-used apps.
  - o Usage patterns throughout the day.
  - o Pick-up frequency.
  - o Your procrastination loops (recurrent distractions).

Step 3: The Reality Check.

For the next three days, you'll track every 20 minutes of your day. Yes, every 20 minutes. I know this sounds boring. And it is. But I would not ask you this if it was not incredibly powerful.

Use your notebook or use the tracking sheet template provided inside the Resource Hub. Just like Nicole, who found 12 hidden hours in her first week, or Chris, who discovered his "quick social media checks" were eating 40% of his prime morning hours, you might be surprised by what you find.

A few non-negotiables:

- Record in real-time, not from memory.
- Include everything, even the stuff you'd rather not admit to.
- Stay honest. This is your private data.
- Don't try to behavior-hack yet. We want your true baseline.

Step 4: The Deep Dive (Optional).

If you have a wearable device (Oura Ring, Whoop, Apple Watch, etc), track these bonus metrics:

- Heart Rate Variability (HRV).
- Sleep quality scores.
- Stress levels.
- Recovery indicators.

No wearable? No problem. The CEP scores and time tracking will give us plenty to work with.

Additionally, if you're pursuing specific goals beyond pure performance—maybe you want more family time, better health, or space for creativity—consider tracking those metrics, too. Want to spend more time with your kids? Track those hours. Working on your health? Take measurements and photos of your body. The key is choosing metrics that align with your personal definition of success.

Remember: This isn't about tracking for tracking's sake. It's about creating a clear picture of where you are now so we can map the most efficient path to where you want to be.

FROM DATA TO DESTINY

Now that you have your performance coordinates locked in, you might be wondering, "Okay, but what do I actually do with all this data?" It's a bit like being handed a detailed genetic report without any explanation of what those genetic markers mean for your health. The data itself isn't the solution. It's what we do with it that matters.

Remember when we talked about blood work and treatment plans? Well, we've just completed your performance blood work. Those CEP scores, device data, and tracking sheets? They're about to become your transformation roadmap.

But before we dive into solutions, I want you to appreciate something remarkable: by completing these assessments, you've already separated yourself from 99% of high performers. Most people spend years trying to optimize their performance without ever establishing a baseline. They're essentially trying to navigate with their eyes closed, hoping they're moving in the right direction.

You're different. You now have precise coordinates for where you're starting from.

In the next chapter, I'm going to show you exactly how to use this data to create lasting transformation through the four pillars (or 4Ps, between us) of Holistic Performance.

Ready to turn your data into destiny? Turn the page, and let's decode the framework that's going to change everything.

RESEARCH & RESOURCES

As mentioned earlier, please visit the Holistic Performance Resource Hub to access the research and additional materials mentioned in this chapter.

To do so, go to hplink.org/resourcehub or scan the QR code below.

CHAPTER 4
THE FOUR PERFORMANCE PILLARS

"When we try to pick out anything by itself, we find it hitched to everything else in the Universe."

– John Muir

If you've ever had a comprehensive health check-up, you know that gathering the data is only half the equation. You don't just get a list of numbers and stats. You get a treatment plan based on what the data reveals.

That's precisely what we're about to do with your performance audit.

So far, you've identified where your time goes, how your energy fluctuates, and how effectively you turn effort into results. But raw data alone doesn't create change. It's what you do with it that matters.

Now, we need a framework to make sense of it all—a structured way to take the insights from your assessment and turn them into meaningful action.

This is where the Four Pillars of Sustainable High Performance come in. Think of your performance as a living ecosystem. Just as nature requires specific conditions to thrive—the right balance of water, sunlight, nutrients, and temperature—peak human performance depends on four essential elements working in harmony. I call these the 4 Ps of Holistic Performance, and they're about to transform how you think about productivity.

THE 4 PS AS YOUR PERFORMANCE OPERATING SYSTEM

Your performance data, both subjective and objective, tells us what's happening in your system. But why are those numbers where they are? And, more importantly, how do we fix them?

The answer lies in the 4 Ps of Holistic Performance, which form the foundation of peak productivity:

- **Prioritization:** Directing effort toward what truly matters so you're not just busy, but productive.
- **Physiology:** The biological foundation that determines your energy, focus, and resilience.

- **Psychology:** The mindset and identity shifts that enable consistency, confidence, and deep focus.
- **Performance Systems:** The structure that makes high performance effortless and repeatable.

If one of these pillars is off, the entire system suffers.

Remember Ashley from Chapter 1? When she first came to me, her productivity metrics were off the charts. She was getting more done than ever. But her Energy and Cognitive scores told a different story. Like many high performers, she had optimized one part of her system (Performance Systems) while unknowingly depleting another (Physiology).

"I thought I was crushing it," she told me, "but I was actually crushing myself. My HRV was tanking, my sleep quality was terrible, and my ability to access flow states? Practically non-existent."

Three months after implementing the 4 Ps framework, Ashley's story looked very different. Not only was she maintaining her high output, but her biological metrics showed a system in harmony rather than crisis. Her HRV improved by 40%, her deep sleep doubled, and most importantly—she started experiencing regular flow states without forcing them.

Think of these pillars as the essential systems in your body. Your circulatory system can't function without your respiratory system, which depends on your digestive system, and so on. They're not just connected—they're interdependent. Similarly, each of the 4 Ps supports and enhances the others, creating a "Performance Multiplier Effect."

For example, you might have strong prioritization skills but constantly feel drained because your physiology isn't supporting your cognitive demands. Or perhaps you've developed a remarkable mental resilience but struggle with execution because your systems aren't structured for efficiency. Many clients come to me with high physical energy but still feel scattered because their psychology and focus are misaligned.

This is why your raw performance data is so critical. It helps us pinpoint exactly which pillars need attention.

CONNECTING YOUR PERFORMANCE DATA TO THE 4 Ps

Your performance audit wasn't just about getting a general sense of where you stand. It was about gathering both subjective self-assessments and objective tracking data to diagnose the root cause of performance gaps.

Here's how each metric maps to the 4 Ps of Holistic Performance:

1. Cognitive Function Score → Psychology + Physiology

If your Cognitive Score was lower than expected, it's likely due to a combination of physiological and psychological inefficiencies. Your Physiology might be compromised if you're experiencing frequent energy crashes, poor sleep quality, or constant brain fog. Even without advanced measurements, these symptoms tell us something is off in your biological foundation. Your Psychology could be misaligned if you're experiencing mental fatigue, focus inconsistency, or emotional volatility during challenging tasks.

For those who tracked optional biological markers, low HRV readings or poor sleep quality data provide additional confirmation of these physiological challenges, but they're not required for diagnosis.

2. Energy Score → Physiology

A low Energy Score is a clear signal that your Physiology needs serious work. This includes your subjective experience of energy stability throughout the day, recovery between demanding tasks, and overall physical resilience. Most people can feel when their battery is consistently running low, even without sophisticated measurements.

If you did choose to track advanced metrics like HRV, resting heart rate, or detailed sleep data, these provide additional layers of insight into your physiological state. They're valuable supplementary information that can help fine-tune interventions, but the foundation of your Energy Score comes from your lived experience of how consistently energized you feel throughout your days.

3. Productivity Score → Prioritization + Performance Systems

A low Productivity Score means you're either spending too much time on low-value tasks (a Prioritization issue) or experiencing unnecessary friction in your workflows (a Performance Systems issue). Your manual time-tracking logs and digital activity reports tell us exactly where these inefficiencies exist.

If your logs revealed excessive context-switching, social media usage, or admin-heavy tasks, it means your Prioritization strategy needs refinement. If you find yourself constantly reinventing workflows instead of leveraging systems, templates, and automation, your Performance Systems require an upgrade.

The beauty of this mapping process is its flexibility. You don't need every possible measurement to identify your performance gaps. Even with the basic CEP scores and time tracking, patterns emerge that point clearly toward specific pillars that need attention. The optional biological data simply adds resolution to this picture, like moving from standard definition to 4K – the image is clear either way, but extra data can reveal finer details.

THE MOST COMMON PATTERNS & THEIR FIXES

By now, you might already recognize some patterns in your data. Here's what some of the most common profiles look like—and what they tell us about what to fix first.

Pattern 1: The Hustler (High Productivity, Low Energy & Cognitive Scores)

When you're operating as a Hustler, you're grinding through tasks, but at the cost of your energy, clarity, and well-being. Your Physiology is completely misaligned with your output demands—which means burnout isn't a distant possibility but an inevitable outcome. The first fix here is straightforward: we need to optimize your energy rhythms, sleep architecture, and nervous system recovery to transform your productivity from unsustainable grinding to something that can endure over time.

Pattern 2: The Overthinker (High Cognitive, Low Productivity & Energy Scores)

As an Overthinker, you possess great ideas, deep thinking capabilities, and strong knowledge—but your execution tends to be slow or scattered. What you're missing isn't intellectual horsepower but rather Prioritization clarity and efficient energy management that would allow you to channel your cognitive abilities into meaningful output. Our first intervention will focus on building high-impact prioritization frameworks and optimizing your energy systems so your brilliant ideas can translate into tangible results rather than remaining trapped in your mind.

Pattern 3: The Spinning Wheels (High Energy, Low Cognitive & Productivity Scores)

If you identify with the Spinning Wheels pattern, you have physical energy in abundance but struggle with focus, clarity, and meaningful progress. This profile calls for a Psychology & Prioritization reset to properly channel your energy into high-leverage work. We'll develop focused protocols, minimize the distractions currently fragmenting your attention, and align your workflow to match your natural deep work rhythms.

Pattern 4: The Foggy Performer (Low Scores Across All Dimensions)

When you're experiencing the Foggy Performer pattern, challenges appear across all three dimensions simultaneously. Your cognitive function feels sluggish, your energy levels are depleted, and your productivity has noticeably dropped. This pattern typically emerges after prolonged stress, major life transitions, or when multiple systems have been neglected for extended periods. The good news is that even when everything seems compromised, we have a clear pathway forward that starts with creating the essential space needed for recovery and optimization. By mapping your personal data onto these Four Pillars, we're no longer guessing what you need to improve. We have a precise starting point for your performance transformation.

HOW WE'LL APPLY THE FOUR PILLARS

Now that you've mapped your starting point, it's time to optimize each of these pillars one by one. Think of it like tuning an instrument—we'll adjust each string until they're all working in perfect harmony.

In the following chapters, we'll take a deep dive into each of the Four Pillars. You'll discover the key leverage points for optimizing Prioritization, Physiology, Psychology, and Performance Systems, and you'll get science-backed strategies to apply them in real-time. More importantly, you'll learn how to create the conditions for consistent flow states—those magical moments of peak performance that we discussed earlier.

But first, we start where most people go wrong—and where the most significant transformation often begins—Prioritization. Just like in biology, sometimes the order of operations makes all the difference.

Ready to turn your performance ecosystem from surviving to thriving? Let's dive in.

CHAPTER 5
THE BIOLOGY OF PRIORITY

"The most important thing is to keep the most important thing, the most important thing.

– Jim Kwik

Think about the last time you got sick. What's the first thing your body did? It didn't try to optimize your athletic performance or enhance your cognitive function. Instead, it ruthlessly prioritized survival—redirecting energy from non-essential functions to power your immune response. Your body knew exactly what mattered most: fighting the infection. Everything else became secondary.

This isn't just clever biology—it's a master class in high performance. And it's precisely what separates sustainable growth from eventual burnout.

Nature always prioritizes before it optimizes or adds something new. When resources are limited, your biological systems don't attempt to grow bigger or stronger—they allocate energy to what ensures survival. An organism under stress doesn't try to build new capabilities—it focuses entirely on maintaining core functions.

This is why prioritization forms the foundation of our Holistic Performance Framework. Just as your body has evolved sophisticated mechanisms to direct resources where they're needed most, you need a system to direct your time, energy, and focus toward what truly moves the needle.

Remember Veronica's transformation that we discussed in Chapter 1? Her shift from relying on energy drinks to achieving natural peak performance wasn't about adding more productivity hacks—it was about understanding what truly deserved her attention. And just like Andreia discovered when finally launching her business, the secret wasn't developing 'superhuman productivity powers,' but rather learning how to eliminate what doesn't matter.

Most productivity systems try to help you do more, when the real secret is doing less—but better. We've already seen the Energy Paradox in action—how productivity doesn't scale linearly with time invested. However, the research goes even deeper than we initially explored.

While the Stanford study we discussed in Chapter 2 showed how productivity plummets after 50 hours per week, the Melbourne Institute's research on 6,500 professionals revealed something even more counterintuitive: peak cognitive performance occurred at just 25 hours per week. That's not a typo—25 hours. Working beyond that actually led to measurable cognitive decline.

This aligns with what Alex Pang discovered after years studying elite performers: most people are only truly productive for 4-5 hours per day. The remaining hours? They're filled with what I call 'productivity theater'—busy work that feels productive but creates minimal impact.

The myth of 'more hours = better results' isn't just incorrect—it fundamentally misunderstands how human performance actually works. Just as your body intelligently redirects resources away from non-essential functions during stress, you need a strategic approach that channels your finite time and energy into high-impact activities that deliver meaningful outcomes.

It's time for a fundamental shift in how we think about performance. Instead of asking "How can I get more done?" we need to ask "How can I eliminate everything that isn't moving me forward—so I can focus on the few things that actually matter?"

This shift in thinking changes everything. But here's the catch. It's not always obvious what deserves our attention and what doesn't. Think about your typical workday. Between emails, meetings, notifications, and that ever-growing to-do list, everything can feel urgent. Everything can seem important.

That's why we started with performance tracking in Chapter 3. Without a clear picture of where your time and energy are going, you're essentially trying to optimize in the dark. It's like trying to cut your spending without looking at your bank statements. You might have a general idea of the problem, but you'll miss the small leaks that are draining your resources.

Research shows that up to 40% of our daily actions are unconscious habits. That means nearly half of what you do each day happens on autopilot. You're not actively choosing—you're just running familiar patterns.

I've heard it countless times: *"I track my time. I know exactly where my hours go."*

That's exactly what Nicole thought before she discovered twelve hours of hidden time in her first week of proper tracking. And she's not alone. The data tells us something fascinating: Most professionals overestimate their productive time by 5-10%. We convince ourselves we're being productive because we're busy. But being busy isn't the same as creating impact.

Let's get real for a moment. Take a quick look at your calendar for the past week. How many of those meetings actually moved the needle on your most important goals? How much of your "productive time" was spent on tasks that someone else could have handled? How many of those "urgent" emails could have waited without any real consequences?

This isn't about guilt—it's about awareness. And more importantly, it's about opportunity.

THE OPPORTUNITY COST OF TIME

Ever notice how we treat time differently than any other resource? If someone asked for $100, you'd immediately think about what else you could do with that money. But when they ask for an hour of your time for "a quick meeting," you might say yes without considering what you're really giving up.

Every time you say yes to something, you're unconsciously saying no to something else. You can't be in a flow state and multitasking at the same time. You can't be fully present with your family while checking work emails. You can't be recovering and pushing your limits simultaneously.

Let's make this simple. Take a look at these numbers:

- 30 minutes of daily social media scrolling = 182.5 hours per year (that's 22 full workdays!).
- 90 minutes of Netflix each day = 547 hours annually (enough time to learn a new language).
- 60 minutes in unnecessary meetings = 365 hours (you could write a book in that time).

"But wait," you might be thinking, "I need some downtime. You're not suggesting I turn into a productivity robot, are you?"

Absolutely not. Remember what we learned about recovery in Chapter 2? Rest isn't just important—it's essential. But there's a difference between intentional recovery and mindless time waste.

Think about it this way: We all start with the same 168 hours each week. The difference between extraordinary success and mediocrity isn't about having more time—it's about being ruthlessly clear about how we invest those hours.

Let's do a quick reality check:

- Do you often feel like you "never have time" for what matters most?
- Are you setting goals but struggling to make real progress?
- Is your schedule full but your actual impact questionable?

If you're nodding along, don't worry—you're not alone. But here's the good news: Just like Nicole discovered those hidden 12 hours, you're about to find pockets of time you didn't even know you had.

THE SCIENCE OF WORKING LESS

Here's a radical idea that's actually backed by science: What if working less could help you achieve more? I know we already saw some data suggesting this but in a world obsessed with "hustle culture" and 80-hour workweeks, this sounHere's a radical idea that's actually backed by science: What if working less could help you achieve more? I know we already saw some data suggesting this but in a world obsessed with "hustle culture" and 80-hour workweeks, this sounds almost heretical. But this isn't just theory—it's being proven in real-world experiments across the globe.

Take Perpetual Guardian in New Zealand. They did something that would make most productivity gurus clutch their pearls: They moved their entire company—more than 240 employees—to a four-day workweek. The twist? They kept the same salaries and expected the same output.

The results? Not only did people get the same amount of work done in four days instead of five, but they also reported a 24% improvement in work-life balance and a 7% drop in stress levels. Employees weren't just more productive—they were more present, more focused, and more energized.

Far from being an isolated example, even the prestigious Boston Consulting Group—a company known for its demanding work culture—experimented with enforced time off. Consultants were required to take predictable, uninterrupted time off each week while still meeting ambitious client demands. The outcome? Team effectiveness improved, collaboration increased, and their work product actually got better—not despite working less, but because of it.

Most compelling is the world's largest four-day workweek trial conducted in the UK in 2022. This wasn't a small experiment—it involved 61 companies and approximately 2,900 workers across various industries. When the six-month trial ended, 92% of the companies decided to continue with the shortened workweek. Productivity remained stable or improved in every organization, while revenue actually rose by an average of 1.4% during the trial period. Meanwhile, resignations dropped by 57% as employee well-being significantly improved.

And it's not just about reducing weekly hours—the benefits of strategic rest extend to broader time scales as well. Harvard Business Review's analysis revealed a pattern that reinforces this principle: Employees who took more than 10 vacation days per year had a 65.4% chance of receiving a raise or bonus, while those taking fewer than 10 days saw their chances drop dramatically to just 34.6%. This counterintuitive finding further confirms what the research consistently shows—strategic disengagement is a performance enhancer, not a liability.

"But how is this possible?" you might be wondering. This is where Parkinson's Law comes into play—the principle that work expands to fill the time available for its completion. Give yourself a week to complete a project, and mysteriously, it takes a week. Give yourself two days, and you'll likely get it done in two days.

Think about your own experience. Ever notice how much you get done the day before vacation? Or how productive you become when you have to leave early for an appointment? That's not coincidence—it's your brain cutting through the fluff and focusing on what actually matters.

This is why I love the Law of Triviality: It states that we often give disproportionate attention to trivial matters while neglecting more critical issues. Ever spent an hour perfecting a PowerPoint slide while postponing a major strategic decision? That's the Law of Triviality in action.

Remember that Melbourne Institute study we mentioned earlier? There's a reason they found peak cognitive performance at 25 hours per week. Your brain, like any high-performance engine, needs the right balance of acceleration and rest.

The key isn't to work less randomly—it's to work less strategically. It's about creating what I call "productive constraints" that force you to focus on what truly moves the needle.

THE COGNITIVE FOUNDATION OF PRIORITY

Back in 1956, a cognitive psychologist named George Miller discovered something that might change how you think about your daily to-do list. He found that our brain can only hold about 7 (plus or minus 2) items in our working memory at once. Think of it like your phone's RAM—try to run too many apps, and everything starts to slow down.

"But wait," you might be thinking, "I juggle way more than 7 things at once!"

And that's exactly where things get interesting. When you try to push beyond this limit, your brain doesn't politely tell you it's full—it starts dropping balls without you even noticing. It's like trying to stream Netflix, join a Zoom call, and edit a document all at once. Sure, technically, all those windows are open, but are you really catching the plot of that show?

John Sweller, another brilliant scientist, took this even further with his Cognitive Load Theory. He found that our brain's processing power gets divided into three types of mental effort:

- Intrinsic Load: The fundamental complexity of the task (like solving a math problem).
- Extraneous Load: All the unnecessary distractions and complications we add.
- Germane Load: The actual mental work of learning and processing.

The cost of ignoring these limits? It's more severe than you might think. When your working memory is constantly full, it creates a cascade of adverse effects: decision quality plummets as your brain struggles to process competing inputs, stress levels spike in response to this cognitive overload, focus becomes increasingly fragmented with each additional demand, and performance drops across the board as these effects compound each other.

This isn't just theory. Cambridge University researchers discovered that the average person makes about 35,000 decisions daily. No wonder we feel mentally exhausted by afternoon! Even something as simple as deciding what to eat involves about 226 decisions (thanks, Cornell University researchers, for making us aware of that overwhelming fact!). This constant decision-making taxes our limited cognitive resources, gradually depleting our mental energy throughout the day.

But decision fatigue is only part of the cognitive cost. When we attempt to manage too many tasks simultaneously, we trigger another drain on our mental resources. Neuroscientist Sophie Leroy identified this phenomenon as "Attention Residue"—every time you switch tasks, part of your brain stays stuck on the previous activity. Studies show it takes a full 23 minutes to regain complete focus after a single interruption. Think about that: one quick email check could cost you nearly half an hour of deep work time.

Consider Manuel's transformation. As a high-performing executive who initially resisted the idea of single-tasking, he discovered something remarkable when he started respecting his brain's processing limits. "What I didn't realize," he shares, "was that by trying to do everything at once, I was actually getting less done. Once I started working with my brain's natural capacity instead of against it, everything changed. My focus improved, my stress dropped, and most surprisingly, I started getting more done in less time."

The goal isn't to eliminate all cognitive load. Instead, it's about being strategic with your mental energy, just like an athlete is strategic with their physical training.

THE 80/20 RULE: SCIENTIFIC PRIORITIZATION

Not all work is created equal. Some tasks create massive results, while others keep you busy but lead nowhere. The challenge? Most people can't tell the difference.

This is where the Pareto Principle—also known as the 80/20 rule—becomes crucial. It's not just another productivity concept; it's a fundamental pattern that shows up everywhere in nature and human behavior. For high performers, understanding this principle isn't optional, it's essential for sustainable success.

The principle states that 80% of results come from just 20% of efforts. However, recent research reveals an even more striking pattern: 64% of results actually stem from just 4% of activities, and an astounding 52% of outcomes come from merely 0.8% of efforts.

Think about that for a moment. A tiny fraction of what you do each day is responsible for almost everything meaningful you achieve. This isn't just theory; it's a mathematical reality that most people ignore at their own peril.

This principle forms the foundation of what I call Needle Mover Tasks (NMTs). The vital few activities that create disproportionate progress toward your most meaningful goals. Just like a needle on a gauge that dramatically shifts when certain conditions are met, these tasks fundamentally change your trajectory when completed. They're not just important tasks—they're game-changers.

To identify exactly which activities fall into that crucial high-impact percentage, we can use what some authors call the Task Accuracy Framework.

This approach helps distinguish between work that merely keeps us busy and work that genuinely moves the needle, using four distinct levels of impact.

At the lowest level, Accuracy 1 represents tasks that consume time without creating value—endless email checks, unnecessary meetings, or social media scrolling disguised as "networking." Accuracy 2 includes work that feels productive but rarely moves the needle—like endless research without action or tweaking minor details on already-completed projects.

The real impact begins at Accuracy 3 with significant contributions—strategic project execution, key relationship building, meaningful skill development. But it's Accuracy 4 where transformation happens. This is where your true Needle Mover Tasks live—revenue-generating activities, game-changing decisions, and high-impact creation that fundamentally move your life or business forward.

Remember those tracking exercises from Chapter 3? This is where they become invaluable. When you map your activities against these accuracy levels, patterns emerge that might surprise you. Most high performers discover they're spending their peak energy hours on Accuracy 1 and 2 tasks, while their most important work gets squeezed into whatever time remains.

But numbers only tell part of the story. The real power of the Pareto Principle emerges when we look beyond pure metrics to examine what truly matters in your life and work. This is where the subjective audit becomes crucial.

Think about your most important goals right now. If financial success is a priority, are you actually spending time on revenue-generating activities? If health matters most, do your daily actions reflect that? This isn't about guilt—it's about alignment.

I love what Ryan, an entrepreneur I worked with, discovered when he finally ran this analysis. "I was doing what every business book told me to do," he shares. "Sixty, seventy-hour weeks, constant meetings, always being 'on.' I thought that's what building a successful business looked like." He pauses, then laughs. "Turns out I was just really good at looking busy."

When Ryan mapped his activities against the accuracy framework, he discovered something that changed everything: He was spending 80% of his energy on tasks that generated less than 20% of his results. His most productive hours were consumed by low-impact work, while his highest-leverage activities got whatever energy remained at the end of the day.

Here's where it gets interesting. Instead of trying to optimize everything, Ryan flipped the ratio. He ruthlessly eliminated Accuracy 1 tasks, delegated Accuracy 2 work, and protected his peak hours for Accuracy 3 and 4 activities only. The result? "I cut my working hours in half but tripled our company's growth rate. More importantly, I finally had energy left for what matters outside of work."

This isn't just about working less—it's about ensuring your effort creates a meaningful impact. In the end, success isn't measured by how busy you look but by what you actually achieve.

Now, please take a moment and grab your notebook. Look at your tasks from the audit you did in Chapter 3 and place them into these four different accuracy rows (grading them according to your goals). Take your time. I'll wait.

THE GLASS JAR PRINCIPLE

Order matters. Whether in chemistry, biology, or mathematics, sequence determines success. Mix ingredients in the wrong order, and your recipe fails. Initiate biological processes out of sequence, and systems break down. Execute mathematical operations incorrectly, and your answer is wrong—no matter how precise your calculations.

You've probably heard the story of the professor and the glass jar—it's a classic illustration in time management circles. When presented with a jar, rocks, pebbles, and sand, most people instinctively start with the smaller elements. It seems logical—sand and pebbles flow easily, filling spaces efficiently. Yet this apparently sensible approach guarantees failure. Only by starting with the rocks, then adding pebbles, and finally pouring sand can everything fit.

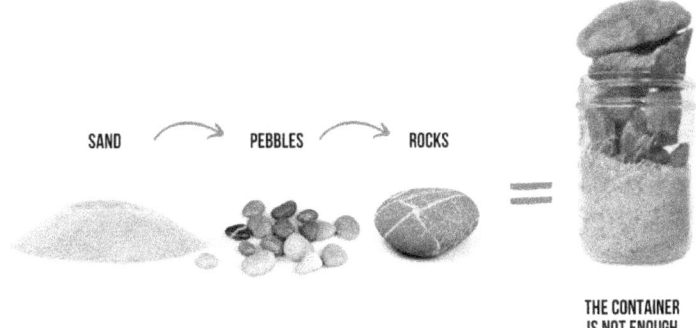

SAND → PEBBLES → ROCKS =

THE CONTAINER
IS NOT ENOUGH

ROCKS → PEBBLES → SAND =

THE CONTAINER
IS ENOUGH

The brilliance lies not in the objects, but in the sequence. Each element finds its place precisely because of the order of operations. The sand flows around the pebbles, which have settled between the rocks. Try any other sequence, and you create artificial constraints.

Think about how a tree grows. It doesn't try to develop leaves before establishing roots, or attempt to produce fruit before building strong branches. Nature follows a precise sequence that can't be rushed or rearranged. Yet in our pursuit of high performance, we often ignore this fundamental principle.

This is where most high performers go wrong. They make three critical mistakes:

- They fill their days with urgent but unimportant tasks first.
- They try to optimize their schedule before identifying true priorities.
- They treat all commitments as equally valuable, failing to distinguish between rocks, pebbles, and sand.

Jen, a real estate executive, lived this reality. "I was doing everything backwards," she admits. "My calendar was perfect—color-coded, optimized, packed with activity. But I was filling my jar with sand first, then wondering why I could never fit in the work that actually moved my business forward." Her transformation began when she started protecting time for her rocks—those critical, needle-moving activities that create exponential returns—before allowing anything else to claim her time.

The lesson is clear: In performance, as in nature, sequence determines success.

THE AOD3 FRAMEWORK

Think about the last time you felt truly overwhelmed by your workload. That sensation of drowning in tasks isn't just uncomfortable—it's biologically unsustainable. Just as your body has evolved sophisticated mechanisms to eliminate waste products, your performance system needs a method for clearing what doesn't serve your highest potential.

This is where the AOD3 Framework comes in—a comprehensive system for reclaiming your most precious resource: time. The acronym stands for Automation, Optimization, Delegation, Deletion, and Deferral—five powerful strategies that work together to transform your productivity landscape.

But how do you know which strategy to apply to which tasks? This is where most performance systems fall short—they give you tools without a diagnosis method. It's like having a cabinet full of medicine without knowing which remedy treats your specific ailment.

To bridge this gap, I've developed a color-coded waste classification system that serves as the diagnostic tool for our AOD3 treatment plan. Think of it as your performance MRI—revealing precisely what's consuming your time and how to address it:

Red Waste: Activities that create no meaningful value but persist through habit or inertia. These aren't just distractions—they're performance parasites that consume energy while giving nothing in return. The danger lies in how easily they disguise themselves as legitimate work—those recurring meetings that continue simply because "we've always had them," those reports everyone creates but nobody reads, those processes that exist only because "that's how it's done."

Orange Waste: These tasks create genuine value but don't require your specific expertise. Think of administrative work that could be systematized, routine client communications that could be templated, or operational tasks that don't leverage your unique abilities. The key isn't that these tasks lack value—it's that they're not the best use of your particular talents and energy.

To put this into practice, look back at your time-tracking journal and the Accuracy 1-4 classifications you created earlier. Take a red marker and highlight all the tasks that produce little to no real value—your Accuracy 1 tasks and any Accuracy 2 tasks that don't genuinely contribute to your goals. Next, use an orange marker to identify tasks that create value but don't require your specific expertise—these might be scattered across your Accuracy 2 and 3 categories. This simple color-coding exercise makes waste immediately visible, transforming abstract concepts into concrete targets for action.

With your tasks properly classified, let's integrate this diagnosis system with our AOD3 treatment plan:

Step 1: Identify and Eliminate Red Waste (Deletion)

Start by examining each task's actual necessity. Not whether it feels important or has always been done, but whether it genuinely contributes to your core objectives. This requires brutal honesty about what creates genuine value in your specific context.

Those recurring meetings that continue purely out of habit? Gone. Reports nobody actually uses? Eliminated. Excessive communication channels that fragment your attention? Consolidated or removed entirely. When you apply this filter rigorously, you'll be shocked at how much of your calendar is consumed by activities that contribute absolutely nothing to your core objectives.

The Deletion component of AOD3 is your scalpel for removing these parasitic activities permanently. Unlike Deferral or Delegation, Deletion is about acknowledging that some tasks simply shouldn't exist in your ecosystem.

Step 2: Redirect Orange Waste (Automation, Optimization, Delegation)

Now, turn your attention to those valuable tasks that simply don't need your personal involvement. These deserve a more nuanced approach than simple elimination:

Automation transforms repetitive tasks into systems that run without your constant attention. Think about the activities you repeat daily or weekly—scheduling meetings, sending follow-up emails, processing routine data, etc. By creating automated systems, you free up cognitive bandwidth for deeper, more impactful work. For instance, implementing a scheduling tool might save you 15 minutes per meeting setup. If you schedule eight meetings per week, that's two hours redirected from email ping-pong to focused strategic work.

Optimization removes unnecessary friction from processes that can't be fully automated. This isn't about working harder or faster—it's about streamlining workflows, batching similar tasks, and eliminating unnecessary steps. The goal isn't perfection—it's progress.

Delegation transfers tasks that require human attention but not specifically your attention. Many high performers struggle here, telling themselves "it's faster if I just do it myself" or "nobody else can do it as well." But here's the reality: If someone else can do a task 80% as well as you, it shouldn't be on your plate. Your energy needs to be reserved for work that indeed requires your unique expertise.

Step 3: Strategically Schedule What Remains (Deferral)

Finally, there's Deferral—the strategic postponement of tasks that matter but don't require immediate attention. Not everything important needs to be done right now. By creating systems to track and revisit deferred items, you maintain control while focusing on what's truly urgent or important in the present moment.

What makes this integrated approach so powerful is how the diagnosis informs the treatment. Red Waste points directly to Deletion. Orange Waste flows naturally into Automation, Optimization, and Delegation. The small portion that remains—work that truly deserves your personal attention—can then be strategically managed through Deferral or immediate action.

When applied consistently, this process yields extraordinary results. Most professionals I work with discover at least 10 hours of recoverable time in their first week alone. One unnecessary meeting eliminated each day recovers five hours weekly. A few well-chosen delegations might free up another three to four hours. The time-saving potential is enormous—and it doesn't require working faster or pushing harder.

THE MODIFIED EISENHOWER MATRIX

After implementing the AOD3 Framework and waste classification system, you'll have significantly reduced your task load. But a critical question remains: How do you organize and protect what's left?

If you've ever seen The Matrix (the movie, not the framework we're about to discuss), you remember that scene where Neo has to choose between the red pill and the blue pill. Well, President Dwight D. Eisenhower faced similar decisions daily—though with slightly higher stakes than choosing between digital illusions and reality. As the five-star general who oversaw D-Day and later became U.S. President, he had to constantly distinguish between what felt urgent and what was truly important.

His solution? A simple but powerful framework that separated tasks into four categories based on urgency and importance. However, what Eisenhower intuited through experience, modern neuroscience has confirmed through research: Our brains process urgent and important tasks through entirely different neural pathways.

When something urgent demands attention, it triggers your limbic system—the same circuit that handles fight-or-flight responses. But when something is important but not urgent, it engages your prefrontal cortex—the part responsible for long-term thinking and complex decision-making.

The traditional Eisenhower Matrix organizes tasks into four quadrants:

1 Urgent and Important
2 Not Urgent but Important
3 Urgent but Not Important
4 Not Urgent and Not Important

While this framework correctly identifies the importance of Not Urgent But Important activities, it typically suggests merely scheduling these for "later." The problem? In the daily battle for your attention, the urgent consistently overpowers the important, and "later" often never arrives.

Our Modified Eisenhower Matrix makes a subtle but powerful shift: it elevates NUBI work (Not Urgent But Important) from "schedule when possible" to "prioritize strategically now." This reframes these high-leverage activities as deserving of your peak cognitive hours rather than whatever time remains after handling urgencies.

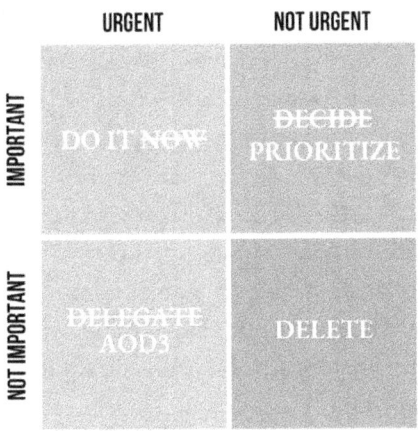

Let's examine each quadrant through this biological lens:

NUBI—Not Urgent But Important: This is where exponential results live. These activities create massive leverage—strategic planning that prevents future emergencies, relationship development that opens opportunity doors, capacity-building projects that multiply your effectiveness, and high-impact creative work that drives real innovation. These tasks engage your prefrontal cortex, allowing you to access your most sophisticated thinking.

U&I—Urgent and Important: These are legitimate "Houston, we have a problem" situations that require immediate attention. True client emergencies, critical deadlines, and genuine crises belong here. Your brain processes these differently from other urgent matters, triggering focused attention while maintaining access to strategic thinking.

UNI—Urgent but Not Important: If you've properly applied the AOD3 Framework, you should have very few tasks remaining in this quadrant. Any that persist are prime candidates for revisiting your Orange Waste strategies— can these be further automated, optimized, or delegated?

NUNI—Not Urgent and Not Important: Similarly, thorough application of the Red Waste elimination should leave this quadrant nearly empty. Any tasks that remain here deserve one final scrutiny—they're likely candidates for complete elimination.

The power of using these frameworks in sequence becomes apparent when you see how they reinforce each other. The AOD3 Framework and waste classification dramatically reduce your task load, while the Modified Eisenhower Matrix helps you protect and organize what remains.

When implementing the MEM, grab your notebook and draw the traditional quadrant matrix. Then, place your remaining tasks in the appropriate quadrants, paying special attention to those that might be disguising themselves as more urgent than they truly are. If you find your NUBI quadrant sparsely populated while UNI is overflowing, that's a clear signal to revisit your waste classification—you're likely still holding onto Orange Waste, which could be redirected.

The completed matrix becomes a biological alignment tool that reveals where your highest leverage opportunities truly lie. As you practice this approach in your planning process, you'll develop an increasingly intuitive sense of what deserves your attention. Just as your body automatically prioritizes essential functions during stress, your matrix will help you automatically direct your focus toward what creates sustainable high performance.

This integrated performance system—from diagnosis (waste classification) to treatment (AOD3) to ongoing management (MEM)—forms the foundation for everything else we'll cover. The space you create isn't just empty calendar blocks—it's the opportunity to implement the deep work practices, recovery protocols, and flow state triggers that drive extraordinary performance.

OVERCOMING IMPLEMENTATION OBSTACLES

Now that we've established our powerful frameworks—the waste-eliminating AOD3 system and the priority-protecting Modified Eisenhower Matrix—we face the critical challenge of implementation. Understanding these systems is valuable, but actually living them requires overcoming two fundamental obstacles: our biological decision-making limitations and the constant pressure of external demands.

Let's address these implementation bridges before diving into your weekly execution system.

The Biology of Better Decisions: Systems Over Willpower

Perfect frameworks aren't enough if they can't survive contact with reality. And this is where biological understanding becomes crucial to implementation success.

Have you ever wondered why you can make perfect decisions in the morning but find yourself scrolling social media by evening, despite your best intentions? Or why you can maintain a new productive habit for a few days before sliding back into old patterns?

This is where most productivity advice falls short. It assumes that knowing what to do automatically translates into doing it. But there's a fascinating biological reality we need to address: willpower alone isn't enough to maintain any system, no matter how well designed.

Dr. Roy Baumeister's groundbreaking research on decision-making revealed something that changes everything we think we know about discipline: willpower isn't just a character trait—it's a biological resource that depletes with use. Think of it like your phone's battery. Every decision you make throughout the day, from what to wear in the morning to how to respond to that urgent email, drains a little more power. By evening, you're not making poor decisions because you're lazy; you're making them because your brain's decision-making battery is literally running on empty.

This isn't just theory. When researchers measured glucose levels in the brain during decision-making tasks, they found that difficult decisions literally consume more energy than simple ones. Your brain, being the energy-efficient organ that it is, begins to conserve power by defaulting to the easiest option available—regardless of whether it's the best choice.

This biological reality explains why even the most disciplined people eventually fail when relying on willpower alone. It's not a moral failing; it's simple biochemistry. Just as you can't consciously decide to lower your heart rate or speed up your digestion, you can't simply choose to have more willpower when your biological systems are depleted.

But here's where it gets interesting. Nature has a solution for this very problem: automation. Your body doesn't rely on conscious decision-making for crucial functions like breathing or maintaining your heartbeat. Instead, it creates automated systems that operate without requiring constant attention or effort.

This insight gives us a blueprint for maintaining our prioritization system through three key elements:

First is decision elimination. Just as your body automates essential functions, you need to automate or eliminate unnecessary choices. This might mean having set responses to common situations or predetermined criteria for what deserves your attention. Instead of debating whether each email needs an immediate response, you have clear rules: client emergencies get handled now, everything else waits for designated email time.

Second is choice architecture, which is the strategic structuring of how decisions are presented and made. Think of it like designing a building where the stairs are more prominent than the elevator. You're not removing choices, but you're making the better option the easier one. In practice, this means setting up your task management system so that high-priority NUBI work is the first thing you see each morning, not your inbox full of UNI tasks.

Third, is environmental design. The deliberate optimization of your physical and digital workspace. While choice architecture focuses on how decisions are structured, environmental design shapes where and how you work. This means creating specific zones for different types of work, eliminating visual distractions, and using physical cues to trigger desired behaviors. It's the difference between trying to focus in a cluttered space with notifications constantly popping up versus working in a clean environment specifically designed for deep work. But, more on this later in the book.

These three elements—decision elimination, choice architecture, and environmental design—come together to create what I call "non-negotiable rules." But before we dive into that framework, you might be noticing something interesting: we're talking about systems again, aren't we? Just as we discussed automation in our AOD3 Framework and environment design in our prioritization strategies, these concepts keep resurfacing. That's because our Four Pillars—Prioritization, Physiology, Psychology, and Performance Systems—aren't really separate entities. They're interconnected aspects of the same performance ecosystem.

Think about how Veronica's transformation illustrates this interconnection. When we first met her in Chapter 1, she was relying on energy drinks to power through her afternoons. But her shift to sustainable performance wasn't just about better energy management (Physiology) or stronger willpower (Psychology). It came from building systems that made good decisions automatic.

"The real game-changer," she explains, "wasn't finding more discipline. It was creating an environment where I didn't need discipline." By restructuring her workspace, establishing clear decision protocols, and designing her environment to support focus, she created a system that naturally guided her toward peak performance.

The key to non-negotiable rules is making them exactly that—non-negotiable. Just as you don't debate whether to brush your teeth each morning or which side of the road to drive on, your performance protocols should be automatic. This might mean:

- No email checks before completing your most important task.
- No meetings during your peak cognitive hours.
- No phone in your workspace during deep work sessions.

Notice how these rules don't require willpower once they're established. They're not choices you make daily—they're just the way you operate. It's like having a biological immune system for your productivity, automatically protecting you from performance-draining distractions and decisions.

These non-negotiable rules become particularly powerful when they form complete protocols. Rather than isolated decisions, they create entire sequences of behavior that protect your performance state. For instance, instead of just having a rule about checking email, you might establish a complete morning protocol:

- Your phone stays in airplane mode until your most important work is done.
- Your workspace is prepared the night before, eliminating morning decision fatigue.
- Your first two hours are reserved for NUBI tasks, without exception.

Think of it like your body's wake-up sequence. You don't consciously tell your organs to start functioning each morning. Your body has an automatic protocol that handles everything from adjusting your blood pressure to regulating your temperature. Your performance protocols should work the same way.

But here's what's fascinating about these systems: once established, they actually expand your capacity for willpower rather than tax it. It's like building an energy-efficient home—the initial investment in good design and infrastructure leads to effortless conservation later.

This is the ultimate paradox of systems over willpower: Structure, properly designed, creates freedom. When you don't have to rely on willpower to make every decision, you preserve that mental energy for what truly matters—the creative, strategic thinking that drives real results.

The Art of Strategic No: Protecting Your New Performance System

With your decision-making biology optimized, we face the second implementation challenge: protecting your system from external demands. Because let's face it—the moment you create space in your schedule, the world will rush to fill it with more of the same low-value activities you just eliminated.

This is where the art of the strategic no becomes not just useful, but essential for your performance transformation.

You see, setting up ideal systems is one thing. Maintaining them in a world of endless requests, impromptu meetings, and "quick favors" is another entirely different thing. This is where the art of the strategic no becomes crucial—not just as a time management tool, but as a biological necessity.

The Science of Boundary Setting isn't just about psychology—it's about physiology. When you fail to protect your boundaries, you're not just compromising your schedule; you're disrupting your entire biological rhythm. Research shows that constant interruptions don't just break your focus—they trigger a stress response that can take hours to reset.

Harvard's William Ury, in his groundbreaking work on negotiation, developed what he calls the "Positive No" framework. But what makes this approach particularly engaging is how perfectly it aligns with your brain's natural processing patterns. Instead of triggering the defensive responses that typically come with rejection, a Positive No actually helps maintain social bonds while protecting your boundaries.

The framework works in three parts:
- First, affirm the relationship and acknowledge the request.
- Then, protect your boundary with clear, firm limits.
- Finally, offer an alternative that maintains connection without compromising your priorities.

Think of it like your body's immune system—it doesn't just reject foreign substances; it maintains a complex balance of acceptance and protection. Your boundaries need to work the same way.

Different situations require different approaches, just as your body responds differently to various types of threats.

Let's break this down:

With superiors, the key is to frame your no in terms of maximizing value. Instead of simply declining, show how protecting your focus time actually serves their objectives better: "I can take this on, but it would mean delaying Project X. Would you prefer I prioritize this new task?"

With peers, clarity and reciprocity become crucial. Establish clear protocols for when and how you can be interrupted, and respect the same boundaries for others. This creates what I call a "mutual performance pact." For instance: "I've blocked off 9-11 AM for deep work, but I'm fully available for collaboration after that. This helps me bring my best thinking to our shared projects."

Client relationships require a different approach entirely. Here, the focus is on demonstrating how your boundaries actually serve their interests: "To ensure you get my absolute best work on this project, I dedicate focused blocks of time specifically for complex tasks like yours. I can dive deep into this tomorrow between 2-4 PM, when you'll have my complete attention."

In personal relationships, authenticity matters most. These are the people who care about your well-being, not just your output. Help them understand that your boundaries aren't about avoiding them—they're about being more present when you are together: "I'm working on being fully present when we spend time together, which means I need to complete this work first. Can we plan for quality time this evening when I can give you my undivided attention?"

The Art of Saying No becomes particularly challenging when we face what psychologists call FOMO—the Fear of Missing Out. Our brains evolved in an environment where saying no to social opportunities could mean missing critical resources or life-saving information. This explains why declining invitations, opportunities, or requests can trigger a stress response that feels disproportionate to the actual stakes involved.

But here's where modern neuroscience offers an interesting twist. Research shows that saying yes to everything actually reduces our capacity for meaningful engagement and impactful work. When we never say no, we're never fully invested in our yes.

This is where we can transform FOMO into something remarkable— JOMO, the Joy of Missing Out. Just as your body needs to say no to certain functions to prioritize others during stress, your performance requires strategic nos to protect your most valuable yeses.

Think about the last time you were in a state of flow, completely absorbed in meaningful work. You achieved that state precisely because you said no to distractions, interruptions, and lesser priorities. Your best performance came not from saying yes to everything, but from choosing deliberately what to decline.

The key to mastering the art of no lies in understanding this biological reality. Every no to a non-essential commitment is actually a yes to something more important—whether that's deep work, genuine recovery, or fully present time with those who matter most.

This isn't about becoming someone who always says no. It's about being strategic with your yeses, so that when you do say yes, you bring your full capacity to what matters most.

THE 15-MINUTE TIME SAVER PROTOCOL

After establishing our frameworks and addressing implementation barriers, we arrive at perhaps the most crucial practice: weekly planning. This isn't just another productivity tip—it's where everything we've discussed comes together into a practical, repeatable process.

Most people don't set aside time to plan their week, which is why they waste so much time during the week itself. Think about it: Would you start a cross-country road trip without looking at a map? Yet most of us start our weeks exactly this way—reacting to whatever comes at us first, allowing the urgent to overpower the important.

The best time to plan is before your week begins—ideally Sunday. This provides a clean transition from the previous week and allows you to start Monday with absolute clarity. But the specific day isn't what matters. What matters is that you have a set time for planning before your week begins.

Why is pre-week planning so crucial? Because it removes decision fatigue by creating a clear roadmap, prevents urgent tasks from hijacking important ones, gives you confidence and control from the start, and ensures balance between performance and recovery.

Here's how the 15-minute process flows:

1. Review & Reflect

Start by examining the week that just ended. What were your biggest wins? What didn't work as planned? Where did you get distracted or slowed down? What small improvements could make next week better? This reflection builds self-awareness and helps you identify patterns that might be limiting your performance or opportunities you could leverage more effectively in the coming week.

2. Set Your Priority

Instead of creating a massive to-do list, identify one central focus—the task or goal that would make the biggest impact if accomplished. Ask yourself: What's the single most important thing I need to achieve this week? What would make everything else easier or unnecessary? How can I break this down into clear, actionable steps?

Your focus should ideally come from your NUBI quadrant—those exponential activities that create massive leverage despite not screaming for immediate attention.

3. Block Your Foundational Routines

Protect the core activities that maintain your biological rhythm. Block your sleep schedule first—when you'll wake up and when you need to wind down for optimal rest. Next, reserve time for your morning routine that bridges the gap between waking and peak performance. We'll dive deep into optimizing this sequence in the next chapter, but for now, just ensure you've blocked off this crucial transition time.

Schedule your end-of-day shutdown ritual—that 5-10 minute period when you review what worked, what didn't, and what needs adjustment for tomorrow. Think of it as preparing the runway for your next takeoff. Finally, protect those 15 minutes for next week's planning session.

4. Schedule Recovery & Relationships

Your day needs consistent recovery points: dedicated meal breaks, intentional movement sessions that might include exercise or walking meetings, and moments for mental renewal through meditation or brief walks.

Weekly recovery requires longer blocks: extended exercise sessions, perhaps a massage or other bodywork, and time for deeper engagement with hobbies or outdoor activities. These aren't indulgences—they're investments in your sustained performance.

Relationships deserve the same strategic attention. Plan for both daily moments with family and weekly events. Make time for social connections, whether that's friends, mentors, or networking. Consider community engagement through volunteering or mastermind groups. These connections provide the emotional foundation for peak performance.

Note: If you have a traditional 9-5 job, start by blocking your work hours first, then build these elements around them. The goal isn't to watch Netflix at 11 AM—it's to create sustainable balance within your existing commitments.

5. Design Your Deep Work Periods

This is where you align your calendar with your Modified Eisenhower Matrix. Your morning blocks deserve special attention. When your energy is typically highest, reserve 90-120 minute focused sessions for your NUBI tasks. These aren't just any focused periods—they're your power hours for tackling your most challenging cognitive work. Remember to build in buffer zones between these sessions; they're essential recovery periods that maintain your peak performance state.

Allocate midday blocks for collaborative activities. This is when to schedule your important meetings, handle U&I tasks that require coordination with others, and engage in work that benefits from group energy. Don't forget to include strategic breaks between these sessions—they maintain mental clarity throughout the day.

By afternoon, shift to "maintenance mode." This is the ideal time for administrative tasks, batch processing emails, and handling routine work that survived your AOD3 elimination process. Your physical energy naturally dips in the afternoon, and so does your capacity for intense focus work.

Match your work-rest ratios to your tasks and energy levels:

- The Traditional Pomodoro (25/5) works well for getting started.
- Extended Focus (50/10) helps build concentration
- Deep Work (90/20) aligns with your brain's natural ultradian rhythm
- Maximum Intensity (120/30) suits complex problem-solving sessions

6. Buffer & Finalize

Create strategic buffer zones between major activities to prevent the continuous context-switching that destroys deep focus. Review your entire plan for balance and feasibility. Make any final adjustments to ensure your highest leverage activities have adequate protection from potential interruptions.

DAILY EXECUTION: MAINTAINING COURSE

Even with a perfect weekly plan, daily refinements are essential. Think of it like navigation—your weekly plan is your map, but you still need to make small course corrections as you travel.

Start each day by reviewing your plan before diving into work. Don't open your email, don't check your phone—take five minutes to get clear on your priorities: your most important task for the day, two to three supporting tasks that move your weekly goal forward, and any potential obstacles you need to prepare for.

Throughout the day, maintain your focus by using the ABC prioritization method:

- **A Tasks:** Must be completed today—these directly impact your most important goals.
- **B Tasks:** Should be done if possible—they support your progress but aren't critical.
- **C Tasks:** Could be done—nice to have but can be deferred if necessary.

End each day with a strategic shutdown. This isn't about closing your laptop; it's a deliberate process of review and preparation: What progress did you make today? What adjustments does tomorrow's plan need? Are you still aligned with your weekly priorities?

This daily rhythm of review-execute-adjust keeps you focused on what matters while maintaining the flexibility to handle reality. It transforms your performance frameworks from theoretical concepts into lived experience, ensuring that the space you created through the AOD3 Framework and the priorities you established with your Modified Eisenhower Matrix actually manifest in your daily life.

MAKING YOUR SYSTEM SUSTAINABLE

One of the biggest reasons people fail at time management isn't lack of motivation—it's overcomplication. They get caught up in searching for the perfect app, the ideal productivity tool, or the most sophisticated scheduling system. But here's what decades of performance research tell us: the best system is the one you'll actually use.

This is why I advocate for starting simple. A basic notebook and pen might seem old-school in our digital age, but there's profound wisdom in this approach. When you remove the distractions of notifications, updates, and endless features, you create space for genuine focus and clarity.

If you're using a notebook, structure it with these essential elements:

- Weekly Review: Your lessons and insights from the past week.
- Priority Focus: Your single most important goal plus 2-3 supporting objectives.
- Time Block Layout: Your deep work periods and recovery blocks.
- Daily Framework: Today's most important task and supporting activities.
- End-Day Notes: Quick insights and adjustments for tomorrow.

The key is simplicity. Create a structure you can maintain without feeling overwhelmed. Think of it like building a habit; start with the minimum effective dose, then expand as the practice becomes natural.

If you're looking for a structured, optimized tool to make this process effortless, I recommend *The High Performance Daily Planner.*

When I first designed *The High Performance Daily Planner*, it wasn't meant to be something I sold. I created it for myself because I couldn't find a planner that actually aligned with the way high performers think and work.

Most planners focus solely on tasks and appointments, assuming that productivity is just about filling your calendar. But I knew from experience that high performance isn't just about doing more—it's about doing what matters, at the right time, in the right way.

So, I built a planner that reflected that reality. One that didn't just track tasks but helped me structure my energy, protect deep work, and stay consistent with the habits that drive long-term success.

I quietly published it on Amazon, not because I intended to market it, but because I wanted my coaching clients to have access to a tool that worked. It's something I still use every day—not just for time management, but to ensure my focus, health, and energy are aligned with what actually moves the needle.

If you're using a simple notebook, that's perfectly fine. The principles in this book work no matter what tool you use. But if you want a done-for-you structure that integrates everything we've covered (and more that we'll explore later), my planner is an option.

At the end of the day, what matters most isn't the tool itself—it's the system you build around it.

To learn more about *The High Performance Daily Planner*, please visit hplink.org/hpdp or scan the QR code below.

Digital Tools as Support Systems

While your core planning should stay analog, certain digital tools can enhance your system:

- Google Calendar for coordinating meetings and time blocks.
- A digital notebook (like reMarkable) if you prefer a paper-like feel without paper storage.
- Note-taking apps (like Notion or Evernote) for capturing ideas and tracking long-term projects.

Remember: These are supplements, not replacements. Use digital tools only where they genuinely add value without adding complexity.

Weathering Reality: Making Your System Adaptable

The biggest hurdle isn't creating your plan—it's maintaining it when reality hits. Your carefully structured week will inevitably meet unexpected demands, urgent requests, and seemingly immovable obstacles. This isn't a failure of the system; it's simply life happening. More importantly, it's an opportunity to implement strategic adaptation.

Think of your planning system like a suspension bridge: rigid enough to maintain its structure, yet flexible enough to move with external forces. Without sufficient rigidity, a bridge collapses. Without flexibility, it cracks under pressure. Your performance system requires this same balance of stability and adaptability.

When unexpected demands arise—and they will—don't abandon your system. Adjust it. Shift time blocks while maintaining their integrity. If a client emergency demands your morning attention, move your deep work block to the early afternoon rather than canceling it. This preserves both the commitment and the cognitive value of uninterrupted focus.

Another effective adaptation involves rearranging tasks within their designated categories. If your planned NUBI work gets displaced, swap it with another NUBI task that better fits your new time constraints rather than defaulting to less important work that feels more urgent. This category integrity protects your long-term performance even when short-term plans change.

Your system should bend, not break. This distinction makes all the difference between sustainable performance and constant frustration. Moving your deep work block to a different time maintains the principle that focused work deserves protection. Fragmenting it into small pieces scattered between meetings abandons the principle entirely. One approach preserves the biological value of deep focus while accommodating reality; the other sacrifices performance on the altar of reactivity.

Remember those buffer zones we built into your schedule? This is where they prove their worth. When an urgent client need arises, you can tap into these predetermined spaces without disrupting your entire day's structure. Your deep work might move to a different slot, but it doesn't disappear completely.

The key isn't to avoid disruptions—they're inevitable. The key is to handle them without letting them derail your entire performance ecosystem. Each challenge becomes an opportunity to refine your system, making it more robust and better suited to your specific needs. Just as biological systems grow stronger through appropriate stress, your planning system becomes more resilient with each adaptive challenge it successfully navigates.

PERFORMANCE ECOSYSTEM TAKING SHAPE

As we conclude our exploration of prioritization—the first pillar of our Holistic Performance Framework—you might notice something fascinating happening. The lines between prioritization, physiology, psychology, and performance systems are starting to blur. This isn't accidental. Just as your body's systems work in concert rather than in isolation, these pillars support and enhance each other.

Think about the journey we've traveled together. We started by understanding the biological foundations of priority and focus—how your brain literally processes different types of tasks through distinct neural pathways. We explored the science of strategic elimination through our waste classification system and AOD3 Framework. You've learned the art of saying no as a biological necessity, not just a productivity trick. And we've established a practical system for weekly planning that aligns with your natural rhythms rather than fighting against them.

But here's what makes this approach fundamentally different from traditional productivity methods: We're not just managing time—we're optimizing your entire performance ecosystem. When you prioritize effectively, you create space for proper recovery. When you protect your energy through strategic planning, you enhance your cognitive capacity. When you eliminate unnecessary demands, you reduce stress and improve decision-making quality. Each element reinforces the others in an upward spiral of sustainable performance.

This integrated approach means your Red Waste elimination creates space for strategic deep work. Your Modified Eisenhower Matrix protects your highest leverage activities. Your 15-Minute Protocol translates these frameworks into daily reality. And your adaptive strategies ensure the system bends rather than breaks when life inevitably happens.

As we move into Chapter 6, where we'll explore the power of habits and routines, remember: Prioritization isn't just about getting more done. It's about creating the conditions for sustained excellence across every domain of your life. You're not just optimizing your calendar—you're optimizing the biological foundation that powers everything you do.

Your next step is simple but powerful: Set aside those 15 minutes this Sunday. Start your weekly planning practice. Don't aim for perfection—aim for progress. Because every journey toward peak performance begins with a single, intentional step.

RESEARCH & RESOURCES

By following the steps outlined in this chapter carefully, there's no reason why you won't be able to reclaim 10+ hours from your work week. The frameworks, strategies, and implementation guidance provide everything you need to transform your relationship with time and priorities.

If you've already joined the Holistic Performance Academy course mentioned in the introduction, we cover these prioritization concepts in depth during our implementation modules, along with the complete journey through all four pillars.

If the full Academy felt like too big a time investment right now, I created *The 10-Hour Advantage* mini-course for you. Why? Because reclaiming your time is the essential first step that makes all other optimizations possible. Without those extra hours in your week, implementing the physiological, psychological, and systems improvements we'll cover in upcoming chapters becomes nearly impossible. This course includes my specific templates and a guided walkthrough of my exact prioritization process, allowing you to implement these time-reclaiming systems in less than two hours. As a reader of this book, use the coupon code **HPREADER** for **80% off** at hplink.org/10hour-advantage or scan the first QR code below.

As always, all the scientific research, frameworks, and additional materials mentioned throughout this chapter are also available in the Holistic Performance Resource Hub. Visit hplink.org/resourcehub or scan the second QR code below.

CHAPTER 6
AUTOMATING GOOD BEHAVIOR

"First we make our habits, then our habits make us."

– John Dryden

"I know what I need to do. I just can't seem to make myself do it consistently." I hear this from clients all the time, and for years, I thought the solution was simple: more discipline, better planning, stronger willpower. After all, we'd already determined their priorities, created perfect schedules, and designed optimal systems. Why weren't they following through?

I had to learn this the hard way. And, even lost some clients in the process.

The more complex the system, the more likely it was to fail. There was no point in optimizing everything in their lives if these changes were never going to stick. At least with the flawed approach, I had back then.

One client, a successful executive, had everything perfectly mapped out—her Modified Eisenhower Matrix was spot-on, her time blocks were precisely arranged, her priorities were crystal clear. Yet three weeks in, she was back to her old patterns of reactive work and scattered focus.

This is where most performance advice falls short. In Chapter 5, we learned that systems beat willpower. But there's a crucial next step: those systems need to become automatic. They need to transform from conscious decisions into unconscious habits.

Think about driving a car. Remember when you first learned? Every action required intense focus—check mirrors, signal, brake smoothly, watch for traffic, try not to kill anyone. Now, you do it all automatically, leaving your conscious mind free to think about more important things. This is the power of habit formation, and it's exactly what we need to achieve with our performance systems.

But here's what captivates me about habits: They're not just about productivity. They shape every dimension of your life. This is why some life coaches often use the Wheel of Life—a framework that helps us examine eight crucial life domains: Business/Career & Finances, Physical Health, Emotional well-being, Personal Development, Family and Friends, Fun and Recreation,

Romance, and Contribution to Society. These interconnected areas collectively form the foundation of a balanced and fulfilling life, each one influencing and being influenced by the others.

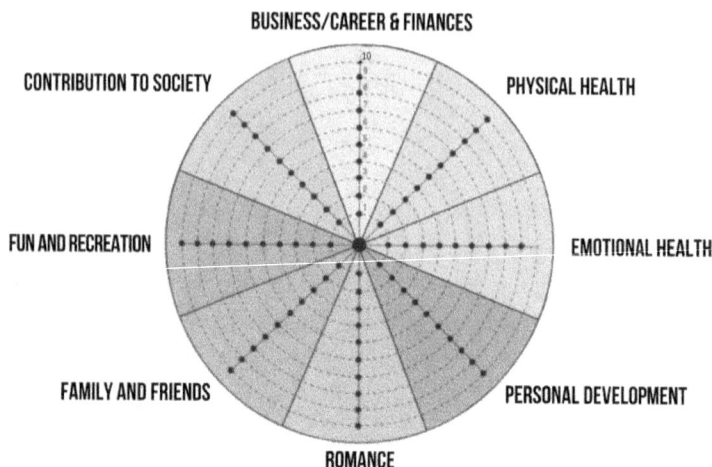

That executive I mentioned? Her real breakthrough came not from perfecting her schedule, but from understanding how habits in each of these areas influence all the others. Poor sleep habits don't just impact your energy—they affect your decision-making, relationships, and professional performance. Similarly, positive habits in one area often create unexpected benefits across the entire wheel.

The solution isn't more complexity—it's strategic simplicity. It's about understanding how your brain naturally forms habits, then using that knowledge to make the right behaviors automatic. Just as we learned to align our planning with our biology in Chapter 5, we need to align our habit formation with how our brains actually work.

This is why we're tackling habits now, even though systems are technically the last pillar of our framework. Because without the ability to make good behaviors automatic, even the best strategies will eventually fail. We need to build the foundation for sustainable change before we dive deeper into optimizing our physiology, psychology, and performance systems.

In this chapter, we'll explore exactly how to do that—not through willpower or complexity, but through understanding and working with your brain's natural habit-forming mechanisms. We'll learn why some habits stick while others fail, how to select the habits that create the biggest impact, and most importantly, how to make high performance your default state rather than your constant struggle.

THE SCIENCE OF AUTOMATIC BEHAVIOR

Remember how we discussed in the last chapter that up to 40% of our daily actions are unconscious habits? This isn't just a quirky fact; it's your brain's brilliant performance optimization strategy. By automating routine behaviors, your brain conserves precious cognitive fuel for more complex thinking.

Take a moment and reflect on your day so far. How many decisions did you actually make consciously? From brushing your teeth to brewing your morning coffee, most of your early actions were habits—behaviors so deeply ingrained they happen without a moment's conscious thought.

This remarkable automation happens through what scientists call the Habit Loop—a three-part neural process that transforms repeated behaviors into automatic routines. Every habit, whether it's grabbing your phone first thing in the morning or your evening wind-down ritual, follows the same neurological pattern:

1. **Cue** (Trigger): An environmental or internal signal that initiates the habit.
2. **Routine** (Action): The actual behavior you perform.
3. **Reward** (Outcome): The benefit your brain associates with the action.

Consider a common morning scenario: You wake up (cue), check social media (routine), and get a dopamine hit from new notifications (reward). Over time, this cycle becomes so automatic that your brain executes it without any conscious deliberation.

Here's where most habit advice goes off the rails: The popular belief that it takes exactly 21 days to form a habit is nothing more than a scientific urban legend.

This myth originated with Dr. Maxwell Maltz, a plastic surgeon in the 1960s who noticed his patients typically needed about 21 days to adjust to physical changes. Somehow, this casual observation morphed into a widely repeated "rule" about habit formation.

The reality? Research by Phillippa Lally and her team at University College London reveals a far more nuanced picture. They discovered that habit formation is a highly individualized process, typically taking anywhere from

18 to 254 days, with an average of 66 days for a new behavior to become genuinely automatic.

The timeline varies dramatically based on the habit's complexity, your unique environment, and individual neural wiring. Some habits might feel natural within weeks, while others require months of consistent practice.

This isn't meant to discourage you. It's about setting realistic expectations. Just as sustainable performance isn't about quick fixes, lasting habit change isn't about hitting an arbitrary 21-day mark. It's about understanding and working with your brain's intricate habit-forming mechanisms.

The goal isn't perfection. The goal is progress, one neural pathway at a time.

ELITE HABITS: THE POWER OF STRATEGIC SELECTION

Not all habits are created equal. While every automated behavior serves a purpose, certain habits create a "cascade effect"—triggering positive changes across multiple areas of your life simultaneously. These are what I call Elite Habits, known in research circles as keystone habits.

Think of them like precisely arranged dominoes. Knock over the right one, and you create a chain reaction of positive change. The wrong one? Nothing meaningful happens. This is why adding another productivity app might feel good but doesn't transform your life. However, establishing a consistent sleep schedule can revolutionize your energy, focus, relationships, and performance.

Elite Habits work because they create a ripple effect. When you establish one of these fundamental behaviors, other positive changes often follow naturally—without requiring additional willpower or conscious effort. For instance, when someone starts exercising regularly, they often spontaneously make better food choices, sleep more consistently, drink more water, feel more energetic, and become more productive at work. None of these additional changes were the original goal, but they happened automatically because one Elite Habit shifted their entire behavioral ecosystem.

But here's the crucial question: How do you identify which habits will create this cascade effect in your life? Most people get stuck trying to change everything at once instead of focusing on the one or two habits that could transform everything else. This is where the strategic life audit comes in—not the surface-level evaluation most productivity experts recommend, but a deeper examination through the lens of our Wheel of Life framework.

Drawing from the weekly planning data you developed earlier, examine your life beyond just work tasks. For each dimension of the Wheel—from

Physical Health to Relationships, from Career to Personal Growth—ask yourself three critical questions:

- What automatic behaviors are already serving you well?
- Which habits might be holding you back?
- Where do you see the biggest gaps between your current reality and your aspirations?

Let's say Physical Health emerges as your focus area. Perhaps your energy levels are consistently low, stress runs high, and these issues are bleeding into every aspect of your life—from your work performance to your family relationships. Instead of attempting a complete health overhaul, we look for that one Elite Habit capable of triggering a cascade of positive changes.

As a busy professional, your options might include a 15-minute morning walk, a post-work stretch routine, or twice-weekly strength training. But remember—we're not just evaluating direct benefits; we're looking for habits with the potential to transform multiple areas of your life simultaneously.

Consider the morning walk. On the surface, it offers clear physical benefits—improved fitness and energy. But dig deeper, and you'll discover a wealth of indirect benefits: enhanced mood through natural light exposure, increased vitamin D production, improved mental clarity, and a natural transition into your workday. The stretching routine, while beneficial, might offer more limited cascade potential across other life domains. Similarly, strength training provides significant physical benefits but demands more initial commitment, potentially creating resistance to consistent implementation.

I witnessed this exact selection process in action recently with a client who chose the morning walk as her Elite Habit. Some might consider this choice "too basic," but it was precisely what she needed at that point in her life. The ripple effects were remarkable: she naturally adjusted her bedtime to accommodate the morning walk, her food choices improved because she didn't want to undermine her new habit, and her work focus sharpened thanks to this clear transition into her day.

Perhaps most surprisingly, her relationship flourished when her partner began joining these morning walks.

This is the essence of Elite Habit selection—finding what's both impactful and achievable for you, right where you are. There's no universal solution.

While some might thrive with an elaborate morning routine, others might find transformative power in something more straightforward.

The key is choosing the habit you'll actually maintain—because the most impressive routine means nothing if it doesn't become part of your daily life.

Remember, the goal isn't to completely overhaul your life overnight. It's about identifying those fundamental behaviors that can create a subtle yet profound cascade of positive change. Like a skilled gardener, you're not trying to force growth, but creating the optimal conditions for natural transformation.

UNDERSTANDING YOUR HABIT CATALYSTS

As we've seen before, every habit, good or bad, begins with a trigger. Think about how some instinctively start brewing coffee the moment they step into the kitchen, or how the sight of running shoes by the door might prompt others to exercise—or make them feel guilty for not exercising. These triggers aren't just random cues; they're the entry points to our habit loops.

What intrigues me about triggers is how they operate on multiple levels of our consciousness. Some are obvious—like a calendar reminder for your daily planning session. Others are subtle but powerful—like how the afternoon slump might trigger a quick snack break that turns into a 30-minute social media scroll.

Research shows that triggers generally fall into three categories:
- Temporal (time-based).
- Environmental (location-based).
- Emotional (feeling-based).

A temporal trigger might be that mid-afternoon slump that sends you searching for a snack. An environmental trigger could be walking into your office and feeling a sudden wave of anxiety, or passing the kitchen and experiencing an immediate urge to grab a coffee. An emotional trigger might be the stress that prompts you to scroll through social media.

But here's where it gets interesting: not all triggers are created equal. Some are "hot triggers"—immediate and actionable. Others are "cold triggers"—reminders without opportunity for action.

Let me show you the difference. Imagine you're driving to work and see a billboard advertising a gym. That's a cold trigger. You can't act on it immediately. But what if you placed your workout clothes next to your bed the night before? That's a hot trigger. The opportunity for action is immediate and clear.

This distinction matters because your brain responds differently to each type. Cold triggers often lead to what psychologists call "intention-behavior gaps"—those frustrating spaces between what we plan to do and what we actually do. You might feel motivated by that gym billboard, but by the time you get home, that motivation has evaporated.

Hot triggers, on the other hand, create what neuroscientists call "action potentials"—immediate pathways to behavior. When your running shoes are by the door and your workout clothes are laid out, you've essentially removed the gap between intention and action.

Why do cold triggers consistently fail where hot triggers succeed? The answer lies in how our brains process behavioral cues. Every cold trigger is essentially a cognitive check that never gets processed. That billboard advertising a gym? It's a suggestion without substance. The online course you bookmark? A wish without a pathway.

Cold triggers are like unfinished circuits in our neural network. They generate a spark of intention but lack the complete connection needed to trigger action. Your brain receives the signal but finds no immediate route to execution. The result? Motivation evaporates, and the intended behavior never materializes.

Converting these cold triggers into hot triggers becomes a matter of strategic design. It's about creating what I call "action bridges"—those immediate, low-friction pathways that transform passive intentions into active behaviors.

Imagine you want to start a meditation practice. A cold trigger might be downloading a meditation app and leaving it buried among your other apps. A hot trigger? Placing your meditation cushion directly next to your morning coffee maker, with an automation to open the app on your phone at that particular time. Trust me. The success rate difference will be profound.

The key is understanding that your brain doesn't respond to good intentions. It responds to clear, immediate, and low-resistance opportunities for action.

DESIGNING EFFECTIVE TRIGGERS

The key to leveraging the difference between hot and cold triggers lies in deliberately designing your environment to favor hot triggers. It's about creating a landscape where success requires less willpower and more automatic response.

Think about what actually triggers your current habits. Not the actions themselves but the cues that set them in motion. The ping of a notification. The sight of your coffee maker. The feeling of stress. The 3 PM energy crash. These are real triggers—they prompt specific behaviors automatically.

When designing new triggers, specificity is crucial. "After lunch" isn't a trigger; it's a vague time period. But "When I put my lunch plate in the dishwasher" is a precise moment that can reliably cue your next action. The sound of the dishwasher closing becomes your signal to transition into focused work mode.

The most effective triggers are both visible and immediate. Your brain responds to clear "hot" signals, not abstract "cold" concepts. Environmental triggers—things you can see, hear, or touch—tend to be more reliable than mental reminders.

The most potent triggers don't just signal the start of a habit; they create a natural pathway through the entire routine. Think of it as designing a behavioral cascade. When you set out your workout clothes the night before, place your water bottle by them, and queue up your workout playlist, you're not just creating a trigger—you're building a bridge that carries you from intention to action with minimal resistance. Each element becomes both a trigger for the next step and a removal of potential friction points.

Managing Digital Triggers

Our devices present a fantastic paradox when it comes to triggers. The same smartphone that can derail your focus with constant notifications can also become a powerful ally in building better habits.

Digital environments are rich with potential behavioral cues—each notification, app icon, and message alert represents a pathway that can either distract or guide your performance. The key insight is recognizing that you have agency over these digital triggers.

Later in this book, we'll dive deep into specific strategies for optimizing your digital environment. For now, the fundamental principle remains: every ping, notification, or alert is a potential trigger, and you get to decide whether it serves or sabotages your goals.

MANAGING DIGITAL TRIGGERS

Our devices present a fantastic paradox when it comes to triggers. The same smartphone that can derail your focus with constant notifications can also become a powerful ally in building better habits.

Digital environments are rich with potential behavioral cues—each notification, app icon, and message alert represents a pathway that can either distract or guide your performance. The key insight is recognizing that you have agency over these digital triggers.

Later in this book, we'll dive deep into specific strategies for optimizing your digital environment. For now, the fundamental principle remains: every ping, notification, or alert is a potential trigger, and you get to decide whether it serves or sabotages your goals.

BUILDING BETTER DEFAULTS

Now that you understand how triggers initiate behavior, let's explore what happens next. After all, a trigger is just the first domino in this cascade.

Your brain doesn't really care about your good intentions or carefully crafted plans. It cares about efficiency; about turning complex sequences of actions into automated routines that require minimal cognitive effort. This is why some habits seem to run on autopilot while others remain stubbornly resistant to change.

The "decision-maker" upstairs, doesn't distinguish between "good" and "bad" habits at a neural level. It only cares about the strength of the pattern. That morning exercise that energizes your day? Neurologically, it's no different from the social media scroll that derails your focus. Both are simply well-worn neural pathways that your brain has learned to execute automatically.

Complexity is the enemy of consistency. Every additional step in a routine creates another potential point of failure. Those elaborate morning routines promising to transform your life? They look great on paper, but they're almost designed to fail.

Your brain prefers simple, clear sequences. It's like teaching a child to tie their shoes. You break it down into small, manageable steps that flow naturally from one to the next. The same principle applies to building any new habit.

Remember Chris, our digital agency owner? When he first tried implementing deep work sessions, he designed an elaborate system with specific music playlists, perfect lighting conditions, and complex preparation rituals. "I thought more structure meant better results," he admits. Instead, he created so many prerequisites that he rarely got started at all.

The breakthrough came when he simplified his approach. Instead of perfect conditions, he focused on one key sequence: closing unnecessary browser tabs, setting his phone to Do Not Disturb, and opening only the documents needed for his current project. Three steps, no complexity. Within weeks, this simple routine became his automatic signal for focused work.

This is where the power of compound gains becomes evident. Each small action, consistently repeated, creates momentum. Your brain strengthens these neural pathways with every repetition, making the sequence increasingly automatic. It's not about dramatic changes; it's about tiny improvements accumulating over time.

This principle of simplification extends beyond just removing steps—it's about understanding how your brain automates behavior. When you break down any complex habit into its smallest components, you'll find natural connection points where one action flows into the next. These behavioral sequences become stronger with each repetition, like a path becoming more defined with each footstep.

For instance, if you want to develop a consistent exercise habit, don't start with an ambitious hour-long complex routine. Begin with 15 minutes of basic movements you can do anywhere. Once that becomes automatic, you can gradually increase duration or complexity. Think of it like learning to play guitar. You don't start with a face-melting Eddie Van Halen solo; you learn a few basic chords first.

But here's what makes this process truly powerful: your brain's reward system responds to completion, not complexity. Every time you complete a sequence—even a simple one—your brain releases dopamine. This chemical reward strengthens the neural pathway, making it more likely you'll repeat the behavior.

The timing of these rewards matters more than their size. Your brain makes stronger connections between actions and rewards that happen close together in time. This is why waiting for long-term benefits rarely drives consistent behavior. The gap between action and reward is too large for your brain to make a strong connection.

Instead of relying on distant outcomes like "better health" or "increased productivity," build immediate micro-rewards into your habits. After completing your morning planning routine, take a moment to enjoy your favorite coffee. When you finish a focused work block, step outside for fresh air. These small wins compound over time, creating an upward spiral of consistent behavior. Each successful repetition makes the next one more likely, building momentum naturally rather than forcing it through willpower.

Think of it like building blocks. Each small action stacks on the previous one. A client who wanted to improve his sleep hygiene didn't start with a complete bedtime overhaul. He began by just closing his laptop at 9 PM. Once that became automatic, he added a 5-minute stretching routine. Then reading a few pages of a book. Each addition was small, but they combined into a powerful sleep routine that transformed his energy levels.

The critical insight is that your brain doesn't distinguish between impressive-looking habits and simple ones. It only recognizes patterns of consistent behavior. A meticulously planned two-hour morning routine that you abandon after two weeks is far less effective than a simple five-minute ritual you maintain for months.

This approach requires a fundamental shift in perspective. Instead of viewing habit formation as a heroic transformation, see it as a series of incremental, almost imperceptible adjustments. Like a skilled sculptor chipping away at a block of marble, you're gradually revealing the performance potential that already exists within you.

The most successful habit designers understand that sustainability trumps intensity. Your goal isn't to create the most impressive routine, but to create a routine that actually becomes a part of your life.

THE FOUR FOUNDATIONAL ROUTINES

Most people think of habits as individual actions, but real transformation happens when habits are organized into structured routines.

A habit is a single action you repeat, like drinking water in the morning. A routine is a sequence of habits performed in a specific order, like a morning routine that includes drinking water, stretching, and journaling.

Routines reduce decision fatigue and make it easier to stay consistent. Instead of remembering individual habits, you follow the routine as a whole.

Everyone's optimal routine will look different based on their goals, lifestyle, and natural rhythms. A CEO with young children will need different morning patterns than a freelancer who works late. What matters isn't copying someone else's routine, but understanding the fundamental routines that create a foundation for peak performance.

After studying high performers across industries for years, I've noticed a pattern. While the specific details vary widely, most consistently successful individuals structure their days around four key routines. These four foundational routines serve as anchors throughout your day, making everything else easier:

1. *Morning Routine: Prime Your Mind and Body for the Day*

How you start your day determines your energy, focus, and momentum. A well-designed morning routine ensures you're proactive, not reactive, from the start.

Here's my morning routine:

- Cold plunge to wake up.
- 60 minutes of Hatha yoga to get calm and centered (outside if possible for some grounding).
- 30 minutes of journaling writing down what I dreamed about and what I want for my life.
- 20 minutes of affirmations with uplifting music in front of my Red Light Therapy panel.
- 45 minutes of reading to get my mind right for the day while lying on my PEMF mat.
- 7-kilometer jog to toughen up my mind and body.
- 30 minutes to eat and get ready for work.

Just kidding! Of course, I'm joking. This would be absolutely nuts. But believe it or not, this is actually similar to the morning routine that a well-known productivity "expert" proudly shared with his audience.

Don't get me wrong. It's quite easy to fall into this trap of spending 2 hours trying to do the perfect morning routine. I've been guilty of this myself.

And even nowadays, I regularly do some of the things listed above, and my life is better because of it. However, doing it all during the morning is a waste of our most precious and peak cognitive hours trying to "get ready or optimized" to work.

The truth is that 90% of morning routines shown on the internet are designed as a perverse form of procrastination. They create the illusion that you're making progress because they feel good. But there's no actual work being done.

For most high performers, it's more productive to keep the morning routine focused and efficient, saving these wellness practices for other times of day when your brain isn't at its cognitive peak.

Take the approach that entrepreneur Marie Forleo advocates with her "Create Before You Consume" principle. She discovered that structuring her morning to prioritize creation rather than consumption dramatically improved her productivity and focus. Instead of starting her day by checking messages and consuming information, she begins by creating—working on her most important project before allowing any external inputs to influence her thinking.

This principle can be adapted to fit various morning routines, whether they're wellness-focused or work-focused. The key is intentionality—ensuring that whatever you do first serves your priorities rather than someone else's agenda.

Here are a few components to consider for your Morning Routine:

- Hydration: Start with water (bonus: add electrolytes or a pinch of salt)
- Movement: Light stretching, a short walk, or quick mobility work
- Mental Clarity: Journaling, meditation, or visualization
- Focus Primer: Review your key priorities for the day
- Resilience Booster: A challenge that strengthens discipline (e.g., cold shower, breathwork)

But remember, you don't need all of these. Pick what makes sense to you.

Take Alex Hormozi—coffee and straight to work. Tim Ferriss? Making his bed, meditation, journaling, then deep work. Your morning routine should support your goals, not slow you down.

If you want something more structured, consider Hal Elrod's popular "Miracle Morning" routine. It consists of six 5-minute activities, remembered by the acronym SAVERS:

- Silence (meditation or prayer).
- Affirmations (positive statements about oneself).
- Visualization (imagining achieving goals).
- Exercise (physical activity).
- Reading (educational or inspirational material).
- Scribing (journaling).

While this framework has helped millions, remember—the best routine is the one that aligns with your primary goal:

Business focused? Prioritize your Needle Mover Tasks (NMTs). Fitness focused? Lead with exercise. Spiritually focused? Start with meditation and visualization.

Focus on what matters to you.

2. Workday Startup Routine: Transition into Deep Work Mode

This will change substantially depending on what you do and your particular goals. For some, it may be merged into their morning routine. Its goal is to transition you from "personal mode" to "work mode," ensuring you're mentally prepared and focused.

Most people start their workday by checking emails and reacting to urgent (but unimportant) tasks. This kills momentum before real work begins. A Workday Startup Routine ensures you start with intention.

Key Elements to consider:

- Review Goals for the Day: Review the key priorities and tasks defined the day before.
- Organize Workspace: Ensure everything needed is ready and reduce possible distractions.
- First Deep Work Block: Use the fresh energy in the morning to focus deeply.

As mentioned before, for some, this blends into their morning routine. Others start this routine after morning responsibilities like family or exercise. The key is to begin work with clarity, not chaos.

3. Workday Shutdown Routine: Mentally Log Off and Reset

A workday shutdown routine is crucial to ensure separation between work and personal life, reducing anxiety and enhancing recovery.

Most of us have experienced finishing work but feeling mentally stuck in "work mode." You struggle to be present with family, keep thinking about unfinished tasks, and feel guilty when relaxing yet overwhelmed when working. This mental carryover doesn't just affect your evening—it compromises your recovery and sets you up for decreased performance the next day.

The shutdown routine solves this problem by creating a clear mental separation between work and personal time. Start by reviewing your day—what did you accomplish and what needs adjustment? Then, plan tomorrow's priorities, making sure to define your most important assignments. Take time to close out any lingering tasks, answering final messages, and tying up loose ends.

The physical act of shutting down is equally important. Close your laptop, turn off notifications, and engage in a disconnecting activity like a workout, hobby, or time with family. This complete disconnect signals to your brain that work mode is over.

This small habit reduces stress and ensures you don't carry unfinished work into your evening. Think of it as creating a mental boundary that allows you to fully engage with your personal life and properly recover for tomorrow.

4. Evening Routine: The Gateway to High-Performance Recovery

Peak performance isn't just about working harder—it's about recovering better. A strong evening routine is the foundation of high-quality sleep, which impacts cognitive function, mood, and productivity.

Your evening routine sets the stage for how well your brain and body recover during sleep. While most people understand the importance of sleep, they often sabotage their recovery by how they spend their evening hours. Scrolling through social media until midnight, answering work emails from bed, or binge-watching shows might feel relaxing, but these habits actively work against your body's natural wind-down processes.

An effective evening routine focuses on transitioning from a high-energy work state to a relaxed recovery state. Start with a digital detox, include some reflection and gratitude, and consider light movement or reading to help your mind wind down. Most importantly, maintain a consistent sleep schedule to optimize your circadian rhythm.

We'll dive deeper into the science of sleep and recovery in the next chapter, but for now, understand that your evening routine is crucial for sustained high performance.

Remember, these aren't rigid prescriptions but flexible frameworks. The key is finding versions of these routines that align with your goals, schedule, and natural rhythms. Start small, focusing on consistency over complexity. As these routines become automatic, you'll find yourself spending less energy on decisions and more on what truly matters.

Now that we understand these foundational routines, let's explore how to implement them effectively in your life, stack them with existing habits, and create the environment that ensures their success.

ADVANCED HABIT IMPLEMENTATION

The difference between knowing how habits work and making them work for you often comes down to implementation. Let's explore the advanced strategies that turn understanding into lasting change.

The Power of Habit Stacking

Your existing habits are like well-worn paths in your brain. Instead of creating entirely new neural pathways, you can leverage these existing routes by attaching new habits to them. This process, known as habit stacking, makes building new behaviors significantly easier.

Think about your current morning routine. You probably perform certain actions in the same sequence without thinking. Perhaps turning off your alarm, using the bathroom, and brushing your teeth. Each action flows naturally into the next. By identifying these existing sequences, you can strategically insert new habits where they're most likely to stick.

For example, instead of creating a new trigger to review your calendar, stack it with your first cup of coffee: "After I take my first sip of coffee, I will review today's three most important tasks." Or "After I put my phone on the charger each night, I will meditate to relax for sleep."

The power lies in attaching new behaviors to reliable anchors in your day—those moments that already happen consistently without fail, like brushing your teeth, making your bed, or starting the coffee machine.

Combining and Overlapping Habits

While habit stacking creates sequential patterns, habit combining allows you to maximize your time by layering compatible behaviors. This isn't multitasking—it's strategic alignment of complementary activities.

Think about your morning routine. Instead of treating exercise and learning as separate activities, you might listen to industry podcasts during your workout. Or combine your team check-ins with a walking meeting, simultaneously addressing both movement and management needs. The key is to identify habits that can naturally coexist without diminishing each other's effectiveness.

But here's where most people go wrong: they try to combine habits that compete for the same mental or physical resources. Writing emails while in a meeting, for instance, typically compromises both activities. The secret is to pair habits that use different types of attention or energy.

Lowering the Activation Barrier

World-renowned choreographer Twyla Tharp revealed a powerful insight about habit formation: the hardest part is often just starting. Her solution? The 2-Minute Rule. If a habit takes less than two minutes to start, you're far more likely to do it.

This isn't about completing the entire habit in two minutes. It's about making the initiation so easy that your brain doesn't have time to resist. Want to write for an hour? Commit to opening your document and writing one sentence. Need to work out? Just put on your gym clothes. The momentum of starting often carries you through the full activity.

The Goldilocks Rule

When it comes to building lasting habits, there's a fascinating paradox at play. Most people either aim too high, setting themselves up for frustration and failure, or too low, creating habits so easy they provide no sense of achievement. The secret lies in what behavioral scientists call the Goldilocks Rule—finding that sweet spot where challenge meets capability.

Think about learning a new language. If you start by attempting to read complex literature, you'll likely give up in frustration. But if you stick to basic greetings for too long, you'll lose interest. The magic happens when you push just slightly beyond your current level—perhaps learning one new phrase each day, then gradually increasing complexity as your confidence grows.

This principle applies to every habit you're trying to build. A client of mine wanted to establish a meditation practice but kept failing at her goal of 30 minutes daily. When we adjusted the target to 5 minutes—challenging enough to require commitment but not so daunting it triggered resistance—she not only maintained the habit but naturally extended the duration as her practice developed.

The key is to start where you are, not where you think you should be. New to strength training? Master bodyweight exercises before touching heavy weights. Want to develop a writing habit? Begin with a few sentences rather than forcing yourself to fill pages. These seemingly modest beginnings create the foundation for sustainable growth.

The Bamboo Effect

Most people abandon their habits too soon, quitting right before their breakthrough moment. This is where understanding the Bamboo Effect becomes crucial for lasting personal transformation.

Imagine a Chinese bamboo farmer meticulously nurturing seemingly barren soil for years. Nothing appears to change. No sprouts, no growth, just patient cultivation. Then, in the fifth year, something extraordinary happens: the bamboo shoots up 90 feet in just six weeks. But here's the fascinating part: during those seemingly inactive years, the plant was quietly building an elaborate underground root system, establishing the foundation for explosive growth.

Your habits follow an identical pattern.

In the beginning, you might feel like you're spinning your wheels. You meditate daily but don't feel more centered. You write consistently but haven't produced anything remarkable. You exercise regularly but don't see dramatic physical changes. This is precisely where most people surrender—during what I call the "underground phase" of habit formation.

The critical insight? Progress isn't always visible, but it's always happening.

Research in neuroplasticity reveals that habit formation is less about dramatic external changes and more about subtle internal rewiring. Each repetition, even when it feels inconsequential, is strengthening neural pathways, creating microscopic shifts that eventually culminate in significant transformation.

This is why tracking habits matters more than measuring immediate outcomes. Just as the bamboo farmer focuses on consistent care rather than visible growth, your focus should be on maintaining the habit, trusting that results will emerge when your foundational infrastructure is robust enough.

Staying consistent during this "underground phase" requires more than motivation. It demands a fundamental understanding that meaningful change is a cumulative process, not an overnight miracle. That being said, let's explore the most powerful approaches behavioral science has validated for maintaining long-term consistency.

Implementation Intentions

One particularly powerful strategy in habit formation is what behavioral scientists call Implementation Intentions. These are precise plans that specify exactly when, where, and how you'll perform a specific behavior. Think of it as the difference between a vague wish and a strategic blueprint.

Consider this exercise study that revealed the profound impact of implementation planning. When participants simply tracked their exercise, only 31% stuck to their routine. Adding coaching about exercise benefits barely moved the needle, pushing adherence to just 33%. But something remarkable happened when participants wrote specific Implementation Intentions detailing exactly when, where, and how they would exercise— adherence skyrocketed to an impressive 90%.

Why such a dramatic difference?

When you form an Implementation Intention, you're essentially pre-deciding your behavior, eliminating the critical gap between intention and action. Instead of relying on motivation or hoping you'll remember to do something, you're creating what neuroscientists call an "action trigger"—a precise cue that bypasses conscious decision-making.

The magic lies in specificity. Compare these statements:

- "I want to exercise more"
- "Every Tuesday and Thursday at 6 AM, I will do a 30-minute strength training session in my home gym, immediately after drinking my morning coffee"

See the difference? The second statement leaves no room for ambiguity or negotiation with yourself.

Implementation Intentions work because they leverage our brain's natural preference for clear, executable instructions. By removing decision friction, you transform a potentially overwhelming task into an automatic response.

The Power of Feedback Loops

While Implementation Intentions tell you when and where to act, feedback loops determine whether those intentions become lasting habits. Think of it like a thermostat that constantly monitors and adjusts room temperature. Your habits need similar monitoring systems to stay on track and evolve.

The science here is compelling: A University of California study found that people who tracked their food choices lost twice as much weight as those who didn't. But it wasn't just the tracking itself; it was how immediate feedback transformed their relationship with the behavior.

Your brain craves evidence of progress, much like a video game player watching their score increase. This creates what psychologists call a "progress narrative"—a story of your development that becomes a powerful motivator, especially during the initial "underground phase" of habit formation when external results aren't yet visible.

When it comes to creating effective tracking systems, different methods serve distinct psychological needs. Visual trackers, like marking X's on a calendar, tap into your brain's pattern recognition systems, making abstract progress tangible. This is the principle behind Jerry Seinfeld's famous "Don't Break the Chain" method, where marking a calendar each day he wrote jokes created a compelling visual incentive to maintain his streak. A similar approach was used by Trent Dyrsmid, a young stockbroker who credited his success to a simple system—moving paperclips from one jar to another after each successful sales call. This small, physical feedback loop made his progress feel immediate and tangible.

Digital tools offer another powerful approach, leveraging our desire for achievement metrics while automating the data collection process. But perhaps their greatest strength lies in their objectivity. They show us exactly what we're doing, not what we think we're doing. This is why fitness trackers, habit-tracking apps, and even simple spreadsheets can be so effective. They replace subjective perception with clear, irrefutable data.

Accountability partnerships also add a crucial social dimension to habit tracking. When we share our commitments with others, we activate powerful social circuits in our brains that make us more likely to follow through. A good accountability partner doesn't just check your progress; they provide perspective and create positive pressure that keeps you moving forward.

Finally, celebration rituals play a vital role in reinforcing habits through positive association. These aren't just empty celebrations; they're strategic moments that strengthen neural pathways and mark meaningful milestones in your journey. The key is to make these celebrations proportional to the achievement. A small reward for daily consistency, a larger one for reaching significant milestones.

The underlying principle across all these methods is making the invisible visible. When you can see your progress (or lack thereof), you're far more likely to maintain momentum. The best tracking system isn't necessarily the most sophisticated one. It's the one you'll actually use consistently. Choose methods that align with your natural tendencies and lifestyle, remembering that you're not just collecting data. You're creating a feedback system that transforms intentions into automatic behaviors.

BREAKING BAD HABITS

Just as we discovered with the Elimination Protocol in our task management, sometimes the most potent change comes not from adding more, but from strategically removing what holds us back. This principle applies perfectly to habit transformation.

When I first encountered Darren Hardy's work in "The Compound Effect," I was struck by the elegant simplicity of his approach to breaking bad habits. While many experts offer complex systems for behavior change, Hardy understood that simplicity leads to consistency, and consistency leads to results.

First, identify the specific habit you want to eliminate. Be precise. Instead of saying, "I want to stop wasting time," specify, "I want to stop mindlessly scrolling social media during work hours."

Next, locate your triggers using the 5 Ws: Why, what, who, when, and where. For instance, you might discover you reach for your phone whenever you feel stuck on a challenging task (why), during mid-afternoon energy dips (when), especially while sitting at your desk (where).

The third step is environmental design. Systematically removing these triggers from your environment. This isn't about willpower; it's about making unwanted behaviors harder to perform. Just as we removed unnecessary tasks from our schedule, we need to remove unnecessary temptations from our space.

Fourth, and perhaps most crucial, substitute the bad habit with a positive one that provides similar rewards. If social media scrolling gives you a mental break and a hit of novelty, you might replace it with a five-minute walking meditation or quick stretching routine. The key is matching the new behavior to the underlying need.

Finally, make a strategic decision about your approach: gradual reduction or complete elimination. Some habits respond better to immediate cessation—like leaving drugs. Others require a more gradual approach to prevent rebound effects.

Think of it like pruning a garden. You wouldn't just randomly cut away at branches; you'd identify exactly what needs to be removed, understand why it grew there in the first place, and ensure the remaining plants have what they need to thrive. The same principle applies to habits. Strategic elimination creates space for positive growth.

This straightforward approach aligns perfectly with what we've learned about performance optimization. Just as we reclaimed hours in our schedule by eliminating low-value tasks, we can reclaim mental energy and focus by eliminating low-value habits. The goal isn't perfection—it's progress toward a more intentional way of operating.

LONG-TERM SUCCESS

Even the most sophisticated machines require regular maintenance, and your habits demand the same systematic upkeep to continue serving your performance goals. Success comes through three key practices that transform fragile behaviors into robust systems.

Monthly Reflection Practices

The most successful performers I've worked with share one common trait: they systematically review and refine their habits. This isn't casual introspection; it's structured evaluation. At the end of each month, they assess three critical aspects of their habit systems: what's working, what's not, and what needs adjustment.

During these monthly reviews, you're looking for specific patterns. Which habits are becoming automatic? Which ones still require conscious effort? Most importantly, which habits are creating the most significant impact on your performance? This data-driven approach allows you to focus your energy where it matters most.

Progressive Upgrades

Once habits become stable, most people make the mistake of settling into comfort. But high performers understand that habits, like muscles, need progressive overload to grow stronger. This doesn't mean making habits more complex. Often, it means making them more refined or efficient.

Take your morning routine, for instance. Once the basic sequence becomes automatic, you might upgrade it by adjusting the timing, adding complementary behaviors, or increasing the quality of execution. The key is to make these upgrades gradual and intentional, never sacrificing consistency for intensity.

Contingency Planning

Life will inevitably throw obstacles at your habits. The people who maintain consistent habits aren't those who magically avoid disruptions—they're the ones who strategically plan for them. This is where the "if-then" protocol becomes your secret weapon.

Develop at least two backup plans for every core habit: one for handling minor disruptions like schedule changes, and another for navigating major interruptions such as travel or illness. These backup plans aren't about giving yourself permission to skip habits, but rather creating modified versions that preserve the essence of your habit while adapting to your circumstances.

These maintenance strategies collectively transform simple behaviors into resilient systems that evolve with you. Month by month, review by review, adjustment by adjustment, you build a foundation of consistency that can withstand challenges and sustain high performance over time.

FROM PLANNING TO BIOLOGY

Throughout this chapter, we've explored the psychological architecture of habits—how they form, how they stick, and how they evolve. We've seen that sustainable habits aren't built on willpower, but on systems that align with our natural tendencies. The frameworks we've covered provide a practical approach to making habits stick:

We examined the science of the Habit Loop, discovered the power of Elite Habits that create cascade effects across your life, and explored how to design effective triggers that make desired behaviors almost automatic. We broke down foundational routines, implementation strategies like habit stacking, and techniques like the Goldilocks Rule that balance challenge with capability.

But here's where our journey takes a fascinating turn. While these psychological frameworks provide the blueprint for habit formation, biology determines our capacity to execute. You can have the perfect habit systems designed, but if your physiology isn't optimized, you'll constantly fight an uphill battle.

RESEARCH & RESOURCES

As always, please visit the Holistic Performance Resource Hub to access the research and additional materials mentioned in this chapter.

To do so, go to hplink.org/resourcehub or scan the QR code below.

LOVING THE BOOK SO FAR?

I hope you're enjoying your holistic performance journey! As you're making your way through these pages, I'd love to hear about your experience so far.

As an independent author without the backing of a major publisher, early reviews are incredibly valuable in helping this book reach others who might benefit from these ideas. Unlike big publishing houses with massive marketing departments, independent work like this spreads primarily through reader support.

Would you take 60 seconds to share your thoughts about what you've read so far? Even a brief review mentioning which concepts are resonating with you most can make a tremendous difference.

What's exciting you? Which ideas are you most eager to implement? Your early impressions help other potential readers discover if this approach might work for them too.

Simply scan the QR code below to leave your review. You can always update it later when you've finished the book.

Thank you for your support—it means the world to me!

hplink.org/review

CHAPTER 7

BIOLOGY OPTIMIZER

"To keep the body in good health is a duty, otherwise we shall not be able to keep our mind strong and clear."

– Buddha

Remember that electric car analogy from earlier? The one where everyone was trying to upgrade the tires and add fancy features while ignoring the dead battery? Well, we're about to pop the hood and really understand what powers your performance engine.

For decades, the personal development world has been like a gym full of people doing bicep curls while completely ignoring leg day. "Mindset is everything!" they proclaimed. "Just think positive thoughts!" they insisted. "Visualize your way to success!" they promised. And sure, like those impressive biceps, the results looked good... for a while.

However, as we discovered in Chapter 2's exploration of performance struggles, something fundamental was missing. While everyone was busy downloading the latest productivity apps and fine-tuning their morning affirmations, their biological batteries were quietly draining. It's like trying to run a marathon while breathing through a straw. No amount of positive thinking will get you to the finish line if your body can't deliver oxygen to your muscles.

This brings us back to the critical distinction between extractive versus regenerative approaches to performance. That insight from our introduction becomes even more crucial now. Because here's what nobody in the productivity space wants to admit: you can't shortcut your biology with quick fixes. While true biological optimization is absolutely possible, you can't strong-arm your neurochemistry into submission with just willpower and a well-organized Notion dashboard. Your body has fundamental needs that no amount of productivity hacks can override.

Enter what I call Physiological Performance Insufficiencies (PPIs)—the hidden handbrakes on your achievement vehicle. These aren't just random energy dips or occasional brain fog moments. They're systematic breakdowns in your body's performance machinery, created by our modern lifestyle and exacerbated by traditional productivity advice that treats humans like computers that just need better programming.

Think about it: When was the last time you felt genuinely energized throughout your entire workday? Not the artificial buzz of your third espresso, but real, sustainable energy? If you're like most people I work with, you probably can't remember. That's not because you lack discipline or need another productivity course. It's because your biological systems are crying out for optimization.

Here's a truth that might sting a bit: You can't outthink a bad physiology. Period. Let's be real. While we're busy studying the habits of ultra-successful entrepreneurs, what we're often seeing is just the tip of the iceberg. Behind every 'superhuman' CEO working 80-hour weeks is usually a small army handling the real workload. But instead of acknowledging this reality, we burn ourselves out trying to match an illusion.

This reality has been decades in the making. While the personal development industry perfected the art of mindset optimization, our bodies were quietly adapting to a world they weren't designed for. Consider this: Our ancient ancestors never had to process 34GB of information daily while sitting motionless under artificial lights, surviving on processed foods and caffeine. Yet here we are, expecting our stone-age biology to handle space-age demands.

The manifestations of these PPIs are as diverse as they are devastating. It starts subtly—maybe you notice you can't focus as long as you used to, or your energy crashes harder after lunch. Then it escalates: chronic procrastination despite strong motivation, decision fatigue that sets in earlier each day, memory gaps that can't be explained by stress alone. These aren't character flaws or mindset issues; they're biological signals screaming for attention.

What makes PPIs particularly insidious is how they masquerade as psychological challenges. When your blood sugar crashes, it feels like a willpower problem. When inflammation clouds your thinking, it presents as procrastination. When your hormones are imbalanced, it shows up as inconsistent motivation. No wonder the quick-fix industry is booming. We're treating the symptoms while ignoring the cause.

The solution isn't another Tony Robbins seminar. As we discussed in the introduction, we need to shift from an extractive model of performance to a regenerative one. This means understanding that every cognitive output has a biological input. Every mental breakthrough requires a physiological foundation. Every peak performance state is, at its core, a biological phenomenon.

UNDERSTANDING YOUR BIOCHEMICAL ORCHESTRA

Think of your brain's biochemistry like a sophisticated symphony orchestra. You don't need to be a musical expert to enjoy the performance, but understanding there's more happening than just "music" can help you appreciate why some concerts move you to tears while others leave you cold.

That's where the **ASCENDO Framework** comes in—an acronym for the seven key biochemical players that drive your performance: Acetylcholine, Serotonin, Cortisol, Endorphins, Norepinephrine, Dopamine, and Oxytocin. Don't worry. I'm not expecting you to memorize these or start micro-managing your neurotransmitters (that would be about as effective as trying to conduct the orchestra by controlling each musician's breathing). As we progress through this and the next chapter, you'll see how our recommended practices naturally optimize these elements in concert.

Let's meet your internal performance team:

Acetylcholine—Your Cognitive Conductor

When this neurotransmitter is optimized, you experience laser-sharp focus, quick learning, and what I call "cognitive flow"—those beautiful moments when complex problems untangle themselves in your mind. But when it's depleted, you might find yourself reading the same paragraph three times or forgetting why you walked into a room (again). Common symptoms of low acetylcholine include brain fog, poor memory retention, and difficulty learning new information.

The good news? Boosting acetylcholine is simpler than you might think. Foods rich in choline, like eggs, fish, and nuts, provide your brain with the raw materials it needs to produce this crucial neurotransmitter. Engaging in mentally stimulating activities—from strategic thinking to learning new skills—helps optimize its utilization. You'll see these elements woven throughout our upcoming recommendations, working alongside other optimization strategies to enhance your overall cognitive performance.

Serotonin—Your Emotional Stabilizer

Often called the "happiness molecule," serotonin is more like your brain's emotional thermostat. When balanced, you experience steady confidence, emotional resilience, and that rare feeling of being unshakably centered. Low serotonin shows up as mood swings, negative thought spirals, and even that dreaded afternoon slump that has you reaching for sugary snacks.

Optimizing serotonin involves a beautiful blend of sunlight exposure (yes, that morning walk you've been putting off), specific proteins containing tryptophan (like turkey, salmon, and seeds), and—surprise—regular movement.

Cortisol—Your Energy Regulator

Despite its reputation as the "stress hormone," cortisol is actually your body's built-in energy management system. When working correctly, it follows a natural daily rhythm—high in the morning to get you moving, gradually decreasing throughout the day. But when dysregulated (hello, modern life), you might feel wired but tired, experience random energy crashes, or lie awake at night with racing thoughts.

Supporting healthy cortisol patterns isn't complicated, but it is crucial. A diet rich in whole foods, especially citrus fruits, berries, fatty fish, and leafy greens (while limiting sugar and caffeine), helps maintain optimal levels. Regular exercise, quality sleep, and mindfulness practices like meditation naturally regulate this crucial hormone.

Endorphins—Your Natural High

Think of endorphins as your body's internal reward system 2.0. They're not just about runner's high. These molecules create that sense of accomplishment and well-being that makes challenging tasks feel worthwhile. When endorphin systems are optimized, you handle stress better, recover faster, and maintain motivation through challenging projects.

The beauty of endorphin optimization lies in its simplicity: regular movement (not necessarily intense exercise), laughing, and even certain spicy foods can trigger their release. These natural highs become part of your daily experience through the practices we'll explore together.

Norepinephrine—Your Alertness Amplifier

This is your brain's natural energizer. When norepinephrine is flowing optimally, you experience heightened awareness, quick reflexes, and that perfect level of arousal that makes you feel alive and engaged. Low levels often manifest as brain fog, low energy, and difficulty maintaining attention—even during tasks you typically enjoy.

The key to optimizing norepinephrine lies in strategic physical activity (especially in the morning), cold exposure (yes, those cold showers have real benefits), and proper protein intake. B-vitamin-rich foods like lean meats, legumes, and whole grains provide the building blocks your body needs to produce this crucial neurotransmitter.

Dopamine—Your Motivation Director

Forget what you've heard about dopamine being just about pleasure—it's actually your brain's motivation and reward predictor. When balanced, dopamine helps you stay focused on long-term goals, find satisfaction in meaningful work, and maintain drive through challenging projects. Dysregulated dopamine can lead to procrastination, lack of satisfaction in achievements, and difficulty initiating tasks.

Supporting healthy dopamine function starts with establishing a healthy reward system: regular exercise, a protein-rich diet, and most importantly, creating what neuroscientists call "positive anticipation" through achievable goals and meaningful work. Tyrosine-rich foods like eggs, fish, and nuts provide the raw materials your brain needs.

Oxytocin—Your Connection Catalyst

Often overlooked in performance discussions, oxytocin is crucial for sustainable success. This "love molecule" doesn't just facilitate social bonds. It helps regulate stress, enhance emotional resilience, and improve cognitive function. When oxytocin systems are optimized, you communicate more effectively, build stronger relationships, and recover better from challenges.

Boosting oxytocin is surprisingly straightforward: meaningful social interactions, physical touch (even just a handshake or pat on the back), and activities that create genuine connection all stimulate its release. Even spending time with pets can boost oxytocin levels—there's a reason successful people often talk about how their dogs keep them grounded.

YOUR BIOCHEMICAL PERFORMANCE PATTERNS

Looking at these seven elements, a clear pattern emerges: while each plays a unique role, they share common optimization pathways. Notice how certain fundamentals—quality nutrition, proper sleep, regular exercise, mindfulness practices, and meaningful social connections—keep appearing?

This is actually great news. It means you don't need to micromanage each neurotransmitter or stress about specific biochemical pathways. Instead, by focusing on these core lifestyle elements in a systematic way, you naturally optimize your entire biochemical orchestra.

Think of it like this: every time you exercise, you're not just boosting endorphins—you're also regulating cortisol, increasing dopamine, and supporting acetylcholine production. When you get quality sleep, you're simultaneously balancing cortisol, supporting serotonin production, and allowing norepinephrine to regulate appropriately.

This brings us to our next challenge: understanding how our modern environment impacts these natural optimization patterns, and more importantly, what we can do about it.

BUILDING YOUR BIOLOGICAL FOUNDATION

Now that we understand how our biochemical orchestra works and how modern life disrupts it, we face an uncomfortable truth: fixing your biology isn't easy. Everything we've discussed—from acetylcholine production to dopamine regulation—depends on having the right biological raw materials, and what comes next might challenge your current lifestyle.

Let's be honest. Some of the nutrition strategies and lifestyle changes we're about to discuss might feel like personal attacks on your current habits. They might question your daily routines or push against the comforts you've grown attached to. But if this wasn't crucial for your performance, I wouldn't bring it up. This isn't about judgment; it's about potential.

Ask yourself: how badly do you want to perform at your peak? You might think you want certain achievements, but are you in love with the idea of success, or are you willing to make the changes success requires?

Consider how much potential income, opportunity, and impact you're leaving on the table by staying comfortable with your current habits. You have far more capacity than you realize, but unlocking it requires stepping out of your comfort zone and embracing necessary changes.

Ready to take that step? Let's begin with the foundation of all high performance: feeding your biochemical success.

THE FUEL OF SUCCESS

While we've explored how our bodies and minds operate as integrated performance systems, there's one foundational element we haven't yet addressed—the fuel that powers it all. Think of this as the most fundamental layer of your performance architecture: before we can optimize output, we need to ensure we're providing the correct input.

The reality is sobering: In the United States alone, 43% of workers report being too tired to function effectively on the job. And while this specific statistic comes from a single country, fatigue and energy depletion have become universal challenges in our modern work environments. This widespread exhaustion isn't just about lack of sleep—it's a symptom of a more profound crisis in how we approach performance optimization.

The scientific evidence remains clear: research consistently demonstrates that our physical condition directly impacts our cognitive function, affecting everything from attention and executive function to decision-making and verbal learning. This isn't about judgment; it's about understanding the fundamental connection between our physical state and our mental capabilities, a biological reality that transcends geographical boundaries.

When we look deeper at this connection between physical health and cognitive performance, multiple factors emerge. While research shows that excess body weight correlates with decreased mental function, this is just one visible aspect of a much larger picture. The truth is that health neglect in any form—regardless of your size or appearance—leads to a critical performance inhibitor: inflammation. This is perhaps the most insidious aspect of poor health habits. Because while obesity is visible, inflammation works as a hidden performance drain.

Even individuals within healthy weight ranges can suffer from inflammation due to lifestyle choices that disregard overall well-being. When your body is fighting inflammation, it's not concerned with helping you achieve your goals or maximize your potential. Instead, it's directing precious resources toward addressing what it perceives as immediate threats to survival. Inflammation stealthily undermines cognitive functions and physical vitality, affecting everything from mental clarity to energy levels.

Research consistently shows that high performers typically maintain lower levels of inflammation, facilitating sharper cognitive functions and sustained energy levels—key components of exceptional performance. Your brain's ability to focus, process information, and make decisions depends entirely on the biological environment you create through your nutrition choices.

What's particularly striking is how this connection is often overlooked in the pursuit of peak performance. We'll invest thousands in coaching programs, spend countless hours optimizing our habits, and chase breakthrough techniques, all while ignoring the biological foundation that makes these optimizations possible. It's like trying to build a skyscraper without first ensuring the ground beneath it can support the structure.

Disclaimer

Before we dive deeper into optimizing your biological performance, let me be clear about something important: Everything you're about to read is based on scientific research and real-world experience, but it's meant for educational purposes only. While I'll share powerful strategies for enhancing your performance through nutrition and lifestyle changes, none of this should be taken as medical advice. Always consult with qualified healthcare professionals about your specific situation, especially before making significant changes to your diet or lifestyle.

This exploration of health's impact on performance isn't meant to shame or judge anyone's personal choices. Instead, it's an invitation to understand how our biological foundation directly influences our capacity to achieve and sustain peak performance. Think of it as a practical toolkit for optimization, not a prescription.

THE PERFECTIONISM PARADOX

Let me share something that fundamentally changed my approach to performance optimization. A couple of years ago, I found myself caught up in the perfectionism culture that dominates the world of biohacking. Like many biohackers, I was constantly chasing the next breakthrough, adding more elements to my routine, getting excited about each "shiny new toy"—while ironically, at times, overlooking the fundamentals.

This hit home when I met a couple at a biohacking conference who had invested over $200,000 in cutting-edge optimization technology over just two years. Their home was a showcase of the latest biohacking equipment—a PEMF machine that cost more than my car, a cold plunge tub that would make Wim Hof cry of joy, and a medical-grade hyperbaric chamber that looked like it could survive a Mars mission. Yet despite all this sophisticated technology and their religious dedication to becoming super-biohackers, they were still eating the same processed junk that got them into trouble in the first place.

Let that sink in for a moment. All that investment in cutting-edge technology while ignoring the most basic upgrade of all: their food. What was the point of biohacking their butts off for two years if they remained exactly where they started? Their story perfectly illustrated a crucial question: What's the value of chasing all these shiny advanced toys if we're ignoring the basic principles of biology?

This experience fundamentally shaped how I approach biological optimization. Rather than chasing every new intervention, I've learned to view human performance like a pyramid, with each layer supporting everything above it. And at the base of this pyramid sits something far less exciting than PEMF machines or hyperbaric chambers: nutrition.

I know, I know—nutrition isn't the sexiest biohack. But here's what's fascinating: when you look at the ASCENDO framework we discussed earlier, almost all those performance-driving neurochemicals are profoundly influenced by what you eat and when you eat it. It's the foundation that either amplifies or undermines every other optimization strategy.

This is where cellular and metabolic performance comes into play. Think of your cells as tiny power plants. They're responsible for your overall energy production (yes, including brain power) and have systemic implications through your hormonal system. When these basic power plants aren't functioning optimally, no amount of advanced biohacking can compensate.

On a practical level, there are just three fundamental aspects of nutrition that drive 80% of your cellular performance:

- Quantity: How much you eat.
- Quality: What you eat.
- Timing: When you eat.

THE BIOLOGY OF NUTRITION AND PERFORMANCE

Your cellular power plants aren't operating in isolation. They're part of an intricate network that connects every system in your body. At the heart of this network lies what scientists call the gut-brain axis, a sophisticated communication system that directly influences your cognitive performance.

Think of this connection like your body's internet—a vast network of neural pathways and chemical signals that constantly transmit information between your digestive system and your brain. This isn't just some minor biological subsystem; it's the backbone of your performance infrastructure. Your digestive tract serves as one of your body's primary lines of defense, protecting your brain from potentially harmful compounds while ensuring proper nutrient absorption.

When this communication highway is functioning optimally, you experience sustained mental clarity, stable energy levels, strong stress resilience, consistent motivation, and enhanced cognitive processing. But when this system becomes compromised, the effects cascade throughout your entire body.

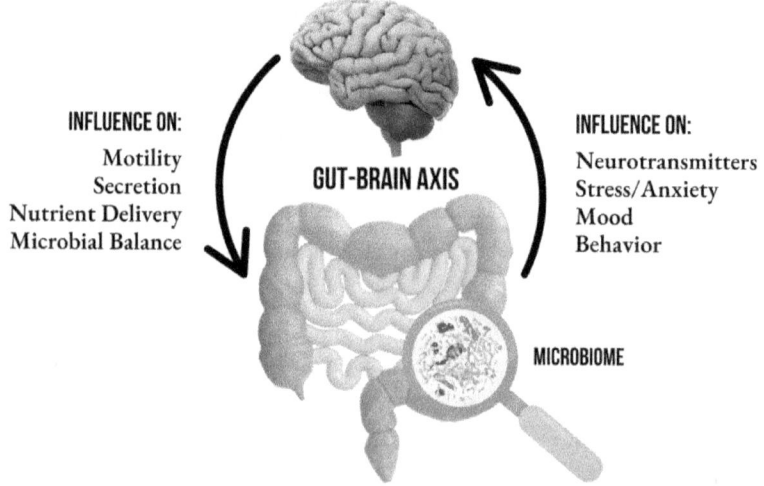

INFLUENCE ON:
Motility
Secretion
Nutrient Delivery
Microbial Balance

GUT-BRAIN AXIS

INFLUENCE ON:
Neurotransmitters
Stress/Anxiety
Mood
Behavior

MICROBIOME

Here's what makes this connection so crucial. Damage to your intestinal barrier, what scientists call "leaky gut," triggers a sequence of events that can devastate your performance. When harmful compounds breach this barrier, they trigger systemic inflammation, leading to autoimmune responses. This inflammation doesn't stay localized; it travels throughout your body, eventually compromising your blood-brain barrier—essentially creating a "leaky brain."

The results are predictable and devastating. Brain fog descends, memory becomes unreliable, headaches become frequent, and mood swings intensify. Many high performers mistake these symptoms for everyday stress or fatigue, but they're actually signs of a deeper biological dysfunction.

But here's where our modern world throws a wrench in the works: The Industrial Revolution didn't just transform our cities and workplaces—it fundamentally altered our relationship with food in ways that directly attack this crucial gut-brain connection. What started as innovations to feed a growing population has evolved into a systematic destruction of our biological infrastructure.

This transformation of our food supply wasn't a single event but a cascade of changes, each more devastating to our biology than the last. It began with the industrialization of agriculture in the late 1800s. These developments were celebrated as progress—higher crop yields and more abundant food—yet they actually marked the beginning of systematic nutrient depletion. As industrial farming practices stripped our soils of minerals, farmers turned to chemical fertilizers and pesticides. These chemicals, along with the later introduction of GMO crops, didn't just change how we grow food. They fundamentally altered our relationship with it. Heavy metals accumulated in our soil and water, while our bodies' natural detox pathways became increasingly overwhelmed by this constant chemical assault.

Then came the post-war boom of the 1950s, when the food industry began converting wartime preservation technologies into consumer products. Chemical preservatives, artificial additives, and industrial processing methods—originally developed for military efficiency—found their way into our daily bread. These weren't just convenient innovations; they were direct assaults on our gut-brain axis. Try this experiment: leave a modern processed snack outside for weeks. It barely changes. That's not food preservation— that's chemistry making something our bodies can barely recognize as food, let alone properly digest. Many of these additives, particularly excitotoxins like MSG, directly disrupt our ASCENDO neurotransmitters—the very chemical messengers that regulate our mood, focus, and cognitive function.

Perhaps the most insidious change came with the replacement of traditional cooking fats. As butter, lard, and tallow—stable fats our bodies evolved to process—became expensive, the industry pushed cheaper alternatives: industrial seed oils. Corn, soybean, and other vegetable oils were marketed for their affordability, but this masked a dangerous truth. These oils were fundamentally unstable at the molecular level, creating cascades of free radical damage and trans fats when heated. These damaged fats trigger inflammation throughout our digestive system and beyond. This wasn't about saving money; it was about maximizing profits at the expense of our biological infrastructure.

The industry's final assault came through packaging. Glass and stainless steel containers were replaced with plastic—cheaper, lighter, and incredibly dangerous to our biology. These plastics don't just hold our food; they leach endocrine-disrupting chemicals into it, creating molecular mimics that confuse our hormonal systems and further compromise our gut-brain communication.

But the food industry wasn't done. In the 1980s and 90s, food scientists made their most calculated move yet: the deliberate engineering of addiction into our food supply. By systematically exploiting our genetic survival mechanisms—our natural attraction to salt, fat, and sugar—they created what they call "hyperpalatable" foods. These products aren't just tasty; they're specifically designed to override our natural satiety signals and keep us craving more.

The result of these systematic changes isn't just a health crisis—it's a performance catastrophe. We're now in a situation where we're simultaneously overfed and undernourished. While consuming more calories than ever before, our cells are starving for the nutrients they need to function. These hyperpalatable, nutrient-poor foods create a vicious cycle: the more we eat them, the more our bodies crave them, not because we're weak-willed, but because our biological systems are desperately seeking the nutrients they need.

This nutritional chaos triggers a constant stress response in our bodies. When your system can't find the nutrients it needs, it interprets this as a survival threat. Your fight-or-flight response activates, directing blood flow away from your prefrontal cortex—the very part of your brain responsible for executive functions like decision-making, emotional regulation, and focused attention. It's a perfect storm: the foods designed to addict us also impair our ability to make better choices.

Consider what happens when you combine this nutritional stress with modern performance demands. Your brain needs stable glucose levels, essential fatty acids, and specific micronutrients to maintain focus and clarity. Instead, it's getting sugar spikes from processed foods, damaged fats from seed oils, and a flood of artificial compounds it never evolved to process. Each meal becomes not just a missed opportunity for optimization, but an active source of biological stress.

The impact becomes painfully clear in real-world scenarios. That 3 PM brain fog that has you reaching for another coffee? It's not normal fatigue— it's your brain struggling to function under a barrage of inflammatory compounds and blood sugar chaos. Those moments of inexplicable anxiety during important meetings? That's not just stress—it's your compromised gut-brain axis sending distress signals. The difficulty maintaining focus during critical tasks? Your prefrontal cortex is literally being starved of the resources it needs to function.

Think about Carla, one of my clients. Her initial assessment revealed something fascinating: despite following what she thought was a 'clean' diet, her food choices were actively sabotaging her performance. Those 'healthy' protein bars between meetings? Loaded with inflammatory seed oils and artificial sweeteners. The 'light' salad dressings? Full of excitotoxins, disrupting her neurotransmitter balance. Even her 'whole grain' breakfast was triggering energy crashes during her most important morning meetings.

What makes this situation particularly challenging is that the very stress of poor performance often drives us toward the foods that make things worse. When you're overwhelmed, behind schedule, or mentally foggy, you're more likely to reach for quick, convenient options—precisely the types of foods that perpetuate the cycle. It's like trying to put out a fire with gasoline.

The solution isn't about willpower or discipline; it's about breaking free from social heredity, those eating patterns we unconsciously adopted growing up. Start with understanding the basics:

- Choose whole foods your grandmother would recognize.
- Avoid industrial seed oils.
- Opt for organic to minimize pesticide exposure.

Here's where the Pareto principle becomes powerful: 80% of those harmful compounds we discussed—seed oils, pesticides, GMOs, artificial additives, and plastics—are concentrated in processed foods. This means by focusing on one simple change—eliminating processed foods from your diet—you automatically reduce your exposure to most of these performance-draining substances.

Look critically at processed foods like packaged snacks, fried foods, sodas, cereals, energy bars, and canned goods. Each one likely contains multiple compounds that compromise your performance.

But here's the crucial mindset shift: elimination alone equals failure. If you just remove these foods without a plan, you'll eventually return to them. The key is replacement. For every processed food you remove, you need a better option ready to take its place.

I've compiled a comprehensive food list that I share inside this chapter's resource hub for those who want to dive deeper. But remember: the goal isn't to memorize lists; it's to understand the principles. Once you grasp these fundamentals, you can use AI tools like ChatGPT to give you ideas of healthy alternatives that work for your lifestyle.

BEYOND CLEAN EATING

It's not just junk food we need to be aware of. Even as you transition to cleaner eating, some supposedly "healthy" foods might be quietly undermining your performance potential.

Conventional wisdom suggests that a predominantly plant-based diet is the way forward to achieve better health and enhanced performance. This perspective has been reinforced through countless books, documentaries, and health associations. While plants certainly play a vital role in our nutrition, the complete picture hasn't always been presented to us.

Both animals and plants have evolved sophisticated defense mechanisms over millions of years. While animals can run, hide, or fight, plants developed chemical warfare systems to protect themselves. These defensive compounds, known as antinutrients, can interact with our biology in ways that impact our performance.

There are numerous antinutrients present in plant foods, including phytates, tannins, saponins, glucosinolates, and several others. However, to keep things practical and actionable, let's focus on two of the most well-documented ones that significantly impact cognitive performance: lectins and oxalates.

Lectins are proteins that can bind to cell membranes, potentially compromising your gut barrier and triggering systemic inflammation. Some lectins, like ricin found in castor beans, are so toxic that a dose the size of a few grains of salt could be lethal. While the lectins in our everyday foods aren't this dramatic, they can still create significant performance issues.

These compounds are concentrated in many foods we're often told to eat more of: grains (especially whole wheat), legumes, the nightshade family (tomatoes, peppers, eggplants), and most seeds. When consumed regularly, they can contribute to brain fog, reduced cognitive function, and compromised energy levels.

Oxalates present a different challenge. These compounds form sharp, crystal-like structures that can deposit anywhere in your body, including your brain and thyroid. They're exceptionally high in foods often celebrated as superfoods: spinach, almonds, many seeds, and even turmeric. What makes oxalates particularly relevant to performance is their ability to disrupt mitochondrial function (your cellular energy producers), which leads to fatigue and reduced mental clarity.

For a comprehensive understanding of antinutrients and detailed protocols to address them, I recommend exploring ***The Neo Diet***, where I dive deep into this fascinating aspect of nutrition. What's important here is grasping the fundamental principle: not all "healthy" foods support optimal performance for everyone.

This knowledge empowers you to make better choices. Whether you're using AI tools to generate meal plans or consulting the resources provided in this chapter, understanding these basic principles helps you navigate toward truly performance-enhancing nutrition choices.

Remember, this isn't about adopting an extreme position or eliminating entire food groups. It's about adding another layer of understanding to your performance optimization toolkit. Just as we learned to evaluate processed foods critically, we can now make more informed decisions about our whole-food choices.

THE DAIRY DILEMMA

For centuries, dairy has been a cornerstone of human nutrition, traditionally consumed without causing the widespread health issues we see today. But something changed. The dairy in your local supermarket bears little resemblance to what our ancestors consumed, and this transformation has significant implications for your cognitive performance.

The story of modern dairy is a perfect example of how food processing can turn a nutritious food into a potential performance disruptor. While pasteurization and homogenization reduce contamination risks, these processes also destroy beneficial components and alter the very structure of milk proteins.

The most fascinating aspect of this transformation lies in the proteins themselves. Through selective breeding of dairy cows, particularly in Northern Europe, we've ended up with cattle producing a different type of milk protein than their ancestors. Most modern dairy cows produce what's called A1 casein, while traditional breeds produce A2 casein. This might seem like a minor detail, but its impact on performance can be significant.

Why does this matter? A1 casein breaks down in your gut to form compounds that can trigger inflammation and affect cognitive function. Meanwhile, A2 casein (still found in Southern European cows, goats, and sheep) tends to be better tolerated and doesn't create these problematic breakdown products.

But there's more to the story than just protein types. Modern dairy processing methods strip milk of its beneficial probiotics and enzymes, alter its natural fat structure, and reduce levels of beneficial compounds called gangliosides—which play crucial roles in brain health and inflammation control.

The solution isn't necessarily to eliminate dairy entirely. Instead, consider exploring better options. Raw dairy from grass-fed cows (where legally available and safely sourced) offers a more complete nutritional profile than conventional options. Fermented dairy products like yogurt and kefir often prove more digestible thanks to their probiotic content and pre-digested proteins. You might also explore milk from traditional breeds (A2 producers), including certain heritage cow breeds, goats, and sheep, which many find easier to tolerate than conventional dairy.

However, it's crucial to recognize that even with these better options, not everyone will tolerate dairy well. Your genetic background, gut health, and overall sensitivity will determine your individual response.

The best way to understand your personal dairy tolerance is to become your own biological detective. Pay attention to how different dairy products affect your energy, focus, and digestion—these subtle signals provide valuable data about your unique response. Consider working with a functional medicine practitioner for proper assessment if you're experiencing persistent issues. For those wanting deeper insights, comprehensive food sensitivity testing or gut analysis can reveal hidden reactions your body might be experiencing.

The key is to make informed decisions based on how dairy affects your personal performance rather than following blanket recommendations. Your biology is unique—your nutrition approach should be, too.

YOUR BRAIN'S RESET BUTTON

We've been exploring eliminating problematic foods, but what about eliminating food altogether—at least temporarily? While this might sound extreme, strategic fasting has emerged as one of the most powerful tools for enhancing cognitive performance.

The science behind fasting's impact on brain function is fascinating. When you temporarily abstain from food, you trigger a cascade of biological processes that enhance mental clarity and cognitive function. Your brain starts producing more BDNF (Brain-Derived Neurotrophic Factor), supporting neuron survival and learning. Your metabolism shifts from glucose to ketones, providing more stable energy. Your cells begin their natural cleaning process called autophagy, while stress hormones like adrenaline and norepinephrine rise just enough to enhance alertness and focus. All this happens while inflammation decreases and your mitochondria become more efficient at producing energy.

But here's the key: you don't need extended fasts to access these benefits. Two particular approaches have proven especially effective for sustainable performance enhancement.

The first is the 16:8 Method. This involves confining your eating to an 8-hour window each day, creating a 16-hour fasting period. Think of it as extending your natural overnight fast. For example, if you finish dinner at 8 PM, you won't eat again until noon the next day.

The second approach is the Biweekly 24-hour Fast, popularized by Brad Pilon. This involves a complete 24-hour fast twice per week, typically from dinner to dinner. Monday and Thursday often work well as fasting days, allowing for normal social eating on weekends.

For both approaches, proper implementation is crucial. Start gradually by pushing breakfast back by one hour at a time. Let your body adapt before extending fasting periods, and pay attention to how your energy and focus respond. Stay well-hydrated during fasting periods with water, and consider adding mineral-rich ancient salt or electrolytes. Herbal teas are acceptable during fasts.

Breaking your fast requires equal attention. Start with easily digestible foods, avoid overwhelming your system with large meals, and focus on nutrient-dense options. Remember: fasting isn't about enduring hunger—it's about optimizing your biology for better performance. If you experience severe discomfort, excessive fatigue, or difficulty concentrating, adjust your approach or consider working with a healthcare professional to find the right fasting strategy for you.

Just as professional athletes have training and recovery cycles, think of fasting as a recovery cycle for your brain. When implemented correctly, it becomes less about deprivation and more about strategic enhancement of your cognitive capabilities.

STRATEGIC MEAL TIMING

Now that we understand when not to eat, let's talk about when (and how) to eat for optimal performance. If you think this is just another lecture about "breakfast is the most important meal of the day," you're in for a surprise. Spoiler alert: your elementary school teacher might have been wrong about a few things.

Understanding your eating window is crucial for peak cognitive function, and it all comes down to insulin's role in your body. Every time you eat, particularly foods high in carbohydrates, your body releases insulin to manage blood sugar levels. When insulin spikes too high, it doesn't just lower blood sugar—it can send it crashing below baseline, taking your energy and focus with it.

Let's start with the morning. If you're following our discussion on fasting, you might skip breakfast altogether. But if you choose to eat it, the standard breakfast of toast, cereal, or other carb-heavy foods essentially programs your brain for an energy crash. Instead, focus on protein and healthy fats for stable energy throughout the morning.

Lunch is where most people really go wrong. The typical high-carb lunch sends your brain a naptime signal—hello, mid-afternoon brain fog. Instead, opt for a high-protein, high-fat lunch with minimal carbs. Think steak and salad rather than sandwiches and pasta. Can't step away for a proper lunch? A protein smoothie can work. However, I'm not talking about those sugar bombs from your local juice bar. Consider a homemade blend with a quality protein powder (like beef isolate or hemp), healthy fats from coconut milk or avocado, and minimal fruit. The key principle here isn't about following specific recipes but understanding that we want to avoid carb-heavy meals that'll crash your energy.

Dinner timing gets interesting. Those warnings about not eating carbs at night? The science tells a different story. A moderate amount of carbs 2-3 hours before bed can actually help with serotonin production, improving both sleep quality and metabolic function.

If you're still hungry after meals, you're probably not getting enough protein, fat, or fiber. And yes, you can eat as many low-carb vegetables as you want. Even if you don't like vegetables, your taste buds will adapt more quickly than you might expect. They regenerate every 10-14 days, meaning those seasoned greens you're forcing yourself to eat now might become craveable in just a few weeks.

While these principles work well as general guidelines, it's essential to understand that we're all unique in how we respond to different foods. A fascinating study from the Weizmann Institute of Science illustrated this perfectly. They asked participants to guess which would spike their blood sugar more: eating a cookie or eating a banana. Most people pointed to the cookie. Yet the results showed surprising individual variations. Some people spiked higher from the banana, others from the cookie, while some maintained stable blood sugar with both.

This isn't to say you need to track every metabolic response to your food. The principles we've discussed will serve most people well. However, for those particularly interested in fine-tuning their nutrition, using a continuous glucose monitor (CGM) can provide valuable insights into your personal responses to different foods. This kind of data can help optimize your diet further, while also revealing important information about your internal ecosystem.

OPTIMIZING YOUR INTERNAL ECOSYSTEM

While we've focused on meal timing and macronutrient balance, there's a crucial piece of the performance puzzle that often gets overlooked: micronutrition. Understanding protein, fats, and carbs is important, but it's the micronutrients—the vitamins, minerals, antioxidants, and other compounds—that truly optimize your brain power and energy systems.

Let's start with your brain's command center—the gut-brain connection. Most people don't realize that about 90% of serotonin is produced in their gut, not their brain. But that's just the beginning. Your gut microbiome—that diverse community of microorganisms residing in your digestive system—influences virtually every aspect of your cognitive function through an impressive array of neurotransmitters.

Your gut doesn't just passively influence your brain; it actively participates in regulating many of the key neurotransmitters we discussed in the ASCENDO Framework. The serotonin for emotional stability, dopamine for motivation, and even acetylcholine for cognitive focus are all directly impacted by your gut health. Beyond these familiar players, your microbiome also produces additional neural messengers like GABA for stress management, glutamate for cognitive enhancement, and histamine for sleep-wake regulation.

Even more fascinating is how your gut bacteria produce short-chain fatty acids (SCFAs) like acetate, propionate, and butyrate through fiber fermentation. These compounds don't just improve gut health; they provide neuroprotection, reduce inflammation, and can significantly impact your mood and cognitive performance.

To leverage this complex internal ecosystem for peak performance, we need to focus on two key strategies: nourishing our existing beneficial bacteria and introducing new ones. The first strategy relies on prebiotics—specific compounds that act like fertilizer for your gut bacteria. While you might not have heard of prebiotics before, you're probably already eating some of them. That subtle sweetness in roasted garlic or caramelized onions? Those are prebiotic compounds. The same goes for that slightly bitter taste in chicory root or the resistant starch that forms when you cool cooked potatoes or rice.

The second strategy involves probiotics—living organisms that enhance your microbiome's diversity. Traditional cultures worldwide have intuitively understood their importance, even without knowing the science behind it. From Korean kimchi to German sauerkraut, from Japanese natto to Russian kefir, fermented foods have been dietary staples for millennia. Now we understand why: these foods introduce beneficial bacteria that can significantly improve our gut-brain connection.

But optimizing your brain chemistry isn't just about gut health. Certain foods act as direct cognitive enhancers through their unique nutrient profiles. Take fatty fish, for example. The EPA and DHA found in salmon, mackerel, and sardines aren't just good for your heart; they're crucial building blocks for brain cell membranes and play a vital role in reducing neuroinflammation.

These omega-3 fatty acids are so important that your brain will literally restructure itself based on their availability.

Eggs represent another fascinating example of nature's brain food. The choline in egg yolks serves as a precursor for acetylcholine, which is crucial for memory and learning. Combined with B vitamins and selenium, eggs provide a complete package of brain-boosting nutrients that can enhance cognitive function.

Perhaps most intriguing are mushrooms, particularly varieties like Lion's Mane and Reishi. These fungi contain compounds that stimulate the production of nerve growth factors—proteins that essentially act as fertilizer for your brain cells. Think about that for a moment: these humble organisms can actually help your brain grow new connections and repair existing ones.

When it comes to putting all this knowledge into practice, the key is strategic implementation rather than trying to overhaul your entire diet overnight. Start by incorporating fermented foods into your daily routine— perhaps some kimchi with your lunch or kefir in your morning smoothie. These small additions can significantly impact your gut-brain axis over time.

For brain-boosting fats, think beyond just fish. Avocados, extra virgin olive oil, and nuts like walnuts and macadamias provide different but complementary fatty acids that support cognitive function. Even grass-fed butter and coconut oil, once demonized by outdated nutritional advice, can play crucial roles in brain health when used appropriately.

Berries deserve special attention in your cognitive enhancement arsenal. Their high flavonoid content doesn't just reduce inflammation; it actively enhances your brain's plasticity, improving its ability to form new neural connections. This isn't just about preventing decline; it's about optimizing your brain's capacity to learn and adapt.

Understanding how to nourish your internal ecosystem is crucial, but there's another fundamental aspect of performance that most people chronically overlook: hydration. While it might seem simple, the way you hydrate can either enhance or undermine all the careful optimization we've just discussed. Let's explore why proper hydration is about much more than just drinking water.

THE FORGOTTEN PERFORMANCE MULTIPLIER

Imagine your body as a complex river system, with water carrying nutrients, signals, and energy to every cell. When water levels drop, even slightly, the flow becomes sluggish, communication breaks down, and waste starts accumulating in the backwaters. This is exactly what happens in your body when you're not adequately hydrated.

The impact is startling: research shows that just 2% dehydration (which can happen before you even feel thirsty) can reduce cognitive performance by up to 20%. In warmer conditions, this impact can spike to 40%. We're talking about measurable decreases in visual vigilance, working memory, and motor skills. Not to mention increased tension, anxiety, and fatigue.

But here's where most people get hydration wrong: it's not just about drinking water. It's about maintaining proper electrolyte balance at a cellular level. Think about it: Drinking excessive amounts of plain water without minerals can actually dehydrate your cells through osmosis. This is why elite performers often start their day with a liter of water and a pinch of high-quality salt.

The timing of your hydration matters, too. That morning liter of water doesn't just rehydrate you after sleep; it kickstarts your metabolism and helps flush out toxins that accumulated during your brain's nighttime cleaning cycle. Throughout the day, consistent small amounts maintain better hydration than large, infrequent quantities.

For enhanced hydration, consider incorporating natural sources of electrolytes. Mineral-rich broths and even certain fruits and vegetables can contribute to your hydration status while providing additional nutrients. If you're a coffee drinker, remember the 3:1 rule—for every cup of coffee, aim for three cups of water to maintain balance.

Whether you're in a high-stakes meeting or deep in creative work, your hydration status is silently influencing your performance. The key is developing a strategic approach that works with your daily rhythm, not against it.

Start your day with a full rehydration protocol. Your body loses significant water during sleep through breathing and perspiration. That morning fog many people feel? Often, it's just dehydration masquerading as tiredness. A large glass of water with a pinch of high-quality salt helps restore cellular hydration quickly.

Throughout the day, aim to drink before you feel thirsty. Thirst isn't a reliable indicator. By the time you feel it, you're already experiencing performance decline. Instead, create environmental triggers: a water bottle on your desk, drinking at the start of each meeting, or setting gentle reminders in between deep work sessions.

But perhaps most importantly, learn to read your body's hydration signals. Subtle signs like decreased concentration, mild headaches, or feeling unusually tired often indicate you need water before anything else. Many people reach for caffeine or snacks when simple rehydration would resolve their energy dip.

Remember: optimal hydration isn't about drinking massive amounts of water; it's about maintaining consistent, quality hydration throughout the day. Your cells need a steady flow, not floods and droughts.

A Note About Alcohol

Speaking of dehydration, we need to address one of the most common performance saboteurs in modern life. Alcohol doesn't just dehydrate you—it's actively neurotoxic. Meaning it can damage brain cells directly. Beyond immediate effects like impaired judgment and reduced reaction time, alcohol disrupts your sleep architecture, particularly REM sleep, which is crucial for memory consolidation and cognitive function. Even moderate drinking can lead to decreased brain volume over time and increased risk of cognitive decline. This isn't about morality; it's about making informed decisions about your performance priorities.

NUTRITION SUMMARY

I understand if you're feeling overwhelmed. After all, this isn't the quick fix or "life hack" most people hope for when they start exploring physiological optimization. Let's be honest. We all wish we could indulge in whatever we want and still perform at our peak. But biology doesn't work that way, and pretending otherwise only delays your transformation.

This is the moment when you need to make a fundamental decision about your priorities. Do you want to think clearly and achieve your goals, or do you want to eat cupcakes?

The nutrition principles we've covered aren't complicated, but they do require commitment. Let's synthesize everything we've discussed into a clear framework for action:

First, embrace mindful eating habits. This isn't just about what you eat, but how you eat. Focus on the quality, quantity, and timing of your meals. A balanced approach includes adequate protein, healthy fats, low-glycemic carbohydrates, and abundant vegetables.

The foundation of your nutrition should be whole, organic foods. This isn't about following trends; it's about minimizing exposure to pesticides in produce and avoiding antibiotics and hormones in conventionally raised meats. Choose organic, grass-fed options whenever possible.

When it comes to essential fatty acids, focus on small fatty fish. While larger fish can accumulate concerning levels of mercury, smaller varieties, salmon and trout provide cleaner sources of crucial omega-3s.

Your brain requires specific nutrients to function optimally. Eggs are nature's multivitamin, particularly rich in choline. Antioxidant-rich berries and mushrooms support cognitive function, while healthy fats from avocados, olive oil, coconut oil, grass-fed butter, ghee, and selected nuts (particularly walnuts, macadamias, and pistachios) provide essential brain-building blocks.

Equally important is what to avoid. Processed and packaged foods, trans fats, artificial sweeteners, refined sugars, and high-glycemic carbohydrates can undermine your performance goals.

Food sensitivities and antinutrients deserve special attention. Many high performers unknowingly sabotage their potential through inflammatory responses to certain foods. Common triggers include dairy and foods high in lectins (including gluten) or oxalates. If you tolerate dairy, opt for raw or fermented varieties. For foods containing antinutrients, traditional preparation methods like soaking and fermenting can significantly reduce their negative impacts.

Hydration remains a cornerstone of performance nutrition. Beyond simply carrying a water bottle, focus on balancing coffee intake with adequate water consumption. Include electrolyte-rich beverages, herbal teas, kombucha, and nutrient-dense broths in your daily routine.

Your microbiome health directly influences cognitive function and energy levels. Support it with prebiotics found in chicory root, garlic, onions, and leeks, along with probiotic-rich foods like fermented dairy and sauerkraut.

Meal composition and timing play crucial roles in daily performance. Strategic carbohydrate timing can enhance both work and sleep: minimize daytime carb consumption to avoid insulin spikes and crashes, but include some with dinner to support serotonin production and sleep preparation.

Intermittent fasting offers another powerful tool for cognitive enhancement. Whether you choose the 16:8 method or biweekly 24-hour fasts, these approaches can reduce inflammation and improve mitochondrial efficiency. The key is maintaining nutrient density during eating windows while staying well-hydrated.

Remember: sustainable change comes through replacement, not elimination. Instead of focusing on what you're giving up, concentrate on finding healthier alternatives that satisfy similar cravings or needs. This approach makes the transition both manageable and lasting.

Finally, develop awareness of your body's signals. Pay attention to how different foods affect your mood, energy levels, and overall well-being. Tools like continuous glucose monitors (CGMs) can provide objective data about your body's responses, helping you fine-tune your nutrition for optimal performance.

MAKING IT WORK IN THE REAL WORLD

Understanding nutrition principles is one thing. Implementing them in a busy life is another entirely. Let's address the practical aspects of turning these insights into daily habits.

The first decision you'll need to make is about food preparation. While home cooking offers complete control over ingredients and can even become a meditative practice, it's time-consuming. Having someone else prepare your meals saves time but requires careful consideration of quality control.

If you choose to outsource your meal preparation, you have several options:

- Hiring a private chef who understands your nutritional requirements.
- Finding a high-quality meal prep service that aligns with your standards.
- Strategically ordering from restaurants while being specific about ingredients.

The key to making any of these options work is eliminating decision fatigue. Rather than facing the paradox of choice every day, predefine your meals. This might mean establishing a weekly meal prep routine, working with a chef to create a rotating menu, or having go-to orders at specific restaurants.

Remember: perfection is the enemy of progress. Instead of seeking the perfect meal every time, establish "good enough" options that align with your performance goals. For example, a couple of years back, I simplified my lunch to a nutrient-dense smoothie that hits all my nutritional targets while requiring minimal time and decision-making.

When eating out, focus on establishments that prioritize quality ingredients. Skip fast food chains in favor of restaurants serving traditional cuisines like the Mediterranean. When ordering, opt for simple preparations—grilled or oven-baked proteins with vegetables or salads. Keep healthy dressings at your office or home to upgrade any basic salad.

For meal prep services, invest time in finding providers who align with your standards. Smaller companies often offer more customization options and are more willing to accommodate specific requirements.

To simplify your food choices, I've created a Food Matrix for my clients—a ranked system of foods that considers antinutrients, pollutants, common sensitivities, and inflammation potential. This tool eliminates the need for constant research when making food choices, whether cooking at home or eating out.

Remember that customization is crucial. While these guidelines provide a framework, your optimal diet depends on your unique physiology, lifestyle, and goals. Pay attention to how different foods affect you. Consider advanced testing—DNA analysis, gut health assessments, or comprehensive blood work—to fine-tune your approach.

A note for vegan readers: Some of the recommendations in this chapter may not align with your dietary choices. While I advocate for an omnivorous diet based on performance optimization research, I respect that personal beliefs and ethics play a crucial role in nutritional decisions. If you follow a vegan diet, I recommend working with a qualified vegan nutrition coach to adapt these principles while ensuring you address potential nutritional deficits through appropriate supplementation.

It's worth noting that what we've covered here represents just the essential 20% of nutrition optimization—the fundamentals that will give you the biggest performance returns. For those interested in diving deeper into the complete science of nutrition optimization, including detailed food matrices, advanced protocols, and comprehensive guidelines, I explore these topics extensively in my book *The Neo Diet*. There, you'll find the other 80% that can help you fine-tune your nutrition for even greater performance gains.

Now that we've established this nutritional foundation, let's translate these insights into immediate action. Knowledge without implementation is just information—but I want you to experience transformation. Here are your three critical next steps to begin optimizing your biological performance:

1. Clean out your pantry of processed foods (and get healthier replacements)
2. Define your weekday meals in advance
3. Establish your food preparation strategy

Each of these steps builds upon the last, creating a cascade of positive changes in your performance ecosystem. Start with the pantry reset to eliminate the most harmful inputs, then move to meal planning to ensure consistent quality, and finally, develop your preparation system to make these changes sustainable.

For detailed implementation tools and resources, check the resources accompanying this book. Remember, sustainable change happens through consistent small steps, not dramatic overhauls.

SUPPLEMENTS AND NOOTROPICS

After optimizing your nutrition, you might be wondering what else you can do to enhance your cognitive performance. While supplements should never replace a solid nutritional foundation, they can serve as powerful tools for optimization when used strategically.

Think of supplements like precision instruments in an orchestra—they can enhance the overall performance, but they can't replace the musicians themselves. Your diet is the orchestra; supplements are the fine-tuning tools that can take the performance from good to exceptional.

The Essential Foundation

Before diving into advanced compounds, let's establish the core supplements that address common deficiencies in modern life:

Omega-3 Fatty Acids: Even with an optimized diet, getting adequate DHA and EPA can be challenging. These essential fats are crucial for brain cell integrity and reducing inflammation.

Vitamin D: The "sunshine vitamin" is chronically low in most people, especially knowledge workers who spend long hours indoors. Beyond bone health, it's crucial for mood regulation and cognitive function.

Magnesium Glycinate: Our modern food supply is notably deficient in this crucial mineral. It's essential for relaxation, sleep quality, and stress management.

Zinc/Copper Balance: Critical for immune function and neurotransmitter activity, this mineral pair needs careful balance for optimal results.

Creatine: While often associated with athletic performance, creatine's cognitive benefits are equally impressive, supporting energy production in brain cells.

Adaptogens

Think of adaptogens as biological shock absorbers. They help your body maintain balance under stress. Just as your car's suspension system prevents you from feeling every bump in the road, adaptogens help smooth out your body's response to daily stressors.

Key adaptogenic compounds include:

Ashwagandha: Perhaps the most studied adaptogen, it excels at reducing stress and anxiety while improving cognitive function. However, be aware that long-term daily use can lead to emotional blunting—cycling is recommended.

Rhodiola Rosea: Particularly effective for mental fatigue, it shines in situations requiring sustained mental performance under pressure.

Panax Ginseng: The grandfather of adaptogens, it offers comprehensive support for both mental and physical performance.

General Performance Enhancers

These supplements form a bridge between basic nutrition and advanced nootropics:

L-Theanine: Often paired with caffeine, it provides focus without jitters. Think of it as turning coffee's jagged energy spike into a smooth, sustained curve.

Bacopa Monnieri: A memory enhancer that requires patience. Benefits typically emerge after several weeks of consistent use.

Lion's Mane Mushroom: This fascinating fungus supports nerve growth factor production, potentially enhancing both memory and concentration.

Alpha GPC: A premium form of choline that crosses the blood-brain barrier efficiently, supporting memory and cognitive processing.

Advanced Nootropics

Here's where we enter the realm of serious cognitive enhancement. These compounds aren't for daily use. Think of them as your cognitive reserve force for when extraordinary performance is required:

Methylene Blue: This compound stands apart from other advanced nootropics. Unlike nootropics meant for occasional use, current research suggests it may be used more frequently to enhance energy production and brain function.

Noopept: Improves memory and learning capabilities by increasing BDNF production. Best reserved for tasks requiring enhanced memory and concentration.

Piracetam: The original nootropic, known for improving memory and cognitive function by enhancing communication between neurons.

Phenylpiracetam: Offers a dual benefit of improved cognitive function and physical performance, making it valuable for demanding situations requiring both mental and physical output.

Pantogam: Combines cognitive enhancement with stress reduction properties, particularly beneficial for memory improvement and anxiety management.

A Note About Medications

Before implementing any supplementation strategy, it's crucial to understand how common medications can impact your performance. Many prescription drugs can create unexpected performance deficits through their side effects. Antidepressants (particularly SSRIs) often affect energy levels and cognitive clarity. Anti-anxiety medications, especially benzodiazepines, can impair memory formation and decision-making. Even less obvious culprits like antimalarial drugs and ADHD medications, including amphetamines, can significantly alter your neurochemistry and energy patterns in ways that counteract your optimization efforts.

As you progress in optimizing your Performance Pillars, consult with your physician about potentially reducing or eliminating certain medications. More importantly, always seek medical guidance before combining any supplements with your current prescriptions. Your biological optimization journey should work in harmony with, not against, any necessary medical treatment.

As we conclude this brief exploration of supplements and nootropics, let's return to our fundamental truth: these are tools, not solutions. Think of them as the finishing touches on a well-built performance foundation, not the foundation itself. While essential supplements can address common deficiencies of modern life, and advanced nootropics might offer an edge during periods of extraordinary demand, they should never replace the basics we've established.

If you're interested in exploring beyond the essentials, particularly with advanced nootropics, work with a qualified healthcare professional who understands your unique biochemistry and performance goals. Remember: the most potent performance enhancers aren't found in bottles—they're found in the fundamentals of nutrition, sleep, and movement, which we'll explore next.

THE WAKE-UP CALL

Think about your last truly great day. One where your decisions were spot-on, your energy was flowing, and everything just clicked. Now, be honest: How did you sleep the night before?

If you're like most high performers I work with, you might notice an uncomfortable pattern. Your best days, those peak performance moments we all chase, often follow your best nights of sleep. Yet somewhere along the way, our culture started treating sleep like a negotiable aspect of success, something to be conquered rather than optimized.

This is where most people hit a fascinating paradox: The more ambitious you are, the more likely you are to sacrifice sleep in pursuit of your goals. It's not because you're lazy or undisciplined. In fact, it's often the opposite—your drive for excellence makes it harder to find that "off button" in your brain.

Remember what we learned about the Energy Paradox in Chapter 2? Just as working longer hours eventually leads to diminishing returns, pushing through sleep debt creates a performance debt that no amount of caffeine or willpower can repay.

What's remarkable about sleep is its role as nature's ultimate performance enhancer. While supplement companies spend billions developing the next miracle pill, your body already has a built-in system for enhancing every aspect of your performance—from memory consolidation to physical recovery, from emotional regulation to creative problem-solving.

The timing of this discussion isn't random. Now that we've optimized your nutrition and understood how to fuel your biological systems, it's time to explore how sleep acts as the master regulator of all these processes. Perfect nutrition without proper sleep is like having premium fuel in a car that never gets maintenance. Eventually, something's going to break down.

This isn't about sleeping longer; it's about sleeping smarter. While we've been busy optimizing every waking moment, we've been largely ignoring the biological reality: sleep isn't just rest, it's your body's most sophisticated performance optimization program.

What makes sleep powerful from a biological perspective is its non-negotiable nature. Your body will force you to sleep eventually, whether you plan for it or not. The only choice you really have is whether you'll do it strategically, harnessing its power for peak performance, or fight against it until you crash.

The cost of fighting this biological imperative is a systematic degradation of every performance metric that matters. When researchers at Stanford studied the impact of sleep debt on cognitive function, they discovered something remarkable: Losing just two hours of sleep was enough to drop cognitive performance to the same level as being legally drunk. Think about that next time you're making crucial business decisions on five hours of sleep.

But here's where it gets exciting: Sleep isn't just about avoiding performance decline; it's about accessing levels of performance you might not even realize you're capable of. When your brain is properly rested, you're not just sharper; you're literally operating with enhanced capabilities for learning, decision-making, and creative problem-solving.

The key insight isn't that sleep is important—you already know that. The insight is that sleep is trainable. Just like we can optimize our nutrition and physical fitness, we can systematically enhance our sleep quality to unlock extraordinary levels of performance. It's about maximizing the effectiveness of everything else you're already doing.

Let's start by understanding what actually happens during those precious hours of sleep—because once you see the sophisticated biological processes at work, you'll never think of sleep as "doing nothing" again.

YOUR BRAIN'S NIGHT SHIFT

Your brain during sleep is like a city after hours. While the streets might seem quiet, behind the scenes, there's an incredible amount of essential work happening. Every night, your brain engages in a complex series of processes that would be impossible during waking hours.

At the heart of this nocturnal activity is your glymphatic system—your brain's dedicated cleaning crew. During sleep, the spaces between your brain cells may expand by up to 60%, creating channels that allow for the removal of metabolic waste products. But this isn't just basic housekeeping; it's a sophisticated detoxification process crucial for your long-term cognitive health and daily performance.

First, it tackles the removal of amyloid plaque, the same substance associated with Alzheimer's and other neurodegenerative diseases. Think of it like preventing rust in a high-performance engine—regular cleaning prevents long-term damage. Next, it systematically eliminates toxins that accumulate during your waking hours, the metabolic byproducts of your daily mental activity. Finally, it creates the optimal environment for brain repair and rejuvenation, allowing your neural networks to be maintained and strengthened.

When this cleanup system is compromised through poor sleep, these waste products accumulate, directly impacting your ability to think clearly and make decisions. It's like trying to run complex calculations on a computer that's never been defragmented—eventually, performance suffers.

This sophisticated maintenance process happens in concert with distinct sleep stages, each playing a vital role in your performance optimization. Think of these stages as specialized teams, each with their own crucial role in preparing you for peak performance.

Light Sleep serves as your entry point into this restorative process. Your heart rate slows, body temperature drops, and your brain begins shifting from active processing to maintenance mode. While some might dismiss this stage as "shallow" sleep, it's actually crucial for memory processing and maintaining neuroplasticity—your brain's ability to adapt and learn.

Deep Sleep is where the real magic happens. This is when your brain waves slow to their lowest frequency, creating the perfect conditions for physical restoration and cellular repair. Growth hormone secretion peaks during this stage, supporting everything from muscle recovery to immune system function. It's no coincidence that athletes and executives who get adequate deep sleep consistently outperform their sleep-deprived counterparts.

REM Sleep takes its name from the rapid eye movements occurring during this phase, but these brief ocular flutters only hint at the intense neural activity happening beneath the surface. This is your brain's innovation lab, where it connects seemingly unrelated pieces of information to generate new insights. During REM sleep, your brain processes complex information, consolidates memories, and even rehearses challenging tasks you encountered during the day.

Research at the University of California has revealed the remarkable role of sleep, particularly REM sleep, in fostering creativity. When sleep stages work in harmony, our brains are significantly better equipped to make innovative connections and find creative solutions to problems that eluded us while awake. Those 'Aha!' moments that seem to appear out of thin air? They're often the product of your brain's nocturnal processing.

But here's what makes this system genuinely remarkable: These stages repeat throughout the night in cycles lasting approximately 90 minutes. Each cycle is an opportunity for enhancement—whether it's strengthening new memories, repairing cellular damage, or generating creative insights. Miss out on quality sleep, and you're not just losing rest; you're missing critical opportunities for biological optimization.

This sophisticated process explains why sleep deprivation is considered a form of torture. It's not just about feeling tired; it's about systematically disrupting every aspect of your biological function. Studies with sleep-deprived subjects show a cascade of effects: inflammation skyrockets, cognitive function plummets, and emotional regulation becomes nearly impossible. Your brain, desperate for the restoration it needs, begins to shut down critical functions—starting with the areas responsible for innovation, complex decision-making, and emotional intelligence.

THE TWO-PROCESS SLEEP SYSTEM

Your sleep system is more sophisticated than what most assume. Instead of a single mechanism controlling when you feel sleepy or alert, your body orchestrates two distinct processes that work in harmony to regulate your sleep. Understanding this dual system is crucial because it gives us precise leverage points for sleep optimization.

Let's start with **Process S**—your sleep drive. Throughout your day, a molecule called adenosine gradually accumulates in your brain. Think of adenosine as your body's sleep accountant, keeping a running tab of how long you've been awake. The longer you stay up, the more adenosine builds up, creating an increasingly powerful urge to sleep.

This is where caffeine enters the picture in a fascinating way. That morning coffee isn't actually giving you energy. In fact, it's blocking adenosine receptors in your brain, essentially hiding your sleep debt from your body's accountant. While this might seem like a clever hack, it comes with a catch: the adenosine keeps building up anyway. When the caffeine eventually wears off, all that accumulated sleep pressure hits at once. That's why you can feel fine all day, then suddenly crash in the late afternoon.

Process C, your circadian rhythm, operates independently of how long you've been awake. This is your body's internal clock, running on a roughly 24-hour cycle. This internal clock orchestrates a complex symphony of biological processes throughout the day. While light is its most powerful regulator, your circadian rhythm responds to multiple cues, from meal timing to exercise, from social interactions to temperature changes. Each morning, even before you see the sun, your body initiates the cortisol awakening response, preparing you for the day ahead. As evening approaches, this process reverses: melatonin production increases, your body temperature drops, and various biological systems begin their nightly transition.

The modern challenge? We're constantly disrupting these natural patterns. Blue light from screens confuses our circadian signals. Irregular meal times throw off our metabolic rhythms. Late-night workouts send mixed messages to our biological systems. Each disruption creates a mismatch between our sleep drive and circadian rhythm.

Borbely & Achermann, 1999

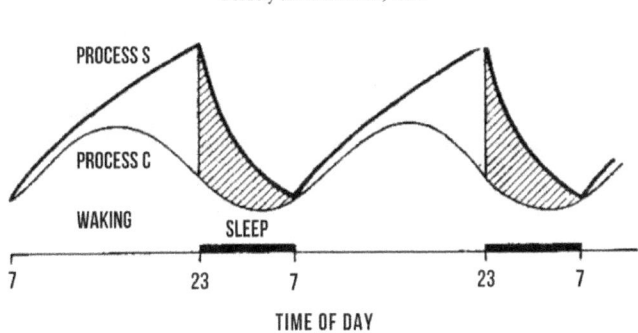

TIME OF DAY

When these two processes align correctly, you experience optimal sleep-wake cycles. When they don't, you get that frustrating experience of being exhausted but unable to sleep, or feeling groggy despite sleeping a full eight hours. The good news? Understanding these processes gives us precise tools for optimization, which we'll explore next.

THE 80/20 OF SLEEP OPTIMIZATION

Optimizing sleep doesn't require mastering fifty different techniques or buying all of the latest sleep gadgets. Like most biological systems, sleep follows the Pareto principle—roughly 20% of the right interventions drive 80% of your results. Let's start with the most fundamental yet overlooked aspect: consistency.

When renowned clinical psychologist and speaker Dr. Jordan Peterson works with depressed patients, he doesn't start with medication, diet changes, or relationship advice. His first prescription? Wake up at the same time every day. The body craves this consistency, and research consistently shows it's more impactful than your bedtime.

This wake-up call anchor becomes even more powerful when combined with immediate sunlight exposure. That morning light isn't just about feeling alert; it's a precise biological signal that sets your entire day's hormonal cascade in motion. Think of it as pressing the start button on your body's daily operating system.

From here, the rest of your day becomes a strategic countdown to optimal sleep. The most crucial checkpoints in this countdown form what some authors call the Reverse Countdown (aka the 10-3-2-1-0 framework)—five specific time markers that systematically prepare your body for high-quality sleep:

Ten hours before bed, cut off all caffeine intake. Remember our discussion about adenosine receptors? That afternoon coffee isn't just affecting your evening; it's actively blocking your brain's natural sleep pressure from building properly. If you're thinking, "But I can fall asleep just fine after coffee," consider this: it's not about falling asleep; it's about the quality of sleep you're getting.

Three hours before bed marks your cutoff for food, drink, and exercise. This is based on your body's metabolic patterns. Late meals force your digestive system to work when it should be winding down. Exercise, while crucial for sleep quality, needs this buffer zone to allow your core temperature and stress hormones to return to levels conducive to sleep.

Two hours before bed, shut down work completely. Your brain needs this transition period. Those "urgent" late-night emails? They're programming your brain to stay in high-alert mode when it should be powering down. This isn't about being unproductive; it's about respecting your biology's need for clear boundaries between performance and recovery.

One hour before bed begins your technology blackout. Recent research from Stanford neuroscience professor Andrew Huberman's lab revealed something fascinating about late-night phone use: it activates a brain region called the habenula, linked to depressive symptoms. Beyond just disrupting melatonin production, this late-night tech exposure can actually suppress dopamine production, leading to decreased motivation and mood the next day.

Zero—the final checkpoint—is your brain dump. Instead of letting thoughts race through your mind in bed, take five minutes to write down everything: tomorrow's tasks, creative ideas, and lingering concerns. A racing mind triggers stress responses that directly oppose your sleep biology.

Now that we've got your pre-sleep countdown sorted, let's talk about turning your bedroom into a sleep sanctuary. Your sleep environment needs to nail three key elements: dark, quiet, and cool. Think of these as the non-negotiables if you want optimal results.

Let's start with darkness. Not the "I can still check my phone" kind of dark. But pitch black, "can't-see-your-hand-in-front-of-your-face dark." That sliver of light sneaking through your curtains isn't just an annoyance; it's actively disrupting your melatonin production. Don't look at blackout blinds or a sleep mask as luxury items but as biological necessities.

When it comes to sound, you've got two options: silence or consistency. Random noise triggers a primitive part of your brain that's still programmed to wake you up in case that sound is a threat. White noise or earplugs help create the acoustic environment your brain needs for deep sleep. And no, falling asleep to Netflix doesn't count as white noise, no matter how boring the show.

Temperature control is where things get interesting. Your body needs to drop its core temperature to initiate deep sleep, which is why you want your room cool—ideally around 65°F (18°C). You can support this natural process with strategic temperature manipulation. A hot shower 60-90 minutes before bed triggers your body's cooling response, essentially preparing your biological systems for sleep.

Most people turn their bedroom into a multi-purpose space—part office, part entertainment center, part sleep zone. Your brain is remarkably good at building associations, and every non-sleep activity trains it to stay alert instead of winding down. Keep technology out of the bedroom. Yes, that means your phone, too. If the thought of being phoneless causes mild panic, that's exactly why you need the separation.

Remember how we discussed your brain's sophisticated cleaning system—the glymphatic system? Here's a powerful way to optimize it: the "Early Dinner Experiment." I know this might sound extreme in our modern world of 9 PM dinners and Netflix binges, but hear me out. Once a week, eat your last meal by 4:30 PM and be in bed by 9:30 PM. Your glymphatic system peaks around 10 PM, and with no insulin response from late eating to interfere, it can work at maximum efficiency.

Look, I get it. This kind of schedule might seem impossible with your current lifestyle. Maybe you have late meetings, family commitments, or social obligations. That's precisely why I'm suggesting just once a week. Think of it as a weekly reset for your brain—one evening where you prioritize biological optimization over social convention. The mental clarity you'll experience the next day might just convince you it's worth occasionally being "that person" who skips late dinner plans.

When it comes to supplements, we can take a strategic approach, starting with natural solutions before moving to more advanced options. Let's begin with herbal teas that have solid scientific backing:

Chamomile tea contains apigenin, a compound that binds to specific brain receptors to promote relaxation and reduce insomnia. Valerian root increases GABA in your brain, helping regulate nerve impulses and calm your system. Lavender tea, with its linalool and linalyl acetate, engages these same GABA receptors while calming your autonomic nervous system. Lemon balm and passionflower teas work through similar pathways, with research supporting their effectiveness for sleep quality.

For those ready to explore more advanced options, here's your supplementation hierarchy:

Start with magnesium glycinate. It's crucial for converting serotonin into melatonin and supports numerous sleep-related processes. Pair it with glycine, which helps lower body temperature and increases calming GABA levels in your brain.

For stress management, consider L-theanine, which increases serotonin, dopamine, and GABA levels, or phosphatidylserine, which helps regulate cortisol. Reishi extract can help you fall asleep faster while supporting broader health markers like immunity and blood sugar control.

CBD interacts with your endocannabinoid system to reduce anxiety and may extend deep sleep phases. Apigenin (yes, the same compound in chamomile) can be taken in supplement form for stronger effects on GABA activity. 5-HTP supports serotonin production, enhancing your natural sleep-wake cycle.

Save melatonin for occasional use only. It's best used as a circadian anchor in specific situations rather than a nightly supplement. When you do use it, opt for a larger dose to create a stronger reset signal.

TRACKING YOUR BIOLOGICAL RESPONSE

All the strategies we've covered so far are based on solid biological principles that work for most people. But here's the reality: you're not "most people." You have unique genetics, lifestyle factors, and biological responses that make your sleep patterns distinctly yours.

This is where sleep tracking becomes a game-changer. Rather than following generic advice, tracking provides a personalized blueprint of your sleep architecture. Modern wearable devices don't just count hours slept; they analyze sleep stages, track heart rate variability, monitor movement patterns, and even assess respiratory quality.

You don't need to invest in expensive tracking technology if you're not ready, but I want you to understand the value it can provide. As of writing this book, several reliable options exist, including the Apple Watch, Oura Ring, and Whoop Band. I'm not recommending any specific model since technology evolves rapidly, but what matters is finding a device that tracks sleep stages and provides consistent data you can analyze over time.

The real value isn't in the data itself but in the patterns it reveals. You might discover that certain foods you thought were harmless are actually disrupting your deep sleep. Perhaps that "relaxing" evening workout is keeping your heart rate elevated for hours. Maybe that highly-rated supplement actually works wonders for you—or does absolutely nothing.

Sleep tracking creates a feedback loop that eliminates guesswork. When you implement a new sleep strategy, you're not left wondering if it worked. You have objective data showing exactly how it affected your sleep architecture. This allows you to double down on what works specifically for your biology and discard what doesn't, regardless of what "should" work according to general principles.

What makes this approach particularly powerful is how it reveals your natural patterns over time. After a few weeks of tracking, you'll likely notice consistent trends that point toward something fundamental about your sleep biology: your chronotype.

UNDERSTANDING YOUR CHRONOTYPE

While we all follow roughly the same biological sleep mechanisms, the timing of these processes varies significantly between individuals. This natural tendency toward certain sleep-wake patterns is what sleep scientists call your "chronotype."

Various frameworks exist for categorizing chronotypes. Perhaps the most famous one is from Dr. Michael Breus. His model identifies four distinct types (Lions, Bears, Wolves, and Dolphins), each with detailed behavioral patterns. However, for practical implementation, I've found Daniel H. Pink's simplified model exceptionally useful. It categorizes chronotypes into three main types, making it straightforward to apply in daily life:

Morning Larks make up about 14% of the population. These individuals naturally wake early, experience their peak energy and focus in the morning hours, and tend to fade significantly by early evening. Their biological rhythms are shifted earlier, with melatonin release beginning sooner and cortisol rising earlier in the morning.

Night Owls represent approximately 21% of people. Their biology runs on a delayed schedule, with later melatonin release and morning cortisol response. They struggle with early mornings but experience their peak cognitive performance in the late afternoon and evening. For Owls, early morning meetings aren't just uncomfortable—they're asking for peak performance during their biological night.

Third Birds comprise the remaining 65%—the reason our standard 9-5 workday exists. These individuals fall between the extremes, typically functioning well in conventional schedules but with some flexibility in either direction.

The implications for performance are profound. Fighting against your chronotype is like swimming against a biological current—possible but enormously energy-intensive. This isn't about creating excuses or avoiding early commitments—it's about strategic energy management. By aligning your most demanding cognitive tasks with your biological prime time, you create natural advantages rather than constant friction.

DETERMINING YOUR CHRONOTYPE

Understanding your chronotype is essential for optimizing your performance. Here's a straightforward process to identify yours:

Step 1: Note Your Natural Sleep and Wake Times

On days without obligations (like vacations or weekends), observe when you naturally fall asleep and wake up without alarms.

- Example: I naturally sleep from 11:00 PM to 7:00 AM.

Step 2: Calculate Your Sleep Duration

Determine your total hours of natural sleep.

- Example: 8 hours.

Step 3: Calculate Your Midpoint of Sleep

Find the exact middle point between when you fall asleep and wake up.

- Example: 11:00 PM + 4 hours (half of 8 hours) = 3:00 AM.

Step 4: Identify Your Chronotype Based on Your Midpoint

Compare your midpoint of sleep to these ranges to determine your chronotype:

- 12:00 AM—3:30 AM: You're a Morning Lark, naturally energized earlier in the day
- 3:31 AM—5:30 AM: You're a Third Bird, with a balanced sleep-wake cycle
- 5:31 AM—12:00 PM: You're a Night Owl, with delayed energy peaks

For the most accurate assessment, track this pattern over several free days—at least three consecutive days when possible. Your body's natural rhythms often take a few days to express themselves after escaping work schedules and social obligations. This isn't a one-time calculation but rather a pattern to observe over time. The more consistent your midpoint appears across multiple free days, the more confident you can be in your chronotype identification.

OPTIMIZING YOUR ROUTINE BY CHRONOTYPE

Knowing your chronotype is only valuable if you apply it strategically. Here's how to adapt your daily patterns to work with your biology:

Morning Larks: Your biological energy and analytical thinking peak early, giving you a natural head start on cognitive tasks. Begin your day with your most demanding mental work—complex problem-solving, critical decision-making, and focused analysis. Your peak cognitive hours are a precious resource, so protect your morning for intellectual rather than physical demands. Schedule important meetings and strategic planning sessions before noon. By mid-afternoon, as your analytical sharpness naturally declines, transition to tasks requiring less intensive focus—administrative work, physical activity, or collaborative projects. For exercise, late afternoon sessions work well when your cognitive capacity is winding down, but your physical coordination remains strong.

Night Owls: Honor your delayed biological rhythm by using morning hours strategically. Rather than forcing deep analytical work when your brain isn't ready, focus on mechanical tasks, routine administration, or preparing for the day ahead. Consider movement or exercise during the morning hours when your body is awake but your peak mental faculties haven't yet come online. Reserve your most critical thinking, analysis, and strategic decision-making for late afternoon and early evening when your cognitive abilities reach their natural performance peak. If possible, negotiate flexible work hours that capitalize on your natural high-performance window.

Third Birds: You have the advantage of natural alignment with conventional timing. After a brief morning routine, you can transition directly into meaningful work, as your cognitive capacity rises quickly and remains steady through midday. The 10 AM to 2 PM window represents your analytical sweet spot for complex problems and focused thinking. Reserve these hours for your most mentally demanding tasks. Exercise is most efficient when scheduled outside your cognitive peak—early morning or late afternoon typically work well. Unlike Larks, who fade early, or Owls, who peak later, you maintain relatively consistent performance throughout the standard day, requiring less dramatic adjustments to conventional schedules.

Evening and Shutdown Routine

Morning Larks: Your analytical abilities decline earlier, making evenings ideal for activities that benefit from reduced cognitive inhibition—brainstorming, creative exploration, and divergent thinking. Avoid caffeine after lunch, as your sensitivity will be higher. Your evening represents an ideal time for reflective activities, gentle movement, and social connection. Begin your wind-down earlier, ideally dimming lights and reducing screen exposure by 7-8 PM.

Night Owls: Your biggest challenge is likely establishing boundaries around analytical work when you're feeling most mentally sharp. Create a non-negotiable shutdown time, even when you feel intellectually productive. Your morning hours might actually be better suited for creative thinking and brainstorming when your analytical mind is less dominant. Implement a structured wind-down routine that includes gradual blue light reduction and transition activities to signal sleep onset despite your naturally later melatonin release.

Third Birds: Your moderate schedule gives you flexibility in the evening but still requires deliberate structure. Set a consistent work end time that allows at least 2-3 hours of wind-down before sleep. Your evenings might benefit from activities that leverage your gradual cognitive decline—creative hobbies, reflective practices, or exploratory thinking that benefits from reduced analytical constraints.

Adapting to Reality

While understanding your chronotype is powerful, most of us face real-world constraints like standard work hours, family responsibilities, and social obligations. Here's how to make practical adaptations:

For Larks forced into later schedules: Protect your mornings fiercely for cognitive work only. Even if you can't control your entire workday, negotiate for meeting-free mornings and refuse to waste these precious peak hours on routine tasks, exercise, or administrative work. If your job requires you to attend morning meetings, arrive early to tackle your most critical thinking work before others begin their day. Accept that you'll have less energy for intellectually demanding activities after work and plan accordingly.

For Owls forced into early schedules: Use weekend recovery days to restore your natural rhythm. During workweeks, focus on maintaining consistent sleep timing rather than fighting your biology completely. Structure your required early activities to be as movement-oriented or routine as possible, saving any critical thinking for later in the day when your cognitive abilities come online. Consider a short afternoon nap, if possible, to address your sleep deficit and strengthen your late-day performance window.

For Third Birds with standard schedules: Your chronotype already aligns well with conventional work hours, giving you a distinct advantage. Your main challenge isn't adaptation but optimization—ensuring you don't squander this natural alignment. Be vigilant about potential time wasters during your prime cognitive window, and resist the temptation to accommodate others' scheduling preferences when it compromises your own performance rhythm. This alignment is a competitive advantage. Treat it accordingly.

RETHINKING SLEEP AS A PERFORMANCE STATE

As we conclude our exploration of sleep, I want to challenge how you fundamentally think about those hours in bed. Most people view sleep as the absence of productivity—time spent offline, disconnected from their goals and ambitions. This perspective couldn't be more wrong.

Sleep isn't downtime. Sleep is a unique performance state where your brain is actively optimizing your biological systems for peak function. During this time, your brain is processing information, consolidating memories, repairing cellular damage, and preparing you for cognitive challenges.

Think about it through the lens of the Tetris analogy: each day is like a game of Tetris, where sleep is one of those unmovable, uncompromisable blocks. You can't reshape it or compress it. You have to build your day around it. High performers don't view sleep as negotiable. They see it as a fixed, essential component of their performance architecture.

This perspective shift leads to what I call "Sleep Forecasting"—planning your life with sleep as a primary consideration, not an afterthought. When evaluating travel plans, scheduling important meetings, or planning intensive work periods, the first question becomes: "How will this affect my sleep quality?" This isn't overthinking; it's recognizing sleep as the foundation that supports everything else.

In a world obsessed with productivity hacks and optimization techniques, quality sleep remains your ultimate competitive advantage. While others push through on caffeine and willpower, you'll be operating with fully restored cognitive systems, enhanced creativity, and superior emotional regulation. You won't just be outworking the competition—you'll be outperforming them through strategic biological optimization.

The science is clear: Sleep isn't just another health recommendation. It's the single most powerful performance enhancer available to you, and it's entirely free. The question isn't whether you can afford to prioritize sleep; it's whether you can afford not to.

YOUR SLEEP OPTIMIZATION PLAN

Now that we've explored the science of sleep and chronotypes, I want you to take a moment to reflect on what you've learned. Open your journal and answer these two simple questions:

1. What's one sleep optimization strategy from this chapter that you could implement this week?

Choose something manageable. Perhaps adjusting your caffeine cutoff time, creating a consistent wake-up routine, or improving your sleep environment. Assess your life and determine what makes the most sense now.

2. How might you better align your most important work with your chronotype's peak performance window?

Even a tiny adjustment, like moving your most demanding cognitive work to match your biological prime time, can yield significant results. So, please do it!

Remember, you don't need to revolutionize your entire sleep routine overnight. One strategic change, consistently applied, will create more impact than a dozen half-implemented optimizations.

Now that we've optimized your sleep, let's turn our attention to another crucial aspect of your biological performance foundation: exercise and movement. Just as sleep rebuilds your systems during rest, strategic movement optimizes your biology during activity. Together, they form the complementary pillars of your biological performance architecture.

THE FITNESS-BRAIN CONNECTION

John F. Kennedy once observed that physical fitness isn't just essential for bodily health; it also provides the foundation for dynamic and creative intellectual activity. Most people associate exercise primarily with physical health or aesthetics. Still, scientific research reveals a far more compelling benefit: your brain might actually be the greatest beneficiary of regular physical activity.

Throughout history, physicians and philosophers have searched tirelessly for a universal remedy, a single intervention capable of addressing multiple ailments. In ancient times, Hippocrates referred to this elusive cure-all as a "panacea." Modern science has uncovered something extraordinary: regular physical activity may be the closest thing we've found to this mythical remedy.

Exercise stands apart from other health interventions because of its comprehensive impact across multiple body systems. Unlike most medications, which typically target specific symptoms or pathways, regular physical activity simultaneously enhances cardiovascular function, metabolic health, musculoskeletal integrity, immune response, hormonal balance, and, perhaps most notably, cognitive performance.

For the high performer, this presents an unparalleled opportunity. Rather than needing separate strategies to improve energy, sharpen focus, boost creativity, and regulate emotions, exercise offers simultaneous enhancement across all these areas through one integrated activity. In this way, exercise becomes the ultimate efficiency hack: one action yielding multiple high-value outcomes.

THE BRAIN LOVES EXERCISE

The Leeds Metropolitan University conducted an illuminating study on office workers who had access to a company gym, uncovering findings that challenge conventional productivity beliefs. On days when employees exercised, they reported enhanced time management abilities, increased productivity, smoother interactions with colleagues, and greater overall work satisfaction.

What makes this discovery particularly compelling is that exercise didn't merely elevate employees' mood; it substantially boosted their cognitive performance. Tasks that typically seemed challenging became more manageable, creative solutions emerged more easily, and sustained focus improved significantly.

Many high performers view exercise as a luxury they can't afford in their packed schedules. Nick, a tech executive with a rapidly growing startup, exemplified this mindset. "Look, I'm already working 60+ hours a week," he explained during our first meeting. "Exercise sounds great in theory, but let's be realistic about priorities."

Six months later, after implementing a modest exercise routine, Nick's perspective had completely shifted. "I've completely reversed my thinking," he now tells fellow founders. "Those 30 minutes of movement give me back two to three hours of improved cognitive performance. It's mathematically the highest ROI activity in my day."

Exercise uniquely activates multiple components of the ASCENDO framework, creating an optimal neurochemical environment for peak cognitive function. Dopamine levels rise, enhancing focus and learning during performance-critical tasks. Norepinephrine, the natural alertness amplifier, increases without stimulant side effects. Serotonin levels are optimized, providing emotional stability crucial for sustained performance. Endorphins released during physical activity foster sustained energy and improved mood. Perhaps most significantly, exercise stimulates the production of Brain-Derived Neurotrophic Factor (BDNF), a vital "brain fertilizer" that rebuilds and optimizes neural networks.

Additionally, regular physical activity leads to structural improvements in the brain, including increased blood flow, hippocampus growth (the brain's memory center), strengthened neural connections facilitating better learning and adaptation, and enhanced temporal lobe function, resulting in improved sensory processing and memory storage.

These physiological changes not only yield immediate cognitive benefits but also offer long-term protection against cognitive decline, optimizing your brain's performance both now and in the future.

CARDIO VS. RESISTANCE TRAINING

A common question I hear is whether cardiovascular exercise or strength training is more beneficial for cognitive enhancement. The truth is that both are essential. Research increasingly highlights the complementary nature of these two training modalities.

Cardiovascular training provides significant advantages, such as improving blood pressure and cholesterol levels, thereby reducing heart disease risk. It enhances mood and energy by efficiently stimulating endorphin release. Cardiovascular activities also improve cerebral blood flow, which lowers Alzheimer's risk, and increase insulin sensitivity—a critical factor for maintaining optimal brain health. Additionally, these exercises support bone density through repetitive weight-bearing movements and significantly boost memory and overall cognitive function.

Resistance training, on the other hand, offers unique cognitive benefits through specific neural adaptations. It helps build lean muscle mass, reduce inflammation-inducing body fat, and enhance metabolic health by improving insulin sensitivity. Strength training also raises baseline energy levels, improves mood regulation, strengthens bones through mechanical loading, and significantly enhances joint stability, balance, and coordination.

Current scientific consensus indicates that the optimal strategy combines both cardiovascular and resistance training. Together, these training methods provide complementary adaptations that neither approach alone can fully achieve. Just as your body thrives on diverse stimuli, your brain adapts most effectively when challenged by a balanced mix of training inputs.

NEAT: ELEVATING EVERYDAY ACTIVITY

While structured exercise is crucial, there's another dimension of movement that might be even more important for your overall health and cognitive performance: Non-Exercise Activity Thermogenesis (NEAT).

NEAT encompasses all the energy you expend outside of sleeping, eating, or formal exercise. From walking to your car to fidgeting during meetings, from gardening to playing with your kids. What makes NEAT particularly interesting from a performance perspective is how powerfully it impacts your overall energy expenditure and metabolic health without requiring dedicated "workout time."

Here's how to strategically incorporate more NEAT into your daily life:

1. Increase Daily Steps: Target at least 10,000 steps daily, tracking with a fitness wearable or smartphone. Simple hacks include parking further from destinations or taking stairs instead of elevators. This isn't just about calorie expenditure; it's about keeping your brain in an active, engaged state throughout the day.

2. Incorporate Movement Into Work: Alternate between sitting and standing using an adjustable desk. Conduct walking meetings instead of sitting in conference rooms. Take brief movement breaks hourly. Even just 2-3 minutes of activity can reset your brain's focus mechanisms and improve cognitive performance.

3. Optimize Your Commute: If feasible, bike or walk to work instead of driving. If you use public transportation, get off a stop early and walk the remaining distance. These small decisions compound into significant cognitive benefits over time.

4. Reframe Household Activities: Approach cleaning, gardening, and home maintenance as opportunities for movement rather than chores. Engage more actively with children or pets through physical play. These activities aren't just "getting things done"—they're opportunities for brain-enhancing movement.

5. Develop Your Optimal Default Workout: Create a simple sequence of bodyweight exercises you can perform anywhere without equipment. Perhaps push-ups, squats, planks, and jumping jacks. Use small windows of time throughout your day to perform these movements. These micro-workouts accumulate significant benefits while maintaining neural activation.

This approach to movement helped transform Miguel's relationship with exercise. As a busy business owner who often worked well beyond full-time hours, he struggled to find time for formal workouts. "I was stuck in all-or-nothing thinking," he explains. "If I couldn't do a full hour-long session, I felt it wasn't even worth lacing up my shoes."

By reframing movement as something that happens throughout the day rather than just at the gym, he achieved better results with less stress. "I still do structured workouts when I can, but now I also accumulate movement all day long. I take calls while walking, do squats while waiting for my coffee to brew, and I walk to work. My energy is better, my focus is sharper, and I no longer feel guilty about 'not exercising enough.'"

THE OPTIMAL EXERCISE PRESCRIPTION

When it comes to formal exercise, a balanced approach yields the most comprehensive benefits for your brain. Current scientific consensus recommends at least 150 minutes of moderate aerobic activity or 75 minutes of vigorous exercise each week, complemented by strength training two to three times weekly. Additionally, it's beneficial to spread your movement evenly throughout the week rather than condensing it into just one or two sessions.

Building Strength

Strength training offers more than just muscular gains; it significantly improves your nervous system efficiency and neural coordination. To maximize cognitive and physical benefits, aim to train two to three times weekly. Choose challenging weights, approximately 85% of your one-rep maximum, and perform three to eight repetitions per exercise. Compound movements that engage multiple muscle groups, such as squats or deadlifts, should be prioritized. Complete three to five sets of each movement, allowing two to three minutes of rest between sets for optimal recovery.

Developing Power

Incorporating power training adds a crucial dimension by focusing on explosive movements that enhance both muscle and nervous system responsiveness. The foundational principle is straightforward: Power equals speed multiplied by force. You can integrate power training into your regular strength sessions or dedicate a separate weekly workout for it. Select lighter weights—around 30% of your one-rep maximum—to facilitate explosive execution. Effective exercises include kettlebell swings, medicine ball throws, or jump squats. Perform three to ten sets of five repetitions, concentrating on maximum explosive effort, and rest two to three minutes between sets to maintain performance quality.

Cardiovascular Training

For a well-rounded cardiovascular regimen, include both moderate and high-intensity training sessions.

Moderate-Intensity Cardio (Zone 3): Maintain your heart rate at approximately 70-80% of your maximum capacity. Aim for sessions lasting about 30 minutes, engaging in activities such as brisk walking, cycling, jogging, or swimming. Afterward, incorporate active recovery methods like walking or stretching.

High-Intensity Cardio (Zone 4/5): Limit these sessions to once per week due to their demanding nature. During intense intervals, target 90-100% of your maximum heart rate. Keep these sessions under 25 minutes in total, using structured protocols such as Tabata intervals (20 seconds of high-intensity work followed by 10 seconds rest) or 30-second maximum effort sprints on a bike followed by one to two minutes of rest, repeated over a 20-minute session.

The Tabata Protocol

The Tabata Protocol deserves special attention for busy high performers. Developed by Japanese scientist Dr. Izumi Tabata, this method consists of just 4 minutes of intense exercise: 20 seconds of maximum effort followed by 10 seconds of rest, repeated 8 times.

What makes Tabata remarkable is its efficiency. In Dr. Tabata's original research, this 4-minute protocol improved both aerobic and anaerobic fitness more effectively than 60 minutes of moderate-intensity exercise. For time-constrained professionals, this represents the ultimate exercise optimization.

A simple Tabata workout might include:

- 20 seconds of burpees, 10 seconds of rest.
- 20 seconds of jumping jacks, 10 seconds of rest.
- 20 seconds of mountain climbers, 10 seconds of rest.
- 20 seconds of bodyweight squats, 10 seconds of rest.
- Repeat this cycle once more.

The key is maximum intensity during work periods—you should feel completely spent by the end of each 20-second interval. If you're not gasping for breath, you're likely not pushing hard enough to trigger the full benefits.

As you progress in optimizing your Performance Pillars, consult with your physician about potentially reducing or eliminating certain medications. More importantly, always seek medical guidance before combining any supplements with your current prescriptions. Your biological optimization journey should work in harmony with, not against, any necessary medical treatment.

A SIMPLE WEEKLY WORKOUT ROUTINE

For busy professionals looking to implement a straightforward exercise regimen, here's a practical weekly template that delivers comprehensive benefits with minimal time investment:

Monday: Strength Training (30-40 minutes)
- 5-minute dynamic warm-up
- 3-4 compound exercises (squats, push-ups, rows, lunges)
- 3 sets of 8-12 reps per exercise
- Focus on proper form rather than maximum weight

Wednesday: Tabata/HIIT Session (15-20 minutes)
- 5-minute warm-up
- 8-minute Tabata protocol (2 cycles of 4 exercises)
- 5-minute cool-down

Friday: Strength Training (30-40 minutes)
- Similar structure to Monday but with different exercises
- Include deadlift variations, overhead press, pull-ups/assisted pull-ups
- Add core-specific work like planks or hollow holds

Saturday or Sunday: Zone 2 Cardio (30-45 minutes)
- Brisk walking, light jogging, cycling, or swimming
- Keep heart rate at 60-70% of maximum (conversational pace)
- Use this session for mental recovery while moving

Daily: Movement Snacks (5 minutes, multiple times)
- Brief movement breaks throughout workdays
- Simple activities like walking, stretching, or bodyweight exercises
- Aim for your 10,000 steps total throughout the day

This approach requires just 2-3 hours of dedicated exercise weekly while delivering comprehensive benefits for brain health, physical fitness, and stress resilience.

Sauna for Cognitive Enhancement

Beyond traditional exercise, sauna therapy has emerged as a powerful complement to any performance optimization protocol. Often found in gym settings, regular sauna use enhances and extends the cognitive benefits of exercise through several fascinating mechanisms:

Cognitive Function Enhancement: Sauna sessions trigger a release of norepinephrine similar to exercise, enhancing attention, perception, and motivation. The controlled heat stress creates conditions that improve mental clarity and cognitive processing—benefits that persist well beyond the sauna session itself.

Stress Reduction and Mood Elevation: The heat promotes endorphin release, creating a state of relaxation and positive mood. For high performers, this provides a valuable reset mechanism between intensive work periods, helping maintain optimal emotional states for decision-making and creative work.

Neurogenesis Support: Perhaps most intriguing, heat exposure stimulates BDNF production, supporting the growth of new neurons and protecting existing ones from degeneration. This makes sauna use particularly relevant for long-term cognitive health and performance longevity.

Beyond these brain-specific benefits, regular sauna use provides complementary advantages for overall performance:
- Improved cardiovascular function.
- Enhanced muscle recovery and flexibility.
- Supported detoxification pathways.
- Strengthened immune system function.
- Potential longevity benefits.

For "ideal" implementation, aim for 2-3 sauna sessions weekly, ideally post-exercise. But if you can only do it once in a while, it's still better than nothing. Each session should last approximately 15-20 minutes, with a gradual increase as your heat tolerance develops. Stay well-hydrated before and after sessions, and always listen to your body's signals regarding heat tolerance.

THE MOVEMENT-STRESS CONNECTION

As we've seen, movement is a powerful tool for cognitive enhancement and biochemical optimization. However, exercise itself is a form of controlled stress. One that makes us more resilient to life's challenges.

This brings us to our next frontier: Stress Mastery. While exercise helps build stress resilience through physical adaptation, we need a comprehensive approach to handle modern life's unique pressures.

In the next chapter, we'll explore how to transform stress from a performance killer into a performance enhancer, building upon the physiological foundation we've established through nutrition, supplementation, sleep, and movement.

RESEARCH & RESOURCES

Once again, please visit the Holistic Performance Resource Hub to access the research and additional materials mentioned in this chapter.

To do so, go to hplink.org/resourcehub or scan the QR code below.

CHAPTER 8
STRESS MASTERY

"Pressure can burst a pipe, or pressure can make a diamond."
– Robert Horry

Imagine, for a moment, that every surge of pressure in your life—every deadline, every unexpected challenge—is not merely a force working against you, but an opportunity to be transformed. Much like carbon under immense pressure transforms into a brilliant diamond, the stress you encounter might become the very catalyst that refines your performance, your clarity, and even your creativity. In this chapter, we unlock the profound science behind stress. Unveiling not only how our bodies and brains respond to threats but also how we can harness that very response as an engine for lasting high performance.

This section does more than just examine stress as a biological anomaly to be subdued; it reframes stress as an adaptive signal built into our biology. As we just discovered in Chapter 7's exploration of nutrition, sleep, and exercise optimization, your biochemistry forms the foundation of performance. Now, we'll see how stress—when properly understood and managed—becomes another powerful lever in your biological optimization toolkit rather than an obstacle to overcome.

Here, we begin our journey by exploring the intricate pathways that govern our stress response. From the vigilant amygdala to the commanding hypothalamus and the dual functions of our autonomic nervous system, we reveal how every cell contributes to a symphony of survival. But this isn't a lecture on dismal stress management. This is a narrative about reclaiming our innate power, setting the stage to integrate practical techniques to help you leverage stress. These tools will serve as part of a multifaceted strategy, helping you convert the energy of stress—whether that energy impairs you or propels you—into a force of improvement and sustainable excellence.

In the rich tapestry of our performance ecosystem, stress is both an inherent challenge and an enlightening guide. Understanding its mechanisms is the first step toward unlocking a more robust, healthy, and dynamic state of being. As we delve into the science behind stress, you'll begin to appreciate how every surge in adrenaline, every spike in cortisol, and every beat of your heart is part of a deeply interwoven system designed not simply to keep you alive but to propel you toward peak performance.

THE TRUE NATURE OF STRESS

At its very core, stress is the body's ancient evolutionary response to threats—a sophisticated alarm system honed over millennia. When we speak of "stress," we are referring to the body's automatic reaction to any kind of demand or danger, whether real or imagined. Think of stress not as an external enemy but as an internal prompt. A call to action that says, "Prepare, react, and adapt." This response, commonly known as the "fight-or-flight" instinct, is our physiological safeguard; it is the process by which our body readies itself for immediate challenges.

The cascade begins in an unassuming structure—the amygdala. Often compared to a watchtower on the outskirts of a bustling city, the amygdala is constantly scanning the environment for even the slightest signal that something is amiss. When it detects a potential threat, it sends a rapid distress signal to the hypothalamus—the body's mission control. In a display reminiscent of a seasoned military commander, the hypothalamus immediately mobilizes the body's resources to confront the perceived challenge.

This activation is executed through the Autonomic Nervous System (ANS), which splits into two distinct branches, each with its own role in managing our internal state. On one side, we have the Sympathetic Nervous System (SNS), the proverbial gas pedal. Once alerted, the SNS springs into action: the adrenal medulla is stimulated to release epinephrine and norepinephrine, hormones that surge through the blood and ignite a series of rapid responses. Your heart rate increases, blood pressure elevates, and a burst of energy floods your system—all critical for those moments when immediate action is required.

Complementing this rapid activation is the Parasympathetic Nervous System (PNS), which acts as the essential counterbalance. Imagine the PNS as the skilled driver who knows when to ease off the accelerator; its role is to calm the body once the immediate danger has passed. By slowing the heart rate, lowering blood pressure, and promoting a state of deep relaxation, the PNS gradually returns the body to balance—a moment of pause that facilitates recovery and lays the groundwork for sustained calm.

In real-world terms, consider the experience of a high-performing executive who, in the heat of a crucial negotiation, feels their heart racing and senses a rush of energy. That surge is the SNS taking charge, arming them for the moment. Yet, once the negotiation concludes, it is the PNS that helps them transition back into a state of clarity and composure, ensuring that the temporary stress does not consume their well-being.

However, the initial burst of a stress response is only the prologue to a more sustained narrative—a deeper, more enduring system known as the Hypothalamic-Pituitary-Adrenal (HPA) axis. As the immediate effects of adrenaline begin to recede, the body recognizes the need for a longer-term strategy to manage the stressor. The hypothalamus, shifting from the role of an emergency responder to that of a long-term regulator, releases corticotropin-releasing hormone (CRH). This hormone sets off a chain reaction: the pituitary gland responds by secreting adrenocorticotropic hormone (ACTH), which in turn travels through the bloodstream until it reaches the adrenal glands. Here, the adrenal cortex produces cortisol, the primary hormone associated with sustained stress.

Cortisol, as you recall, has a complex portfolio. Among its many features, it ensures that your brain has an ample supply of glucose—a critical fuel during demanding times—while simultaneously downregulating nonessential functions such as digestion and reproductive processes. In a sense, cortisol is the body's economizer, reallocating resources to power what matters most in moments of crisis.

Yet, while an acute stress response is both necessary and beneficial, our modern environment often subjects us to chronic stressors that can lead to dangerous levels of HPA activation. Unlike the short bursts of energy designed for immediate survival, prolonged high cortisol levels can disrupt nearly every system in your body—fueling anxiety, impairing sleep, skewing weight balance, and even dulling your cognitive clarity.

This delicate balance—between the immediate, protective burst of the SNS and the controlled, adaptive regulation via the HPA axis and PNS—is what makes understanding stress so essential. It is a biological symphony where every note must be in tune; when one aspect overplays its role, the entire composition of our well-being can unravel.

In the sections to come, we will see how mastering these processes—by harnessing additional tools from cognitive reframing to biofeedback, and not least, to various forms of breathwork—empowers you to modulate your body's responses effectively. As you read on, you'll begin to recognize that stress, often demonized as a destructive force, can actually be reprogrammed into a powerful ally in your holistic performance journey.

THE DUAL NATURE OF STRESS

As you are learning, stress is not a uniform phenomenon but rather a spectrum of responses that can manifest in very different ways. On one end, we have **distress**—a state of overwhelming pressure that impairs performance and degrades well-being. On the other, there is **eustress**—a form of stress that, rather than overwhelming us, actually propels us forward.

Imagine two captains at the helm of a ship. One faces a relentless, roaring storm capable of wrecking even the sturdiest vessel; this is distress. Waves of pressure, uncertainty, and fear batter his ship, leaving him exhausted and struggling to stay afloat. In contrast, the other captain harnesses a favorable wind—a burst of dynamic energy that challenges him just enough to steer his ship with precision toward a promising horizon. This is eustress. It offers the kind of challenge that ignites creativity, focus, and a heightened state of awareness.

Scientific research underpins this duality. The Yerkes-Dodson Law, for instance, graphically illustrates that performance improves with increased arousal, but only up to an optimal point. Too little arousal and our performance languishes in boredom; too much, and our capacity to function deteriorates. This inverted-U curve highlights that not all stress is inherently harmful; the trick lies in finding that sweet spot where the energy derived from stress becomes a catalyst for peak performance.

A critical factor in this equation is perception—the lens through which you view a stressor. How you interpret a situation—a grueling deadline, a high-stakes presentation, or even a challenging personal goal—shapes its impact. When you see a stressor as a threat, your body gears up for a fight-or-flight response, leading to chronic activation of the HPA axis and persistent cortisol elevation. On the other hand, if you reframe the same situation as an opportunity for growth, you can shift its energy to invigorate your mind and body. In this way, stress becomes optional.

You have far more control over your response than you might think. Research shows that with techniques such as meditation, biofeedback, and controlled stress exposure, even those involuntary responses—like fluctuations in body temperature or metabolism—can be consciously moderated. These approaches help reset the HPA feedback loop, empowering you to harness stress as an ally rather than viewing it solely as a destructive force.

This nuanced understanding is essential. It teaches us that mastering stress doesn't mean eliminating it entirely, but rather fine-tuning our systems to respond in a balanced way. In our quest for holistic performance, recognizing and cultivating eustress is as vital as mitigating distress. A well-calibrated system, where our adaptive capacity matches the intensity of a challenge, becomes a crucible for resilience and improved performance.

MASTERING THE AUTONOMIC NERVOUS SYSTEM

Having established that not all stress is created equal, we now turn our attention to one of the body's most promising tools for modulating our stress response—the vagus nerve. Often described as the communication highway between the brain and our organs, the vagus nerve plays a pivotal role in orchestrating the parasympathetic nervous system, effectively acting as the "brake" to the sympathetic surge we discussed earlier.

Think of the vagus nerve as the thermostat for your internal climate. When life's pressures push your system into overdrive, a well-tuned vagal response helps cool things down, restoring balance and preventing overheating. The goal of vagal toning is to enhance the responsiveness of this nerve, essentially raising your threshold for stress and enabling a quicker return to calm. This balance is essential for maintaining a state of adaptive resilience, particularly in the face of chronic stressors.

There are several practical strategies to boost vagal tone, each grounded in both ancient wisdom and modern science:

Diaphragmatic (Belly) Breathing: This practice encourages deep, slow breaths that stimulate the vagus nerve, shifting the balance toward parasympathetic activity. Imagine each breath as a gentle wave, washing over your body and ushering in a sense of calm.

Laughter Yoga and Genuine Belly Laughs: Engaging in hearty laughter doesn't just lighten the mood—it has a measurable impact on vagal activation. The spontaneous bursts of laughter serve as a natural tonic, resetting the body's stress response.

Cold Exposure: Brief, controlled encounters with cold—such as a quick cold shower or splashing cool water on the face—can trigger a beneficial vagal response, much like a quick reset button for your internal thermostat.

Ear Massage and Humming: Simple tactile stimulation, such as a gentle ear massage or the resonant quality of humming and chanting, can activate the vagus nerve. These practices tap into the subtle yet powerful sensory connections that contribute to our overall sense of well-being.

Yoga and Other Mind-Body Practices: Many yoga poses and mindful movement practices are known to enhance vagal tone, seamlessly connecting physical posture with mental balance.

Integrating these tools into your daily routine offers more than just temporary relief from stress; it builds a robust foundation for long-term resilience. Improved vagal tone translates into better emotional regulation, faster recovery after stressful events, and an enhanced ability to maintain clarity even during high-pressure situations. In effect, by mastering vagal toning, you are training your body to view stress not as an insurmountable adversary but as a manageable—indeed, even a beneficial—part of your broader performance ecosystem.

Let me share how Chris, the digital agency owner we met earlier, has been working with these concepts. When we first discussed stress management, he was skeptical.

"I was running on pure adrenaline for years," he told me. "The deadlines, the client emergencies, the team issues... I just powered through it all. When you suggested I try cold showers and breathing exercises, I honestly thought it sounded like new-age nonsense."

Two months later, Chris sent me a text after a particularly challenging week: "That breathing thing you taught me actually worked. Had three client fires to put out yesterday. Did the box breathing before each call. Still felt the pressure but didn't get that foggy panic feeling. Even slept better. Weird but it works."

It wasn't a dramatic overnight transformation, but Chris found that consistently practicing vagal toning, mainly through breath work and occasional cold exposure, gave him a practical tool to handle pressure without burning out. "I'm not saying I'm zen master now," he joked during our follow-up, "but I'm definitely not red-lining all day like I used to."

MASTERING THE PHYSIOLOGICAL RESPONSE WITH BREATHWORK

Breath isn't just that invisible force that keeps you alive; it's also one of your most direct tools for calibrating your internal state. By controlling your breathing, you can switch your body's mode from "panic mode" to "zen mode" in just a few mindful moments. Research shows that targeted breathwork can shift your system from a stress-induced sympathetic overdrive to a calm, parasympathetic balance—and vice versa if you need a boost of alertness. In short, mastering the art of breathing is like having an on/off switch for your internal thermostat.

Breathwork for Relaxation

When you need to dial down the tension after a long day or a challenging meeting, specific breathing techniques can win the day. Consider these advanced relaxation methods:

The Doublet Breath (Physiological Sigh): Promoted by Andrew Huberman, this technique involves a sharp, nasal inhale followed by a forced sniff, then a long, deliberate exhale. This pattern is designed to rapidly reduce stress by quickly expelling carbon dioxide and calming the nervous system.

Valsalva Maneuver: Performed <u>mindfully and with care</u>, this technique momentarily increases internal pressure, thereby stimulating the vagus nerve. The subsequent exhale facilitates a transition into a state of calm. (Note: This is not recommended for those with cardiovascular concerns.)

Box Breathing: Picture drawing a perfect square with your breath: inhale for four seconds, hold for four, exhale for four, and hold again for four. This technique is beneficial for focus and calmness.

4-7-8 Breathing: Gently inhale for a count of four, hold the breath for seven counts, and then exhale slowly through slightly pursed lips for a count of eight. Similar to box breathing in its effectiveness, this technique is particularly useful for reducing immediate stress.

Alternate Nostril Breathing: In this method, you close one nostril while inhaling through the other, then switch for the exhale. This practice is aimed at balancing both hemispheres of the brain while reducing physiological signs of stress.

Breathwork for Activation

Not every situation calls for a full-on relaxation; sometimes, you need to power up and focus. Here are some techniques to energize your system:

Kapalbhati Pranayama (Breath of Fire): This involves rapid, rhythmic inhalations and forceful exhalations through the nose. The focus is on expelling air forcefully while the inhalation happens passively. Start with one round of 30 breaths and, as you build comfort, work up to three rounds with breaks in between.

Wim Hof Breathing: Developed by the "Iceman" himself, this method consists of 30–40 cycles of deep, forceful breathing, followed by a breath-hold at the end of the cycle for as long as possible. Then, release and repeat the cycle. The deep inhalations are the primary focus, with the breath-hold further enhancing the activation effect.

Power Breathing: In this practice, you perform deep, "somewhat" rapid inhalations through the nose followed by quick, forceful exhalations. It is less intense than the previous two methods, making it a more accessible option for a quick energy boost. Start with two to three minutes of continuous breathing, gradually extending the duration to five minutes or more as you become more comfortable.

Surya Bhedana (Right Nostril Breathing): This technique involves inhaling exclusively through the right nostril, believed in yogic traditions to stimulate the body's solar energy channel. It's particularly effective in boosting energy, enhancing focus, and generating internal warmth. Begin with a cycle of 10 breaths and work up to 15–20 breaths per round, completing up to three cycles with brief rests in between.

APPLICATION IN DAILY LIFE, SAFETY, AND INTEGRATION

The real value of these breathwork techniques lies in their versatility and integration with our broader biological optimization strategy. Here's how breathwork complements what we've been building:

Remember the ASCENDO framework we explored in the previous chapter? These breathing practices give you direct control over multiple components simultaneously. Relaxation techniques downregulate cortisol while supporting serotonin production, creating the emotional stability needed for clear decision-making. Activation breathwork, meanwhile, stimulates norepinephrine and dopamine, providing that edge of heightened focus and motivation when you need it most.

This creates powerful synergies with your other biological optimization practices. While quality sleep—as we discussed extensively—provides the foundation for recovery and neural cleaning, breathwork offers on-demand modulation between active and restorative states. Similarly, the nutritional strategies we covered help maintain steady glucose levels and reduce inflammation, creating a baseline of biochemical balance that makes your breathwork even more effective.

Think about how this complements your movement practice too. The cardiovascular conditioning from regular exercise enhances your breathing capacity and vagal tone, making these techniques progressively more powerful. Conversely, strategic breathwork can amplify the benefits of your workouts—whether you're using activation breathing to maximize performance during high-intensity intervals or relaxation techniques to deepen recovery during cool-downs.

Strategically select techniques to balance your current state. Use relaxation methods when feeling tense or overwhelmed, and energizing practices like Kapalbhati when mental fatigue sets in or focus wanes. Match the technique to your immediate need rather than following a rigid schedule. With practice, you'll develop an intuitive sense of what your system needs at each moment.

Although these techniques are highly accessible, it's essential to start slowly, especially if you're new to breathwork or have any health concerns. Listen closely to your body's signals, and don't push yourself beyond comfortable limits. If a method feels too intense, opt for a gentler alternative or seek guidance from an experienced instructor.

The goal of sharing these techniques isn't for you to memorize them all immediately but to experiment and discover what works best for you. Over time, you'll develop the intuition to select the correct technique for your current state. Additional tools and tutorials are provided in Resource Hub to offer further guidance on proper execution.

By incorporating these breathwork practices into your daily life, you can build a resilient and adaptable system that meets both moments of relaxation and activation. The aim is not to follow every instruction perfectly but to practice, adjust, and determine which techniques best align with your personal needs. With time and experience, your breath will become one of your most potent instruments for regulating your body and mind.

YOUR BREATHWORK CHALLENGE

Before continuing to the next section, I invite you to put this knowledge into immediate practice. Take 10 minutes right now to experiment with two contrasting breathwork techniques:

1. First, try the Box Breathing technique for 3 minutes. Notice how your shoulders relax, your mind clears, and your heart rate steadies. Pay particular attention to the transition from mental chatter to focused presence.
2. Then, after a brief pause, experience the energizing effects of Power Breathing for 2 minutes. Observe how your alertness increases, your posture naturally straightens, and your energy shifts.

This mini-experiment serves two purposes: it gives you immediate experience with these powerful tools, and more importantly, it demonstrates the remarkable control you have over your own biology. The difference you feel between these two states, within just minutes of practice, reveals the extraordinary precision with which you can modulate your internal environment.

MASTERING YOUR INNER LANDSCAPE

Imagine fighting an invisible opponent. You feel the impact of every blow, your energy depletes with each exchange, yet you can't quite see what you're up against. That's exactly what battling stress feels like when you lack internal awareness. While we've explored how nutrition, sleep, and movement form the biological foundation of performance, we now face perhaps the most elusive element of all: our internal landscape.

Here's something that consistently amazes me when working with clients: the most debilitating stressors often aren't the external challenges everyone can see. It's not the looming deadline, the competitive market, or the demanding stakeholders that ultimately break performance. It's our internal relationship with these pressures—a relationship most people never consciously examine.

"How can you solve stress when you're not even aware of its cause?" This question sits at the heart of stress mastery, yet about 90% of the population remains blind to their internal triggers at any given moment. Think about it. We invest countless resources optimizing external systems while our most sophisticated instrument—our mind-body connection—operates on autopilot, running outdated programming we never bother to update.

This is where introspection becomes your ultimate competitive advantage. While others remain trapped in reactive cycles, introspective awareness creates a crucial gap between stimulus and response—a space where true performance mastery becomes possible.

Take Manuel, the executive who had already seen remarkable improvements from the single-tasking strategies we discussed in Chapter 5. Despite his productivity gains, he kept hitting an invisible wall. "I'd fixed my external systems, but I was still losing whole days to stress and overwhelm," he admitted. When I suggested developing internal awareness through brief daily check-ins, he was dismissive. "I need practical solutions, not more time-wasting techniques," he said bluntly.

Two months later, Manuel's perspective had changed. "I was dead wrong," he confessed. "For years, I couldn't figure out why I'd suddenly snap at my team or freeze up during important presentations. Turns out I just wasn't paying attention to what was happening in my own body. Now I can tell when I'm about to hit the wall because I actually notice when my breathing gets shallow or my shoulders tense up. It's not complicated—it's just paying attention to signals I was ignoring before."

This shift from operating on autopilot to conscious awareness represents the fundamental first step in stress mastery. Just as we discussed the importance of tracking your biological metrics in previous chapters, developing internal awareness creates your personal dashboard for navigating life's challenges with precision rather than reaction.

Instead of being hijacked by stress, you become its interpreter and, ultimately, its master. And that journey begins with understanding your body's most sophisticated feedback system. One that's been quietly communicating with you all along, whether you've been listening or not.

HRV: YOUR BODY'S BIOLOGICAL FEEDBACK SYSTEM

Remember our discussion of the autonomic nervous system—that intricate balance between sympathetic (fight-or-flight) and parasympathetic (rest-and-digest) responses? While we've explored how nutrition, sleep, and strategic movement influence this system, there's a remarkable metric that offers a window directly into this delicate balance: Heart Rate Variability (HRV).

Despite its technical-sounding name, HRV reflects something profoundly simple yet powerful—the variation in time between successive heartbeats. This isn't about how fast your heart beats but rather how adaptable it is from moment to moment. Think of it like the difference between a metronome rigidly keeping time versus a skilled jazz drummer who flows with the music, adjusting each beat to create something simultaneously stable and responsive.

What makes HRV fascinating from a performance perspective is how directly it connects to our ASCENDO framework. High HRV correlates with balanced cortisol regulation, optimal norepinephrine levels, and enhanced serotonin function—essentially, it reflects your entire biochemical orchestra flowing in harmony rather than discord.

The performance implications are profound. Research consistently shows that individuals with higher HRV demonstrate:

- Superior emotional regulation during high-pressure situations.
- Enhanced cognitive flexibility when faced with complex problems.
- Faster recovery from intense efforts.
- Better sleep quality and efficiency.
- Improved decision-making, particularly under stress.

"But I thought a steady heartbeat was ideal," Nicole, once told me in one of our sessions. This common misconception highlights our cultural misunderstanding of stress physiology. The truth is counterintuitive yet beautiful: variability in heart rhythm indicates flexibility and resilience, not inconsistency or weakness.

Consider the implications: a high HRV suggests your body can efficiently shift between sympathetic activation (when you need focused energy) and parasympathetic recovery (when you need restoration). This adaptability is precisely what allows elite performers to engage intensely when needed, then disengage completely for recovery—rather than remaining stuck in chronic low-grade activation that drains performance and health.

Measuring HRV has become increasingly accessible through wearable technology like Oura Rings, Apple Watches, Whoop bands, and other devices. These tools provide a non-invasive window into your autonomic function, offering concrete data about your stress response and recovery capacity.

What's particularly valuable about tracking HRV isn't just the absolute numbers but the patterns that emerge over time. You might notice, for instance, that moderate alcohol consumption tanks your HRV the following day, or that specific breathing practices substantially improve it. These insights create a feedback loop that allows for increasingly precise management of your internal state.

Beyond measurement, the real question becomes: how do we improve this crucial metric? While we'll explore specific techniques shortly, the foundation comes from developing something more fundamental—your capacity for interoception, your sixth sense that monitors your internal environment.

DEVELOPING YOUR INTEROCEPTION

When you think about your senses, you probably list the classic five: sight, hearing, taste, touch, and smell. But there's another crucial sense that most people overlook entirely—your interoceptive sense—the ability to detect and interpret signals from inside your body.

Interoception is essentially your internal awareness system. A sophisticated network that monitors everything from subtle shifts in heart rate to changes in breathing patterns, from muscle tension to digestive activity. Think of it as your body's internal monitoring system, constantly gathering data that could significantly enhance your performance if only you knew how to access it.

The science behind this internal sensing system is fascinating. Your body contains specialized nerve receptors called interoceptors that detect internal states and relay this information to key brain regions, particularly the insula. This brain area integrates these bodily signals with emotional processing and decision-making. When this system functions optimally, you gain access to what feels almost like a superpower—the ability to detect and respond to subtle internal shifts before they manifest as performance problems.

Consider how this might play out in practice. Most people only recognize stress when it's already overwhelming—when the headache has started, the irritability has emerged, or the focus has completely shattered. However, someone with developed interoceptive awareness notices the first subtle shoulder tension, the slight shift in breathing pattern, or the initial speed-up in heart rate. This early detection creates a crucial advantage—the ability to course-correct before stress cascades into performance breakdown.

"I used to think being 'in tune with your body' was more like something yoga teachers talked about," shared Andreia, our clinic owner. "But developing this awareness completely changed how I handle stress. Now I can feel the tension building in my jaw or my breathing getting shallow, and I address it immediately instead of waiting until I'm completely overwhelmed."

This body-mind connection serves as the foundation for peak performance states. Research from the flow state literature consistently shows that deep embodiment—that sense of being fully present in your physical experience—

often precedes those extraordinary moments of effortless high performance. When you're deeply connected to your internal landscape, you create the conditions for what Steven Kotler calls "total physical awareness," one of the key precursors to flow.

The good news? Interoception is a trainable skill. Here are some evidence-based approaches to enhance this critical capacity:

1. Daily Movement Practices

Activities like yoga, Pilates, and tai chi naturally strengthen the connection between mind and body. The slow, deliberate movements combined with breath awareness create ideal conditions for developing interoceptive sensitivity.

2. Mindfulness Training

Regular mindfulness practice enhances your ability to notice subtle internal signals without automatically reacting to them. Even simple practices like taking three mindful breaths before important meetings can begin developing this capacity.

3. Body Scanning

This structured practice involves systematically moving your attention through different parts of your body, noting sensations without judgment. Research shows that regular body scanning significantly improves interoceptive accuracy.

4. Contrast Experiences

Deliberately exposing yourself to controlled stressors—like brief cold exposure or intense exercise followed by complete relaxation—helps calibrate your internal sensing system, making subtle shifts more noticeable.

The benefits extend far beyond stress management. Enhanced interoception correlates with improvements in emotional regulation, intuitive decision-making, and even interpersonal sensitivity. By strengthening this internal awareness, you develop what amounts to an early warning system for performance threats and opportunities alike.

This heightened internal awareness sets the stage perfectly for our next exploration—the practical application of mindfulness as a performance-enhancing strategy.

THE MINDFULNESS ADVANTAGE

If you've ever rolled your eyes at the suggestion to "just be more mindful," you're not alone. Few terms have suffered more from wellness-industry overexposure than mindfulness. Yet beneath the Instagram hashtags and corporate wellness buzzwords lies something profoundly valuable—especially for high performers seeking a sustainable edge.

Let's start by clarifying what mindfulness actually is, stripped of the cultural baggage. At its core, mindfulness is simply a state of awareness characterized by attention to present-moment experience without judgment. It's not about emptying your mind, achieving enlightenment, or even relaxing (though relaxation is often a welcome side effect). Instead, it's about developing the mental skill of directing and sustaining attention with precision.

The neuroscience is compelling. Regular mindfulness practice correlates with measurable changes in brain regions associated with attention control, emotional regulation, and stress management. Most notably, research shows increased gray matter density in the prefrontal cortex (your executive function center) and decreased activity in the amygdala (your alarm system)—essentially strengthening your brain's "accelerator" while calibrating its "brakes."

What makes mindfulness particularly relevant to our discussion is how it builds upon interoceptive awareness while enhancing your relationship with stress. Remember, stress itself isn't the enemy; it's our relationship with stress that determines whether it enhances or impairs performance.

This relationship transformation happens through what Dr. Daniel J. Siegel calls the "3 O's of Mindfulness":

Openness

Developing the capacity to approach experiences with curiosity rather than automatic judgment. This creates cognitive flexibility, allowing you to consider new perspectives and solutions rather than defaulting to habitual reactions. When facing a challenging negotiation, for instance, openness might help you see past your initial defensive reaction to recognize the underlying interests driving the other party's position.

Observation

Cultivating the ability to witness your thoughts, emotions, and sensations as passing events rather than absolute truths that demand immediate action. This creates a crucial gap between stimulus and response. What psychiatrist Viktor Frankl allegedly called "the space in which our power to choose our response lies." During a high-stakes presentation, observation allows you to notice anxiety arising without becoming overwhelmed by it.

Objectivity

Gaining perspective on your mental and emotional patterns, recognizing that thoughts and feelings are transient experiences rather than defining characteristics. This creates emotional resilience by helping you avoid over-identification with temporary states. When receiving critical feedback, objectivity enables you to evaluate the information usefully rather than experiencing it as a threat to your identity.

These qualities don't just sound nice; they translate directly into performance advantages. A 2018 meta-analysis published in the Journal of Management found that mindfulness training consistently improved job performance across multiple domains, with particularly strong effects on attention, working memory, and resilience to stress.

Chris, our agency owner, initially approached mindfulness with skepticism. "I thought it was just about sitting cross-legged and chanting," he admitted, laughing. "But what changed my mind was learning it's really about mental training, like weight lifting for your attention muscles. Once I understood it that way, I could separate the practical benefits from all the spiritual stuff that wasn't relevant to me."

Let's explore how to implement this training practically. Contrary to popular belief, mindfulness doesn't require hours of meditation or dramatic lifestyle changes. Here are some evidence-based approaches that integrate seamlessly into a busy professional's life:

Mindful Breathing: Several times throughout your day, particularly during transitions between tasks, take 30-60 seconds to focus completely on your breathing. Notice the sensation of air entering and leaving your body without trying to change anything. When your mind wanders (which it will), gently return your focus to the breath.

Mindful Walking: Whether moving between meetings or taking a brief break, pay complete attention to the physical sensations of walking. Notice the pressure in your feet, the movement of your legs, and the rhythm of your steps. For an advanced practice, synchronize your breathing with your stride.

Focused Spot Exercise: Find a specific point on a wall or object and concentrate on it without distraction for two minutes. This deceptively simple practice builds attention control while reducing impulsivity, which is particularly valuable before important decisions or negotiations.

Mindful Listening: During conversations, practice giving your complete attention to the speaker without mentally preparing your response while they're talking. Notice when your mind drifts to formulating replies, judgments, or unrelated thoughts, then gently redirect your focus to simply listening.

The beauty of these practices is their accessibility. You don't need special equipment, extensive training, or even extra time—just moments of intentional awareness integrated throughout your existing routine. With consistency, these brief practices accumulate into significant enhancements to your cognitive function and stress resilience.

As your mindfulness capacity develops, you set the stage for deeper practices that can further amplify your performance potential—specifically, the advanced meditation and visualization techniques we'll explore next.

ADVANCED MENTAL TRAINING

The word "meditation" often conjures images of monks making the "ohm" sound or corporate retreats where executives fidget on overpriced cushions, wondering if they're "doing it right." But strip away the clichés—what if it's just the ultimate biohack for your brain? Not spirituality, but systematic mental reps that upgrade focus, resilience, and biological performance. No chanting required—just think of it as cognitive CrossFit for your prefrontal cortex. This shift in perspective transforms meditation from something esoteric into something practical and doable.

Research consistently shows that regular meditation practice creates measurable changes in brain structure and function. Studies using fMRI and EEG have documented increased gray matter density in regions associated with attention, sensory processing, and decision-making. Simultaneously, meditation decreases activity in the default mode network, often called the brain's "rumination center."

If you've tried meditation before and found your mind constantly wandering, here's a liberating truth: that's actually part of the process. Think of meditation as an attention game. Each time you notice your mind has wandered and bring it back to your chosen focus, you're strengthening neural pathways that support sustained attention. It's like a bicep curl for your executive control center.

Let's explore several meditation approaches, each offering unique benefits for performance optimization:

Focused Attention Meditation functions like interval training for your concentration. By repeatedly directing and redirecting attention to a single point (like your breath), you strengthen neural networks that support sustained focus. This practice typically enhances performance in tasks requiring deep work and sustained attention.

Start with just 5 minutes daily, sitting comfortably with your attention on your breath. When your mind wanders (which it will), simply notice and return to the breath. The power isn't in maintaining perfect focus but in the process of returning your attention again and again.

Open Monitoring Meditation develops a different kind of attention. Rather than narrowing focus to a single point, you expand awareness to observe whatever arises in your consciousness without attachment. This builds cognitive flexibility and enhances creativity by opening your awareness to connections you might otherwise miss.

Begin with 10 minutes of sitting quietly, observing thoughts, sensations, and sounds as they enter your awareness. Notice them without following or suppressing them, like watching clouds pass across the sky. This practice is particularly valuable before brainstorming sessions or creative problem-solving.

Movement Meditation integrates physical activity with mindfulness, making it ideal for those who find sitting meditation challenging. Practices like tai chi, qigong, or even mindful walking engage the body while training attention.

Try a simple walking meditation by moving very slowly, focusing completely on the sensations in your feet and legs. Feel each component of each step. This practice creates a powerful mind-body connection while developing concentration.

Transcendental Meditation (TM), despite its mystical-sounding name, is one of the most researched meditation techniques. It involves silently repeating a mantra (a specific sound or phrase) for 20 minutes twice daily. What makes TM interesting from a performance perspective is its efficiency. Research suggests it creates deeper physiological relaxation in less time than many other approaches.

While learning TM typically requires instruction from a certified teacher, the basic approach involves sitting comfortably with eyes closed, silently repeating your mantra, and gently returning to it whenever thoughts arise.

For implementing any meditation practice into your busy life, consider these practical guidelines:

1. *Start small:* Five minutes daily builds more momentum than 30 minutes once a week. Consistency matters more than duration, especially at first.
2. *Create environmental cues:* Designate a specific location and time for practice. Your brain quickly learns to associate these cues with the meditation state.
3. *Use technology wisely:* While meditation apps can be helpful for beginners, be careful not to become dependent on guided sessions. Eventually, developing the ability to meditate independently builds greater resilience.
4. *Track your results:* Notice how different meditation styles affect your performance, mood, and stress levels. This personalized data helps refine your practice for maximum benefit.

Remember that meditation isn't about achieving some perfect mental state. It's about systematic training that enhances your cognitive functioning and stress resilience. The ultimate goal isn't what happens during meditation but how it transforms your capacity to perform under pressure in real-world situations.

MENTAL REHEARSAL AS A PERFORMANCE TOOL

"I always visualize the run before I do it. By the time I get to the start gate, I've run that race 100 times already in my head, picturing how I'll take the turns."

When Olympic champion Lindsey Vonn shared this insight, she wasn't discussing some mystical secret. She was describing a scientifically validated performance enhancement technique used by elite athletes, surgeons, musicians, and business leaders worldwide.

Visualization, or mental imagery, involves creating detailed mental representations of desired outcomes or activities. What makes this practice compelling from a neuroscience perspective is how it activates many of the same neural pathways as physical practice. When you vividly imagine performing an action, your brain fires similar motor neurons to those activated during actual performance.

The science behind this phenomenon is robust—but there's a catch. You've probably heard about the famous University of Chicago study where basketball players improved free throws through visualization alone. While preparing this book, I went digging for this study... and it appears to be scientific folklore. There's no record of the alleged author "Dr. Blaslotto" or his research at the University of Chicago.

The breakthrough came from Australian psychologist Alan Richardson, published in Research Quarterly (1967). Here's what actually happened:

Richardson took three groups of students. Group 1 practiced free throws daily for 20 days (24% improvement). Group 2 only practiced twice—on days 1 and 20 (no improvement). Group 3 also only practiced twice, but spent 20 minutes daily visualizing: feeling the ball, hearing the bounce, seeing the shot. Result? 23% improvement—nearly matching the daily physical practice group.

Modern research has not only confirmed Richardson's findings but expanded them in crucial ways. A comprehensive 2007 meta-analysis by Feltz and Landers examined 60 studies and found that mental practice produces about half the performance gains of physical training for motor skills—still impressive, though less dramatic than Richardson's original numbers.

Building on this foundation, a 2019 systematic review (Lindsay et al.) analyzed 20 sports studies and confirmed the power of visualization across 12 different sports. Three key findings emerged: combined mental and physical practice consistently outperforms either method alone; longer interventions

(>4 weeks) yield significantly greater improvements; and these benefits extend equally to all skill levels—from novices to elite athletes.

So, how does this work at a neurological level? The science reveals two complementary mechanisms. First, visualization strengthens the same neural pathways used during physical performance. When you mentally rehearse the perfect golf swing or surgical procedure, you're essentially creating and reinforcing the neural firing patterns required for the actual movement. Your brain doesn't fully distinguish between vivid mental practice and physical execution—both build the neural architecture needed for skilled performance.

Beyond this direct neural training effect, visualization also influences your Reticular Activating System (RAS), the filtering mechanism in your brainstem that determines what information reaches your conscious awareness. This is where visualization extends beyond pure motor skills to broader performance enhancement.

Think about the last time you considered buying a particular car model. Suddenly, you started noticing that model everywhere. Those cars were always there, but your RAS wasn't filtering them into your conscious awareness until they became relevant to you. Visualization works similarly for comprehensive performance enhancement, making your brain more attuned to opportunities, resources, and solutions pertinent to your visualized outcomes.

Here are three evidence-based visualization protocols that can enhance your performance:

1. Process Visualization focuses on mentally rehearsing the specific steps required to achieve a goal, not just the result. Research shows this approach is particularly effective for complex tasks requiring precise execution.

For example, before an important presentation, you might visualize each component: walking confidently to the front of the room, making eye contact with key stakeholders, delivering your opening with appropriate pacing, handling potential questions, and concluding powerfully. This mental rehearsal creates neural patterns that support smooth execution when you actually perform.

2. Outcome Visualization involves vividly imagining the achievement of your goal, including the emotions and sensations associated with success. This approach helps strengthen motivation and build confidence.

Before a challenging negotiation, you might visualize reaching a mutually beneficial agreement, feeling confident and satisfied, shaking hands, and implementing the terms successfully. This creates positive expectancy that can significantly impact performance.

3. Obstacle Visualization, contrary to popular belief about "positive thinking," involves deliberately imagining potential challenges and mentally rehearsing effective responses. Research shows this approach significantly increases goal achievement compared to purely positive visualization.

When preparing for a product launch, you might visualize potential technical issues, competitive responses, or customer objections, then mentally rehearse addressing each effectively. This creates psychological readiness that prevents being blindsided by challenges.

For maximum effectiveness, visualization should engage multiple sensory modalities. Don't just see yourself succeeding; incorporate relevant sounds, physical sensations, emotions, and even smells or tastes when applicable. This multi-sensory approach creates stronger neural encoding and more effective performance enhancement.

Practical implementation might look like this:

- **Morning visualization:** Spend 5-10 minutes visualizing your most important tasks for the day, imagining both ideal execution and effective handling of potential obstacles.
- **Pre-performance visualization:** Before important events (presentations, negotiations, difficult conversations), take 3-5 minutes to mentally rehearse the specific process and desired outcome.
- **Evening review visualization:** Reflect on the day's events, visualizing how you'll improve tomorrow based on today's experiences.

This strategic visualization practice creates a powerful complement to the mindfulness and meditation techniques we've explored. Together, they form a comprehensive approach to optimizing your internal landscape for peak performance.

PRACTICAL TOOLS FOR DAILY IMPLEMENTATION

Now that we've explored the foundational practices of mindfulness and visualization, let's turn our attention to practical tools you can implement immediately. Think of these as your everyday mental training equipment—accessible strategies that translate these powerful concepts into your daily life.

Vision Boards: Beyond New Age Wishful Thinking

If you've dismissed vision boards as something from a cheesy self-help seminar, I get it. I felt the same way until I dug into the cognitive science behind them. Vision boards aren't magical manifestation tools; they're sophisticated RAS programming devices.

Unlike the Law of Attraction's focus on mysterious universal forces, vision boards work through concrete neurological mechanisms. When you create visual representations of your goals and place them where you'll see them regularly, you're essentially training your brain's filtering system to notice relevant opportunities, resources, and connections.

The key lies in cognitive activation. Repeatedly exposing yourself to visual representations of your goals strengthens neural pathways associated with those objectives. It's like creating a personalized billboard campaign targeted at your own brain.

To create an effective vision board:

1. Choose imagery that genuinely resonates with your goals rather than generic "success" symbols.
2. Include both process and outcome visuals—not just the beach vacation but also images representing the work that gets you there.
3. Place it where you'll encounter it naturally during your daily routines.
4. Update it regularly as your goals evolve and progress.

Gratitude as a Biological Optimization Tool

Perhaps nothing has been more thoroughly co-opted by wellness influencers than gratitude practices. But beneath the social media buzz lies something neurobiologically powerful—a practice that directly influences your stress physiology.

Research consistently shows that regular gratitude practice creates measurable improvements in HRV and reduces stress markers in the body. Studies examining thousands of participants have demonstrated that gratitude practices positively impact cardiovascular function, enhance autonomic nervous system activity, and even reduce inflammatory biomarkers. These physiological benefits are comparable to those seen from established exercise interventions.

What makes gratitude particularly valuable for performance optimization is how it shifts your autonomic nervous system balance. By focusing attention on positive aspects of your experience, you activate parasympathetic activity while reducing sympathetic dominance. This creates an internal environment more conducive to recovery, clarity, and balanced decision-making.

Consider implementing one of these evidence-based approaches:

- **Morning gratitude priming**: Before tackling your day, take 60 seconds to mentally list three specific things you're grateful for, focusing on the sensations these thoughts create in your body.
- **Gratitude transitions**: Use the space between activities to briefly acknowledge something positive from your previous task before moving to the next. This creates natural reset points throughout your day.
- **Evening reflection**: End your day by writing three things that went well and your role in making them happen. This pattern interrupts the brain's negativity bias and enhances sleep quality.

The Science of Play and Mental Detachment

In our achievement-oriented culture, we often overlook one of the most powerful recovery mechanisms available—play. Yet research shows that deliberate mental detachment from work through playful activities creates some of the most efficient cognitive recovery possible.

Play activates different neural networks than work-focused attention, allowing stress-taxed brain regions to rest while maintaining overall engagement. This selective activation pattern proves more restorative than passive activities like watching TV, which often keep work-related neural networks partially engaged.

Strategic play includes:

- **Skill-building hobbies** that create flow states while being unrelated to your professional domain.
- **Physical play** that combines movement with enjoyment.
- **Social games** that engage interpersonal circuits while providing cognitive variety.
- **Creative exploration** without performance pressure.

The key distinction is intention—approaching activities for their inherent enjoyment rather than instrumental value. This shift in approach activates different neurochemical cascades, particularly boosting dopamine through intrinsic reward pathways rather than achievement-based ones.

YOUR PERSONALIZED REGULATION SYSTEM

With all these tools at your disposal, the question becomes: How do you create your personalized approach to stress mastery? The answer lies in systematic experimentation and personalization.

The reality is that no single technique works optimally for everyone. Your unique neurophysiology, life circumstances, and specific stressors require a customized approach. Think of building your regulation system like creating a personalized medicine cabinet—you need different products for different situations.

If you are just starting in this process... Start by conducting a stress audit. For about a week, track when you experience stress, what triggers it, how it manifests physically, and which coping mechanisms you currently use. This creates your baseline data.

Next, experiment methodically with the techniques we've explored. Try each approach, noting its effects on your subjective experience and, if possible, objective metrics like HRV or sleep quality. This experimental approach reveals which tools work best for your specific biology.

As patterns emerge, you can develop situation-specific protocols. Perhaps breathwork excels for acute stress management, while staring at a wall proves most effective for midday cognitive recovery. Visualization might be your go-to for performance preparation, while gratitude practices enhance your evening wind-down.

To simplify implementation, consider this stress regulation cheat sheet based on specific states:

- **When feeling anxious**: Take a brief walk to deactivate the amygdala while engaging in box breathing (4-4-4-4 pattern).
- **When angry or impulsive**: Dilate your gaze by focusing on the periphery of your visual field while taking three physiological sighs (double inhale, extended exhale).
- **When motivation is low**: Look at your goals, recall a past win, or reflect on something you're grateful for to activate the brain's dopamine

system. If you're feeling sluggish, add a short burst of movement to reset your energy.

- **When you need to focus:** Stare at a single point for 60 seconds to trigger noradrenaline release and sharpen attention. Pair it with a deep inhale and slow exhale to prime your brain for deep work.
- **When experiencing self-doubt**: Engage the logical brain by writing down three specific strengths relevant to your current challenge.
- **When overwhelmed**: Implement a 90-second reset combining heart-centered breathing with hand-on-chest touch to trigger oxytocin release.

The integration of these practices with your existing biological optimization strategies creates powerful synergies. The nutritional foundation you built in the previous chapter enhances neurotransmitter availability for these mental techniques. Your optimized sleep architecture improves the brain's baseline functioning for implementing these practices. Your movement patterns complement and reinforce the benefits of mindfulness and visualization.

Together, they form an integrated performance ecosystem where each element supports and amplifies the others. This is the essence of holistic performance—understanding that physical, mental, and emotional systems operate not in isolation but as an interconnected whole.

MOVING FORWARD MINDFULLY

Now that we've explored these powerful stress mastery techniques, it's time to craft your personal approach. This isn't about adopting every practice at once, but rather developing a customized system that works for your unique biology and circumstances.

Plan Your Introspection Path

Take 10-15 minutes right now to brainstorm how you'll integrate these practices into your life:

1. Select Your Foundational Practice

Choose one core technique (meditation, breathwork, visualization, or gratitude) to implement daily. Which resonated most strongly with you?

2. Define Your Implementation Approach

Ask yourself and define:

- When will you practice? (Specific time of day).
- Where will you practice? (Designated space).
- How will you track consistency? (Journal, app, calendar).

3. Identify Trigger Points

What specific stress situations could benefit from targeted techniques? Match each common stressor with a particular response from the methods we've covered.

This personalized approach ensures you're not just collecting techniques, but actually implementing practices that will create meaningful change in your performance and well-being. Remember, mastery comes through consistent practice, not perfect execution from day one.

ENVIRONMENTAL OPTIMIZATION

You know that feeling when you walk out of a stuffy conference room into fresh air, and suddenly your brain starts working again? That's not just psychological relief; it's your biology responding to environmental cues that we've evolved with for millions of years. While we've been diving deep into internal optimization strategies, now it's time to explore how your surroundings shape your performance in ways you might never have considered.

Think about it: we evolved in natural environments with dynamic light patterns, connection to earth, meaningful social bonds, and natural movement rhythms. Now, we spend 90% of our time indoors, bathed in artificial light, isolated in cubicles, and staring at screens. The mismatch between our evolutionary design and modern environments creates a performance tax most people never even recognize they're paying.

What research consistently confirms is that environmental factors don't just influence your mood; they directly impact your neurochemistry, cognitive function, and stress resilience. The good news? These factors are often far easier to optimize than internal habits, creating some of the highest-leverage interventions available for peak performance.

Let's explore how to create an environment that works with your biology instead of against it—starting with our most fundamental connection to the natural world.

THE HEALING POWER OF NATURE

There's a reason we instinctively seek out parks, beaches, or mountain trails when we need to recharge. Nature doesn't just feel restorative; it physically rebuilds us.

The concept of biophilia, popularized by biologist E.O. Wilson, describes our innate affinity for natural settings. As Wilson puts it, "Nature holds the key to our aesthetic, intellectual, cognitive and even spiritual satisfaction." Neuroscience backs these poetic words up, showing how our brain is wired to respond in predictable ways.

When you immerse yourself in natural settings, remarkable biological shifts occur:

- Cortisol levels drop significantly within just 15-20 minutes of nature exposure.
- Parasympathetic activation increases, enhancing recovery and cognitive function.
- Attention restoration occurs as directed attention fatigue diminishes.
- Creative problem-solving improves by up to 50%, according to University of Kansas research.
- Natural killer cell activity (immune function) increases for up to 30 days following forest exposure.

The Japanese practice of *shinrin-yoku* (forest bathing) has been particularly well-studied. Research published in Environmental Health and Preventive Medicine found that participants walking in forests showed significantly decreased hostility and depression scores compared to those walking identical distances in urban environments. The natural environment wasn't just more pleasant; it fundamentally altered psychological and physiological states.

A client of mine named James, a tech professional who initially scoffed at the idea of "nature therapy," gave me honest feedback after trying morning nature walks: "Look, I'm not gonna lie... I didn't turn into some zen master or anything. But I did notice that after walking in the park for like 20 minutes, I stopped obsessing about the account that was stressing me out. By the time I got back to my desk, I had a solution that wasn't even on my radar before. Weird, but it definitely helps."

Beyond general nature exposure, the practice of grounding (direct physical contact with the earth's surface) offers additional benefits. Research shows that this direct connection facilitates electron transfer from the earth to your body, potentially neutralizing free radicals and reducing inflammation— creating physiological conditions more conducive to peak cognitive performance.

While traditional productivity advice ignores these biological realities, high performers are increasingly recognizing nature connection as an essential performance infrastructure rather than an optional luxury. Here are practical ways to incorporate nature's benefits into your life:

Self-talk walks: Combine nature exposure with positive internal dialogue by taking walks without technology. Use this time to reflect on gratitude, achievements, or creative problems that need solutions. The combination of movement, nature, and constructive thinking creates a powerful cognitive enhancement.

Workspace biophilia: If you can't get outdoors regularly, bring elements of nature inside. Research by the University of Exeter revealed that introducing plants to previously sparse office environments increased productivity by 15%. The Human Spaces global study found that employees in environments with natural elements report a 15% higher level of well-being and are 15% more creative overall. Furthermore, a Norwegian study demonstrated that plant presence in office spaces reduced employee fatigue, headaches, and sick days by over 30%. So, try to position your desk near windows with natural views when possible, and incorporate natural materials, plants, and nature imagery in your workspace.

Microexposures: Even brief nature contacts matter. A study in the International Journal of Environmental Research found that just 40 seconds of viewing a green roof during a mentally fatiguing task significantly improved concentration compared to viewing a concrete roof. Consider taking brief "nature snacks" throughout your day—a moment at the window, a quick step outside, or even looking at high-resolution nature imagery during breaks.

Grounding practice: When possible, incorporate direct earth contact by walking barefoot on grass, sand, or soil. This doesn't require special equipment or extensive time. Even 10-15 minutes several times weekly can provide measurable benefits to inflammatory markers and sleep quality, both crucial for cognitive performance.

The key insight here isn't just that nature feels good—it's that natural environments create the precise biological conditions that support peak cognitive function. By strategically incorporating natural elements into your environment, you're not just improving subjective well-being; you're optimizing the very biochemistry that drives performance.

PROGRAMMING YOUR PERFORMANCE CLOCK

If I asked you to name the most potent regulator of your cognitive performance throughout the day, what would you guess? Food? Sleep? While these all matter, there's an environmental factor with an even more direct impact on your moment-by-moment cognitive function: light exposure.

Your brain contains a master control center called the suprachiasmatic nucleus (SCN), located in the hypothalamus. This tiny region, about the size of a grain of rice, orchestrates virtually every physiological process in your body based primarily on one environmental signal: light. The SCN receives input directly from specialized retinal cells that are particularly sensitive to blue and yellow light wavelengths, using this information to coordinate everything from hormone production to body temperature and alertness cycles to digestive function.

What happens with light exposure isn't psychological; it's biochemical. Morning sunlight exposure triggers a precise cascade of hormonal responses:

1. Melatonin production (your sleep hormone) is actively suppressed
2. Cortisol release (your alertness hormone) increases
3. Serotonin production rises, supporting mood and cognitive function
4. Your circadian rhythm "resets," synchronizing dozens of biological processes

The science here is exciting. Natural daylight provides 10,000 to 100,000 lux. A stark contrast to the 300–1,000 lux found in most office environments. This difference isn't just noticeable; it's biologically significant. Without strong light signals, your SCN struggles to maintain an optimal rhythm, leading to sluggish cognitive function, mood imbalances, and metabolic inefficiencies. Simply put, brighter light isn't just about vision; it's about programming your brain for peak performance.

Beyond general alertness, sunlight exposure directly impacts your vitamin D levels, which research shows plays a crucial role in cognitive function. Studies reveal that optimal vitamin D levels enhance working memory, improve information processing speed, support better mood regulation, and contribute to long-term brain health and neuroplasticity.

What makes this environmental factor particularly powerful is how quickly it can influence performance. While nutritional changes might take days or weeks to significantly alter your biochemistry, light exposure creates immediate hormonal shifts that directly impact cognitive function within minutes.

For practical implementation, consider structuring your light exposure around these principles:

Morning light anchoring
Ideally, you'd spend 10-20 minutes in bright natural light within an hour of waking. This creates a powerful anchor for your circadian system. But let's be real: not everyone can take a leisurely morning sunbath! If you're time-crunched, even 5 minutes while drinking your coffee outside or standing by a bright window counts. Multi-task by making your morning call outside, parking farther from your building, or combining it with a quick dog walk. For those in windowless offices or northern climates during winter, a small 10,000+ lux light therapy device used during your morning email check can be a game-changer.

Workspace light optimization
Position your workspace near windows when possible, ideally with the natural light coming from the side rather than causing screen glare. Research shows that workers near windows experience better sleep quality, more physical activity, and higher subjective well-being—all factors that support cognitive performance.

Evening light management

Remember that light exposure is a double-edged sword. The same blue light that enhances morning performance can significantly impair sleep quality when experienced in the evening. Consider implementing a "technology curfew" two hours before bedtime, or use blue-light-blocking glasses if evening screen use is unavoidable.

THE SOCIAL EDGE

Let's talk about what tends to be the most underrated performance enhancer available—our relationships. While we've been deep-diving into various performance strategies, there's a remarkable powerhouse sitting right in front of us. The people we connect with every day.

If you're thinking, "Wait, this is supposed to be about performance, not friendship bracelets," I get it. But here's the reality: the quality of your relationships might be the single strongest predictor of both your performance potential and your longevity.

When Harvard researchers set out to discover what predicts a well-lived life, they didn't expect relationships to steal the show. Their landmark study tracked 268 Harvard graduates (including future presidents) and later expanded to include 1,300 additional participants, following them for over 80 years.

The shocking conclusion? The quality of your relationships at age 50 predicts your health at age 80 better than your cholesterol levels, blood pressure, or any other biomarker. Let that sink in for a moment.

"When we gathered all our data about these lives for a combined total of 75 years," explains Dr. Robert Waldinger, the study's director, "we asked, 'What did we learn? What are the lessons that came from tens of thousands of pages of information that we generated on these lives?'" The clearest message was that good relationships keep us happier and healthier. Period.

But this isn't just about living longer; it's about performing better right now.

Your social connections are more than just emotionally fulfilling. Positive social interactions play a crucial role in regulating the autonomic nervous system, reducing stress hormones like cortisol and adrenaline. Meaningful conversations, shared experiences, and emotional support activate the parasympathetic nervous system, promoting relaxation, lowering stress responses, and improving heart rate variability.

At the neurochemical level, oxytocin is a key facilitator of these effects. Released during positive social interactions like hugging, touching, or even engaging conversations, oxytocin strengthens social bonds, fosters trust, and counteracts stress hormones. This remarkable neurochemical:

- Reduces cortisol levels, mitigating the harmful effects of chronic stress.
- Enhances heart rate variability, a key marker of resilience and nervous system balance.
- Improves immune function, making the body more resistant to illness.
- Accelerates recovery from stressors, helping you bounce back faster.
- Creates a sense of psychological safety, enhancing creativity, risk-taking, and problem-solving.

In professional environments, fostering a culture of positive social connection acts as a powerful performance multiplier. When team members engage in trust-building interactions, oxytocin release enhances workplace dynamics by improving collaboration and communication. Simple, intentional efforts like celebrating collective wins, practicing active listening, and creating spaces for authentic conversations can profoundly impact both individual well-being and team productivity, transforming the workplace from a mere functional space to a thriving human ecosystem.

However, there's a darker side to this equation. On the opposite end, prolonged social isolation rewires the brain in ways that actively undermine peak performance. Chronic isolation triggers an accumulation of tachykinin, a neurotransmitter linked to fear, anxiety, and aggression. Over time, this neurochemical imbalance doesn't just make people feel worse; it raises dementia risk by 50%, increases the likelihood of heart disease by 29% and stroke by 32%, and accelerates cognitive decline. Even creativity and innovative thinking take a hit, as the brain struggles without the stimulation and perspective that social interaction provides.

BEHAVIORAL OSMOSIS

Here's something wild about human biology: we unconsciously absorb and mirror the behaviors, attitudes, and even physiological patterns of those around us. This phenomenon, called behavioral osmosis, means your social environment shapes your performance capacity whether you're conscious of it or not.

Think about it like a dried raisin placed in water—it expands as it absorbs its surroundings. The question becomes: What kind of water are you soaking in? Are you absorbing pure, performance-enhancing influences, or contaminated ones?

"Show me your friends and I'll show you your future," Mark Ambrose famously observed. This isn't just motivational fluff; it's documented neuroscience. Through mirror neuron activation, hormonal synchronization, and unconscious behavioral modeling, you literally become more like the five people you spend the most time with.

This creates a powerful optimization opportunity. By thoughtfully curating who you spend time with, you leverage behavioral osmosis to naturally pull you toward higher performance states. This explains why joining mastermind groups or high-performance teams often accelerates growth. You're not just gaining knowledge; you're absorbing successful patterns at a neurological level.

BUILDING YOUR PERFORMANCE NETWORK

Once we understand how powerfully our social connections influence our biology, the next logical question becomes: How do we strategically build a social network that enhances rather than undermines our performance?

Behavioral osmosis works whether you're conscious of it or not. But that doesn't mean you should leave it to chance. The most successful performers I've met take an intentional approach to their social environment. They don't just wait for osmosis to happen; they actively seek opportunities to learn from those they admire. In other words, be proactive!

Remember, though, this is a two-way street. While absorbing positive influences is key, striving to be a positive influence for others is also essential. The best social ecosystems feature mutual elevation, where everyone is simultaneously teaching and learning.

One mistake I commonly see is building one-dimensional networks focused entirely on professional connections. Research shows that truly optimized performance requires a multifaceted support system spanning four distinct domains.

Think about the different needs you experience throughout your life. Sometimes, you need someone to vent with; other times, you require practical help; and occasionally, you simply need companionship without any particular agenda. Your network needs this same diversification.

Let's explore the four essential domains every high performer should cultivate:

1. Emotional Support Network

These are the confidantes in your life. People with whom you can be completely authentic. They offer listening, empathy, and unwavering support during challenging times. Equally important, they celebrate your successes without jealousy or reservation.

Strong emotional support connections create psychological safety that allows you to:

- Process difficult emotions without suppression.
- Maintain perspective during setbacks.
- Experience genuine acceptance and belonging.
- Share vulnerabilities that would otherwise consume mental bandwidth.

Without adequate emotional support, even the most successful performers often struggle with isolation, imposter syndrome, and emotional depletion that undermines their cognitive capacity.

2. Informational Support Network

These are your mentors and knowledge providers. Folks who offer valuable advice, guidance, and insights based on their experience or expertise. You trust their judgment and turn to them for reliable information when navigating complex decisions or learning new skills.

Strategic informational connections provide:

- Perspective beyond your current knowledge.
- Shortcut learning that prevents costly mistakes.
- Challenge to your thinking patterns and assumptions.
- Domain expertise across complementary fields.

Most high performers naturally cultivate this domain while neglecting others, creating an imbalance that limits their overall resilience and adaptability.

3. Instrumental Support Network

These are the people you can rely on for tangible assistance. They might lend a helping hand with tasks and errands or contribute specialized skills. They form your practical support system, freeing mental and physical bandwidth for your highest-leverage activities.

Effective instrumental support:
- Reduces cognitive load during complex projects.
- Creates capacity for focus on strengths and priorities.
- Provides specialized capabilities beyond your expertise.
- Offers practical backup during high-demand periods.

Many high-achievers resist developing this domain out of misplaced self-sufficiency, not realizing that the world's top performers invariably have substantial instrumental support systems.

4. Companionship Support Network

These are your fellow adventurers in life. People who share your interests and provide a sense of belonging through shared activities and social connections. They are the ones you enjoy spending leisure time with, creating balance and joy beyond pure achievement.

Quality companionship relationships:
- Facilitate true recovery through enjoyable activities.
- Satisfy fundamental belonging needs.
- Provide contrast that enhances work appreciation.
- Create memories and experiences that enrich life's meaning.

This frequently neglected domain actually creates the psychological foundation for sustained high performance by preventing burnout and maintaining life satisfaction.

BUILDING AND NURTURING STRONG SOCIAL TIES

Now that we understand the four domains, how do we actually build and maintain these crucial connections? The science reveals several evidence-based approaches that can transform your social ecosystem from merely pleasant to genuinely performance-enhancing.

In our digitally connected world, we've been sold a story of networking success measured by follower counts and connection numbers. But psychological research tells a different, more nuanced story. While we can accumulate hundreds or even thousands of digital contacts, our capacity for meaningful connection is far more limited and profound.

Social psychology reveals that the depth of our relationships matters dramatically more than their breadth. A few high-quality connections provide substantially more emotional and physiological benefits than a sprawling network of superficial interactions. Think of it like nutrition. Would you rather graze on empty calories all day or enjoy a few carefully prepared, nutrient-dense meals that truly nourish your body?

These deep connections act like emotional and psychological immune systems. They actively support our resilience, providing a buffer against stress, enhancing our cognitive function, and contributing to our overall well-being in ways that a thousand casual acquaintances never could.

Cultivating these deeper connections requires intentional practice: regular, unrushed interactions where you're fully present; genuine curiosity about others' lives rather than waiting for your turn to speak; appropriate vulnerability that builds trust; and reliable presence during both celebrations and challenges. Think of these practices as relationship investments that compound over time, creating social capital you can draw upon during high-demand periods.

Community engagement extends these benefits beyond individual relationships. Whether you join a volunteer organization, recreational sports league, or professional group, active participation creates a sense of belonging that satisfies fundamental psychological needs. I've watched countless people transform their outlook after finding "their people" through community involvement. Even more fascinating, studies show that community participation correlates with improved cognitive function and lower cortisol patterns—essentially priming your brain for better performance.

Here's something counter-intuitive: the connections that ultimately provide the greatest value often feel uncomfortable initially. Your comfort zone rarely contains the relationships that will elevate you to new levels. This explains why saying "yes" to social invitations despite awkwardness can lead to relationships that transform your trajectory. That intimidating industry event or friend-of-a-friend introduction might just introduce you to your next mentor, collaborator, or source of inspiration.

Developing connector skills amplifies your social impact exponentially. By actively introducing people who might benefit from knowing each other, you create a network effect where your value grows with each connection facilitated. This approach builds a sense of belonging for everyone while positioning you at influential network intersections. As organizational psychologist Adam Grant's research demonstrates, "givers" who connect others ultimately receive more valuable opportunities than those who network solely for personal gain.

High performance requires integration between work and social life, not isolation. Rather than viewing relationships as competing with productivity, consider how they enhance each other. Strategic social connections reduce the stress that undermines cognitive function, improve mood and creativity, provide essential perspective during challenges, and create the recovery capacity that sustains high output. This integration explains why the most successful performers don't sacrifice relationships for work. They leverage relationships to enhance their work.

Technology can either strengthen or undermine these connections, depending entirely on how you use it. The key distinction is intention versus distraction. Use digital tools for meaningful interactions—scheduling regular video calls with distant family or maintaining organized connection with colleagues—while being mindful of how social media's passive consumption affects your mental state. Research shows that active digital engagement (direct messaging, video calls) correlates with well-being benefits, while passive scrolling produces the opposite effect.

By thoughtfully implementing these relationship-building approaches, you're not just creating a pleasant social life—you're constructing the environmental conditions that allow your biological optimizations to express their full potential. Think of it as creating the perfect growing conditions for the performance seeds we've been planting throughout our journey.

YOUR SOCIAL PERFORMANCE SYSTEM

So, how do we transform all this research into something practical? Let's build an integrated approach that enhances both your relationships and performance without overcomplicating things.

The quality of your connections depends largely on how you show up within them. Cultivating active listening and empathy not only strengthens relationships but also enhances your emotional intelligence—a key performance factor across virtually every domain. Small practices make an enormous difference: being fully present during conversations (phone away, notifications off), asking thoughtful follow-up questions that show genuine interest, validating others' perspectives even when they differ from yours, and noticing emotional signals that others send.

I'm always struck by how the highest performers tend to be exceptional listeners. There's a reason for this connection. The same focused attention that drives achievement in professional domains creates relationship depth when directed toward other people.

Just as you schedule important work commitments, carve out specific times for social connection. This isn't about turning friendships into appointments; it's about ensuring these critical relationships don't get crowded out by seemingly urgent demands. Try creating dedicated time for deep one-on-one conversations with your closest connections, community involvement that broadens your network, family rituals that create continuity, and exploration time for developing new relationships.

Remember how we discussed time-blocking for peak cognitive performance earlier? The same principle applies here. By protecting relationship time with the same rigor you protect your deep work sessions, you ensure these crucial connections receive the investment they deserve.

One of the most effective ways to maintain strong connections without constant planning effort is establishing regular traditions. Think weekly family dinners, monthly friend gatherings, quarterly check-ins with mentors, or annual trips with close connections. These standing commitments remove the friction of constant scheduling, build positive anticipation, create shared history, and provide the structure that survives busy periods.

A client who struggled with maintaining relationships while scaling his business found that instituting "Third Thursday" dinners with his closest friends created an anchor point that survived even his most chaotic growth periods. "Having that regular connection in my calendar meant I never went more than a few weeks without seeing my core people," he explained. "It became sacred ground that business couldn't invade."

For those with particularly demanding schedules, some find value in a more systematic approach to relationship maintenance. Just as businesses use CRM systems to track client interactions, you might benefit from a simple personal system that helps you remember important details and touchpoints. This isn't about treating relationships as transactions; it's about being intentional with your social energy when life gets hectic.

A coach I worked with initially rejected this concept outright. "It sounds so calculated," she told me. Three months later, her perspective had completely shifted: "Having reminders for birthdays and conversation follow-ups actually helps me be more present and thoughtful. I'm not constantly worried about who I've neglected because I have a way to ensure these important connections are not neglected."

To start implementing these ideas, take 15 minutes to map your current connections across the four domains we've explored: emotional support, informational support, instrumental support, and companionship. Where do you have strengths? Where are the gaps? Most people discover they're overweight in certain domains (typically informational) while neglecting others (often emotional or companionship).

From this assessment, identify the single relationship intervention that offers the highest potential return for reasonable effort. Perhaps it's scheduling regular one-on-one time with a potential emotional support person, joining a community group, establishing a standing check-in with a mentor, or creating simple reminders for key connections. Focus on implementing that one change consistently for the next two weeks before adding anything else.

Remember that optimizing your social connections isn't separate from the biological foundations we've been building; it's the essential context that allows those optimizations to express their full potential. The nutritional strategies you've implemented create the biochemical foundation for positive social engagement. The sleep optimization enhances your emotional regulation during interactions. The stress management techniques help you maintain presence in relationships.

Everything is connected. Your brilliance doesn't emerge from isolated interventions, but from the complete ecosystem you create. And your relationships form perhaps the most influential aspect of that environment. As we continue our journey toward holistic performance optimization, this perspective remains essential: no biological intervention exists in a vacuum. The true magic happens when your internal biology and external environment work in harmony, creating the conditions for sustained excellence in everything you do.

RESEARCH & RESOURCES

As part of this chapter's focus on helping you reconnect with your own biology, you'll find the **Multidimensional Assessment of Interoceptive Awareness** inside this chapter's Resource Hub. It's a quick but powerful self-assessment that can offer insight into how attuned you are to your internal signals—and help highlight areas that may benefit from more attention.

In addition, the hub includes **guided tutorials for the breathwork techniques** discussed here, along with the usual resources: the research articles that support the concepts covered and the recommended tools to deepen your practice. To access everything, visit hplink.org/resourcehub or scan the QR code below.

CHAPTER 9
THE HOLISTIC PERFORMANCE BLUEPRINT

"The whole is greater than the sum of its parts."

– Aristotle

It was 9 AM on a beautiful March morning in South Florida. That perfect time of year when the sun feels like a warm embrace, not yet the skin-melting inferno of summer. I'd been on the road for nearly two hours, driving between client appointments, my mind churning with numbers.

Last month's earnings were still fresh in my mental calculator. An all-time high that would make most people grin from ear to ear. Each mile I drove felt like another dollar added to that impressive total. Success, I thought, was a simple equation of hours worked and invoices sent.

But the cost of that success was mounting in ways I couldn't yet see.

My body was the first to revolt. Late-night reports meant fast food drive-thrus and energy drinks throughout the day. My once-athletic physique was softening, replaced by constant fatigue and unexplained weight gain. Memory lapses became more frequent—walking into rooms and forgetting why, struggling to recall patient details I'd once tracked effortlessly. The panic attacks started subtly: a racing heart during client meetings and a sense of dread that would wash over me without warning.

Relationships were the next casualty. My girlfriend, who had recently moved in, was watching our connection disintegrate. I was physically present but mentally absent. Date nights became silent affairs, with me checking emails or mentally calculating the next day's schedule. She'd talk, and I'd realize I hadn't heard a word. The vibrant connection that drew us together was being suffocated by my relentless pursuit of what I thought was success.

One evening, she broke. "You're here, but you're not present," she said, her voice a mixture of frustration and genuine pain. "You're so focused on achieving that you're missing your actual life." It was a mirror I couldn't look away from. The high-performer persona I'd constructed was a prison of my own making.

In that moment, I became afraid of losing her. And with startling clarity, I realized I was about to lose myself.

This wasn't just another wake-up call about work-life balance. This was a fundamental reimagining of what success could mean—not as a collection of achievements but as a holistic experience of being fully alive.

Which brings us to this moment in our journey together. You've absorbed an incredible amount of strategies—from prioritization to physiology, from stress management to building connections. But knowledge without integration is just noise.

This chapter is our pause button. Our opportunity to step back and ask: How do all these pieces actually work together? How can we transform information into a life that's not just successful, but meaningful?

Think of what we've covered as pieces of a high-performance puzzle. Individually, each piece offers value, but when connected, they create something vastly more powerful—a complete performance ecosystem where each element amplifies the others.

Are you ready to connect the dots?

THE FOUNDATIONS: YOUR INTEGRATED PERFORMANCE SYSTEM

Remember our 4Ps framework? Let's revisit how everything we've covered fits into this integrated system:

1. Prioritization: We started by clearing the slate—eliminating what doesn't matter so you could focus on what does. You learned to reclaim time through the AOD3 Framework, structure your days with the Modified Eisenhower Matrix, and create space for what truly moves the needle in your life and work.

2. Physiology: We then optimized your biological hardware through nutrition, sleep optimization, strategic movement, and stress regulation. You discovered how to fuel your body for sustained energy, incorporate exercise that enhances both physical and cognitive function, optimize your sleep architecture for recovery, and master your autonomic nervous system through breathwork and mindfulness.

3. Psychology: To be explored in detail soon. However, we've already begun addressing this through stress mastery and relationship optimization, setting the stage for more profound work on mindset, resilience, and emotional regulation.

4. Performance Systems: We've already started implementing systematic approaches throughout our journey. From habit formation to environmental design, from relationship management to recovery protocols—we've been gradually building automated workflows that make high performance your default state rather than something you constantly struggle to achieve. This integration of systems thinking throughout our work reflects the reality that sustainable performance requires structural support, not just individual techniques.

THE HOLISTIC PERFORMANCE DAY

Earlier in this chapter, I shared the reality of a period when my relentless pursuit of success ended up pushing me into burnout. Since then, I've learned to integrate everything we've explored—and will continue to explore—into a practical, realistic framework for a sustainable, high-performance day. Let me share my day with you—not because it's perfect or prescriptive, but as an example of how you might begin integrating the insights you've gained into your own schedule. Of course, there's no one-size-fits-all formula; the goal here is to provide you with a practical starting point. With the knowledge you now have, you can customize this framework to fit your chronotype, preferences, job demands, and personal circumstances.

Morning Launch

My alarm goes off consistently at 6:30 AM. This timing aligns naturally with my chronotype, giving me the best possible cognitive start. Immediately, I hydrate with water infused with electrolytes—not because it's trendy, but because I've found it genuinely improves my mental clarity first thing in the morning. For a while, I was experimenting with cold plunges or showers, but lately, I noticed they weren't enhancing my mornings as they once did. It's a great strategy for many people, but for me, it stopped feeling beneficial. Within about 15 minutes, after a quick hygiene routine and exposure to bright natural or simulated sunlight, I'm already sitting down for my first deep work block.

Deep Work Block One: High Cognitive Impact

From 7:00 to 9:00 AM, I tackle my NMTs—those needle-mover tasks that require my absolute sharpest focus, such as writing, strategic planning, or developing complex training materials. Before diving in, I briefly open my physical daily planner and take a minute to review what I've scheduled for the day, clarifying my priorities. This time is intentionally free from distractions; my phone is on airplane mode, notifications are off, and there's nothing on my screen but the work at hand. To enhance focus, I put on my flow-inducing playlist on Spotify and primarily work using my adjustable stand-up desk, as standing helps me maintain alertness and energy levels. Additionally, if I'm working from home, I often activate my red-light therapy device—something I've found helps not just with energy but also offers several other physiological health benefits. I work in uninterrupted 45-minute intervals, pausing briefly between rounds to stretch or perform a few squats to stay physically active and energized.

Strategic Reset

Around 9:00 AM, I deliberately pause. Instead of jumping straight to emails or mindlessly scrolling, I spend about 15 minutes resetting with a quick walk outside or breathwork exercises. This break also includes grabbing another cup of water, a restroom break, and, if I'm feeling particularly sluggish, doing some pull-ups or jumping jacks to reenergize myself. I've learned this break is essential for maintaining performance throughout the day.

Deep Work Block Two: Sustained Productivity

Refreshed, I transition into my second productivity session from roughly 9:30 AM until 11:00 AM—a 90-minute block. I typically limit this block to 90 minutes, as I've found after the first intensive session, my cognitive stamina naturally decreases slightly. My tasks here often include client work, content refinement, or detailed project execution. The emphasis, as always, is on single-tasking in focused intervals, supported by clear environmental cues: my workspace remains distraction-free and optimized for focus.

Exercise and Recharge

Around 11:00 AM, I shift gears and head to the gym. This dedicated exercise period is crucial, serving as both physical and mental recovery from my intensive morning work sessions. As you've probably noticed, I typically follow a 16:8 fasting schedule—this means I usually haven't eaten up to this point. While I sometimes break my fast earlier if needed, on most days, my first meal comes after the gym. Post-workout, I refuel with a protein and fat-rich smoothie, as I've shared previously. It's practical, quick, easy to digest, and helps maintain steady energy levels. During this time, I connect socially by briefly chatting with my wife, take my dog for a walk to soak up more sunlight, and enjoy some playful interaction with him, which provides that beneficial oxytocin boost we discussed earlier.

Afternoon Work: Practical Flexibility

Afternoons from about 1:00 PM to 5:00 PM are structured for less cognitively demanding activities, often broken into shorter blocks of 60 or 45 minutes. These tasks might include client meetings, emails, administrative tasks, or creative brainstorming. I've found that slight afternoon mental fatigue can actually spark creativity, making this an ideal time for more flexible, collaborative, or imaginative tasks. During one of my short breaks between these afternoon blocks, I set aside around 10 minutes for meditation, which I've found significantly boosts clarity and helps manage stress levels throughout the day. Though less intense than morning sessions, this period still represents productive work time.

Intentional Evening Transition

At around 5:00 PM, I intentionally shut down work. This transition involves opening my physical daily planner to review the day—what worked and what didn't—and jotting down tasks for tomorrow. I also use this time for a formal gratitude practice, reflecting positively on the workday and planning for the next. The key here is psychological closure, knowing I've set myself up for another productive day tomorrow.

Evening Recovery and Wind-Down

Evenings are dedicated to genuine restoration. This typically includes errands, engaging in hobbies, playing sports with friends, enjoying dinner with my wife, or leisure activities that truly disconnect me from work. Following the 10-3-2-1-0 sleep framework (no caffeine 10 hours before bed, no food 3 hours prior, etc.) helps me consistently achieve high-quality sleep—my ultimate recovery strategy.

Adapting to Your Chronotype and Circumstances

This example reflects my personal chronotype, lifestyle, and professional commitments. You can—and should—shift these blocks around using the detailed chronotype guidance provided in Chapter 7, adapting your activities and timings to fit your unique biology, job demands, and lifestyle. Remember, this is about finding what works best for you. Honor your responsibilities, your rhythm, and your preferences. Do what makes sense for your own life.

IMPLEMENTING YOUR HOLISTIC PERFORMANCE BLUEPRINT

Now that you have a practical example of what holistic performance integration can look like, let's shift the spotlight back onto you. It's time to move from theory to action—to translate insights into tangible improvements in your own life. Here's a practical approach to help you do just that:

Step 1: Conduct Your Reality Check

Before bridging theory into action, it's crucial to clearly understand your starting point. Begin by briefly comparing your current typical day with the practical example I provided earlier. Of course, you're not expected to mirror my day exactly. Rather, this exercise is intended to help you identify possible areas of improvement that you're yet to address.

However, if you'd prefer a more structured tool, I've also created a simple checklist below. This will help you clearly see the elements you're already doing well and identify immediate opportunities for growth and improvement. Don't worry—you're not supposed to tackle all these elements at once. Consider this checklist an ongoing resource, something you can revisit regularly as you gradually introduce and solidify changes into your routine.

Holistic Performance Checklist

Biological Foundation:

☐ Morning routine aligned with your chronotype

☐ Strategic meals supporting cognitive function and steady energy levels

☐ Appropriate fasting periods (if suitable for your biology and lifestyle)

☐ Targeted supplementation addressing personal nutritional gaps

☐ Structured movement routine (formal exercise sessions and NEAT)

☐ Evening routine optimized for high-quality sleep

Mental Mastery:
- ☐ Regular breathwork or mindfulness practice
- ☐ Intentional recovery breaks during the day
- ☐ Nature or sunlight exposure
- ☐ Meaningful social connections each day

Performance Architecture:
- ☐ Scheduled deep work blocks aligned with personal energy peaks
- ☐ Clearly defined recovery periods integrated throughout the day
- ☐ Consistent Workday Shutdown Routine (reflection and planning)
- ☐ Clear environmental triggers set up to support habit formation
- ☐ Intentional rewards for successful habit implementation

Note: A downloadable version of this checklist is available in this chapter's resource hub, so you can easily print it or use it digitally.

Step 2: Choose One Keystone Change
Rather than overhauling everything at once, identify the single change that would create the most significant positive cascade through your performance ecosystem.

Step 3: Implement and Track Your Keystone Change
Monitor not just whether you're following through but what effects you're experiencing. To make this easier, I've provided a practical habit tracker template you can download in this chapter's resource hub.

Step 4: Gradually Add New Layers
Once your first change has become relatively automatic, return to your assessment checklist. Identify the next most impactful improvement to introduce and repeat the implementation and tracking process. Gradual, intentional layering ensures steady, sustainable growth.

LOOKING AHEAD: WHAT'S NEXT IN YOUR JOURNEY

Now that we've established this holistic foundation, we're ready to explore deeper dimensions of sustainable performance. In the coming chapters, we'll expand on systematically accessing flow states, further strengthening your mental resilience, designing antifragile systems that automate high performance, and ensuring that your newfound capabilities last a lifetime.

Each upcoming topic builds on this integrated foundation. The prioritization, biological optimization methods, and environmental factors we've explored create the necessary conditions for these more sophisticated performance strategies.

The journey from here gets even more exciting, but this integrated foundation is required to succeed. Reliable flow states depend on optimized biology. True resilience requires a solid grasp of stress regulation. Effective systems demand clarity on prioritization and efficiency. Everything you've learned connects and amplifies each subsequent layer.

Now equipped with your holistic performance blueprint, you're ready to reach extraordinary levels of success, resilience, and fulfillment.

Let's continue this journey together and unlock the next layer of your potential.

RESEARCH & RESOURCES

As you've seen throughout this journey, one of the most effective ways to create lasting change is to track it. As you begin integrating these new habits for physiological optimization and stress mastery, I've included a simple **habit tracker** to help you stay consistent and monitor your progress.

You'll also find the **Holistic Performance Checklist**, a quick-reference guide to help you assess how well you're implementing the core principles covered in this chapter.

Both are available inside this chapter's Resource Hub.

Please visit hplink.org/resourcehub or scan the QR code below.

CHAPTER 10

FLOW ALCHEMY

"Flow is the doorway to the 'more' that most of us seek."

– Tara Brach

Think about the most extraordinary performance of your life. That presentation where the words flowed effortlessly. The creative breakthrough where time seemed to stand still. The athletic achievement where your body moved with perfect precision without conscious thought. These weren't random moments of luck; they were glimpses into what neuroscientists call the flow state, the most powerful leverage point available in human performance.

What if you could access this state not by chance, but by design?

Throughout history, exceptional performers have described this remarkable mental state using different terms. Athletes call it "being in the zone." Musicians describe it as being "in the pocket." Creatives talk about "the forever box." Martial artists refer to it as "mushin" or "no-mind." But while the labels differ, the experience remains strikingly consistent across domains.

This phenomenon isn't new to human experience. In the 1870s, Friedrich Nietzsche introduced the concept of the Übermensch, describing a transcendent state where humans surpass ordinary limitations. By the 1950s, Abraham Maslow had begun to ground this concept in psychology through his research on "peak experiences" among self-actualized individuals. But it wasn't until the 1970s that Mihaly Csikszentmihalyi transformed these observations into a systematic, scientifically verifiable framework—what we now know as flow.

This evolution—from mystical concept to psychological phenomenon to scientific framework—mirrors our own journey in understanding human performance. Like early naturalists who observed flight in birds before understanding aerodynamics, we recognized extraordinary human states long before we could measure the underlying neurophysiology.

What makes flow particularly powerful in our journey toward holistic performance is how it integrates with everything we've explored so far. Remember in Chapter 2 when we discussed flow as the ultimate internal leverage system? We saw those remarkable statistics about productivity, learning, and problem-solving enhancements.

But now that we understand the biological foundations we've built through nutrition, sleep, and stress management, we can see flow for what it truly is—the culmination of all these optimizations working in perfect harmony. Flow isn't just another technique; it's the state where your optimized biology, focused attention, and intrinsic motivation converge to create performance that feels almost supernatural.

This is why I refer to flow as "ultimate leverage"—it multiplies the effectiveness of every other strategy we've discussed. When you enter flow, your prioritization becomes intuitive, your biology operates at peak efficiency, and your psychology aligns perfectly with your tasks. It's the difference between pushing a boulder uphill and guiding it down a perfectly designed path.

UNDERSTANDING THE FLOW EXPERIENCE

To recognize flow, we need to understand its essential characteristics. Csikszentmihalyi identified six main traits:

1. **Intense Focus:** Complete immersion in the present moment, with undivided attention on the task at hand.

2. **Intrinsic Reward:** The activity becomes its own reward, providing deep satisfaction independent of external outcomes.

3. **Altered Time Perception:** Time seems to either speed up or slow down, creating a sense of temporal distortion.

4. **Merging of Action and Awareness:** A seamless integration of thoughts, actions, and emotions during the experience.

5. **Loss of Self-Consciousness:** Diminished self-awareness, where personal concerns and ego temporarily fade away.

6. **Sense of Control:** A feeling of mastery and influence over the activity, despite its challenges.

Another helpful framework comes from researchers Ryan Doris and Steven Kotler, who created the STER acronym to describe flow experiences:

- **Selfless**: Engaging with diminished self-consciousness, fully absorbed in the activity
- **Timeless**: Experiencing a distortion of time perception
- **Effortless**: Performing with a natural ease despite high engagement
- **Richness**: Encountering deep fulfillment and satisfaction from the activity itself

At a neurobiological level, flow represents a dramatic shift in brain function. When you enter flow, your brain transitions from high-frequency beta waves (13-30 Hz) associated with normal waking consciousness to the border between alpha waves (8-12 Hz) and theta waves (4-7 Hz). This alpha-theta borderline state creates the perfect conditions for the seemingly contradictory experience of relaxed high performance.

This shift in brainwave activity corresponds with a fascinating neurological phenomenon called "transient hypofrontality." During flow, activity in your prefrontal cortex—the brain region responsible for self-monitoring, time perception, and analytical thinking—temporarily decreases. This partial deactivation of your conscious "inner critic" allows more automatic, intuitive brain regions to take control, enabling faster processing and more fluid performance.

Simultaneously, your brain experiences a cascade of powerful neurochemicals. Dopamine surges to enhance pattern recognition and create feelings of pleasure, norepinephrine sharpens focus and increases physical energy, and anandamide promotes lateral thinking and novel connections. Meanwhile, endorphins are released to reduce pain perception and foster a sense of well-being, while serotonin stabilizes your mood and reduces anxiety.

Beyond these neurochemical changes, researchers have identified several other physiological markers of flow. Heart rate variability increases, indicating an optimal balance within your autonomic nervous system. Respiration becomes deeper and more synchronized, aligning your breathing rhythm with your heightened state of performance. Additionally, core body temperature slightly decreases as blood is redistributed to prioritize brain and muscle function. Galvanic skin response also intensifies, reflecting a state of heightened engagement and alertness.

Together, these biological shifts create the optimal internal environment for exceptional performance—a state where you're simultaneously relaxed yet energized, focused yet flexible, and challenged yet confident.

THE FLOW CYCLE

One of the most common misconceptions about flow is that it can be maintained indefinitely. The reality is quite different. Flow operates as part of a natural cycle with distinct phases, each serving an essential purpose in the overall experience. Understanding this cycle is crucial for intentionally accessing flow states rather than leaving them to chance.

The complete flow cycle consists of four distinct phases:

1. Struggle
2. Release
3. Flow
4. Recovery

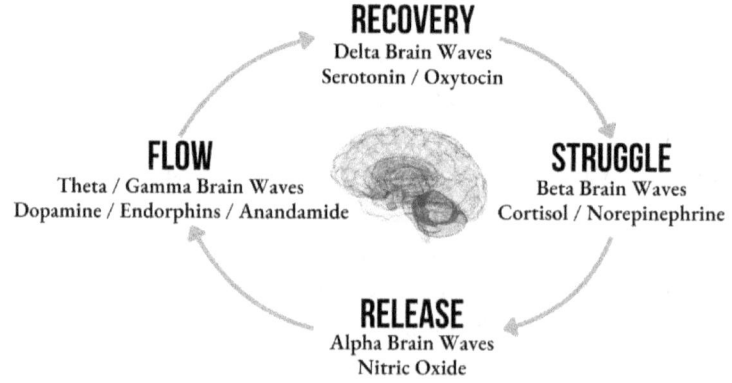

Let's explore each phase to understand how they work together to create the conditions for optimal performance.

Phase 1: The Productive Struggle

The journey to flow always begins with struggle. This initial phase involves confronting challenges, gathering information, and pushing against the boundaries of your current capabilities. The struggle phase activates your sympathetic nervous system, creating the alertness and tension necessary for growth.

Many people misinterpret this necessary struggle as a sign that something is wrong, but this discomfort is actually the gateway to flow. As we discussed in Chapter 8 when exploring stress mastery, productive stress (eustress) serves as a catalyst for growth and adaptation. The struggle phase creates precisely this type of productive tension.

The key insight from Csikszentmihalyi's research is that optimal challenge occurs when a task is approximately 4% beyond your current capabilities—difficult enough to demand your full attention, but not so difficult that it triggers excessive anxiety or frustration. This sweet spot creates what psychologists call "optimal anxiety," the perfect level of arousal for peak performance.

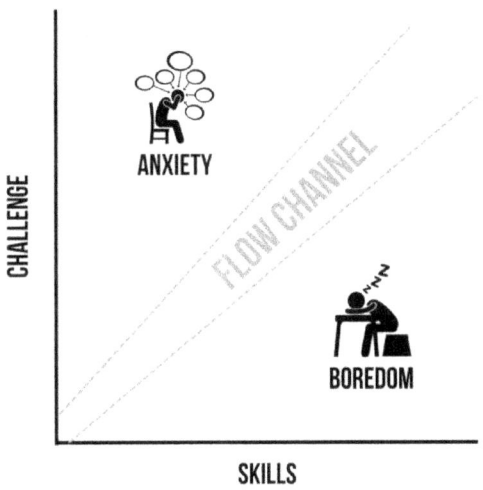

When faced with this phase, resist the urge to escape the discomfort. Instead, remind yourself that frustration is the path to flow. This reframing is more than positive thinking; it's neurologically sound. Research shows that anxiety and excitement share identical physiological signatures. The difference lies entirely in how we interpret these sensations. By consciously relabeling anxiety as excitement, you transform what could be performance-hindering stress into performance-enhancing anticipation.

One powerful technique for navigating this phase is what psychologists call the Problem-Response Gap—the space between experiencing a stressor and choosing your response to it. By recognizing this gap, you gain the opportunity to choose your response rather than being swept away by automatic reactions. When you feel frustration mounting, try this three-step reframing process:

1. Ask yourself: **"Do I have enough information?"** — Assess whether your anxiety stems from a lack of information, and identify what you need to discover.

2. Consider: **"What's the payoff from excitement?"** — Focus on the potential benefits of channeling your energy toward solving the problem rather than avoiding it.

3. Use the **Affirmation + Physical Anchor** technique — Repeat "I am excited about this challenge" three times while using a specific physical gesture (like pressing your thumb and forefinger together). Research shows this simple practice reduces anxiety more effectively than three minutes of focused breathing.

Another key to shortening the struggle phase is breaking larger challenges into smaller components. Instead of tackling an entire project at once, identify the smallest meaningful unit of progress—what productivity expert David Allen calls the "next action." This approach reduces cognitive load and makes the challenge feel more manageable, creating a series of small wins that build momentum.

I've seen this principle transform the productivity of many of my clients. Christine, a health coach struggling with scattered focus, found that breaking tasks into their smallest meaningful units created a clear pathway toward greater productivity.

"Breaking things down made all the difference," she noted after implementing this strategy for several weeks.

By simplifying her focus and experiencing regular small wins, Christine began building momentum that created the conditions where flow could naturally emerge.

Her story is just an example of an essential principle: the struggle phase becomes manageable when broken into digestible pieces, allowing your brain to build confidence through completion rather than becoming overwhelmed by complexity.

Phase 2: The Release Mechanism

The second phase of the flow cycle—release—serves as the critical transition between struggle and flow. During this phase, you temporarily step back from the problem, allowing your subconscious mind to process information and make connections that your conscious mind might miss.

This release isn't about giving up; it's a strategic disengagement that creates space for insight. Neurologically, it allows your brain to shift from focused, analytical beta-wave activity toward the more diffuse alpha-theta state characteristic of flow. This transition can't be forced. It requires temporarily releasing conscious control.

One effective release technique is the MacGyver Method (named after the resourceful TV character known for creative problem-solving). Here's how it works:

1. Clearly define the specific challenge you're working on
2. Engage in a release activity that occupies your conscious mind while allowing your subconscious to work (walking, showering, light exercise)
3. Return to the task with a fresh perspective

This technique leverages what neuroscientists call the "default mode network"—the brain regions that activate when you're not focused on external tasks. During the release phase, this network processes background information and generates new connections, often leading to those "aha!" moments that seem to come from nowhere.

The most effective release activities share a few key characteristics. They provide just enough mental engagement to keep you from fixating on the problem, but they don't require intense concentration or complex decision-making. Many involve light physical movement or sensory engagement, helping to shift focus without demanding too much cognitive effort. Just as importantly, they create a sense of psychological safety—an environment where your brain feels at ease, allowing insights to surface naturally.

Some of the most reliable ways to tap into this state include walking, particularly in natural settings, where the rhythmic movement and change of scenery encourage mental clarity. Light stretching or gentle yoga can have a similar effect, providing subtle physical engagement while letting the mind wander freely. Brief meditation, or the breathwork techniques we explored in Chapter 8, can be particularly effective during this phase, quieting mental noise and making space for fresh ideas. Even simple, repetitive tasks like washing dishes or folding laundry can serve as effective release activities, as their automatic nature allows the mind to process information in the background. Sometimes, a short, non-work-related social interaction is enough to shift perspective and unlock a creative breakthrough.

Many people find it helpful to develop a personalized "trigger list" of reliable release activities that work for their particular physiology and preferences. These become go-to strategies when you notice yourself stuck in a prolonged struggle phase without making progress.

Remember that the release phase isn't about forcing insight; it's about creating the conditions where insight becomes possible. As the pioneering scientist Louis Pasteur famously noted, "Chance favors the prepared mind." The release phase prepares your mind for the flow state that follows.

Phase 3: The Flow State Experience

Following the release phase comes the magical moment we've been working toward—the flow state itself. Think of it as slipping into a different operating mode where everything just... works.

When you're in flow, the experience is unmistakable. Time warps (hours passing like minutes or seconds stretching into meaningful moments). Self-consciousness vanishes. Your actions feel simultaneously effortless yet precise. It's as if you've accessed a hidden gear in your performance engine—one that was always there but rarely engaged.

But here's something fascinating about flow that most people miss entirely: your ability to access this state isn't consistent throughout the day. In fact, it follows a predictable biological rhythm that, once understood, can transform how you approach your most important work.

Enter ultradian rhythms—one of your body's most powerful but least understood performance systems.

While most people are familiar with circadian rhythms (our 24-hour sleep-wake cycle), these shorter cycles operate largely beneath our conscious awareness, yet profoundly influence our cognitive capabilities. I've mentioned them earlier in the book, but haven't fully explained how these cycles specifically impact your ability to access flow states. Let's fix that now.

Ultradian rhythms are recurrent cycles within your 24-hour circadian cycle, typically lasting around 90 minutes. During these cycles, your energy and cognitive abilities naturally ebb and flow—regardless of your caffeine intake, motivation level, or deadline pressure.

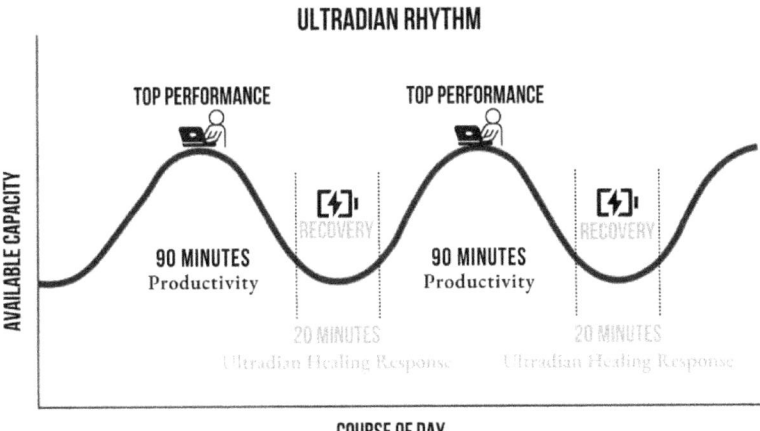

During the peak of each roughly 90-minute cycle, your brain creates the precise neurological conditions that facilitate flow:

- Your prefrontal cortex functions at optimal capacity.
- Your neurochemistry naturally shifts toward flow-friendly states.
- Your attention mechanisms resist distraction more effectively.
- Your working memory expands to hold more information simultaneously.
- Your pattern recognition systems operate with heightened sensitivity.

It's no coincidence that experienced flow practitioners report their deepest states lasting approximately 90 minutes. They've unknowingly synchronized with their brain's natural high-performance windows.

Studies tracking brainwave patterns during peak performance reveal a remarkable correlation: flow states tend to emerge most readily during the first 60-75 minutes of an ultradian peak, when alpha-theta brainwave patterns naturally predominate. As the cycle progresses toward its recovery phase, these optimal patterns become increasingly difficult to maintain.

This biological reality offers a profound insight: flow isn't just about what techniques you use; it's about timing those techniques with your brain's natural rhythm. Think of it like surf. You can have perfect form and equipment, but if you're not catching the wave at the right moment, you'll struggle regardless of skill.

This explains why we structured your day around 90-minute work blocks back in Chapter 5. Those weren't arbitrary time periods; they were deliberately calibrated to your brain's natural processing cycles. When you align your most challenging work with these biological peaks and respect the recovery periods between them, you're essentially harmonizing with your neurophysiology rather than fighting against it.

Phase 4: The Recovery Imperative

The final phase of the flow cycle—recovery—is perhaps the most frequently neglected, yet it's absolutely essential for sustainable high performance. Flow states, while incredibly productive, create what scientists call "cognitive debt"—a depletion of the neurochemicals and energy reserves that make peak performance possible.

Without proper recovery, this debt accumulates over time, eventually making flow states inaccessible regardless of your intentions or techniques. The neurochemical cocktail that powers flow—particularly norepinephrine and dopamine—requires specific recovery protocols to replenish.

Effective recovery after flow involves several dimensions, each playing a crucial role in restoring balance. Active recovery, unlike passive rest, includes intentional activities that accelerate physiological restoration. Low-intensity movement, such as walking or gentle yoga, helps reset the nervous system. Contrast therapy, alternating between hot and cold exposure, supports circulation and reduces inflammation. Light socializing with trusted people provides a sense of connection and relaxation, while time spent in natural settings aids in lowering stress levels. Massage or other bodywork can further facilitate physical recovery by relieving muscle tension and enhancing circulation.

Sleep optimization remains one of the most critical aspects of recovery, allowing for neurotransmitter replenishment, memory consolidation, and cellular repair. As explored in Chapter 7, deep sleep and REM cycles play a key role in cognitive recovery, ensuring the brain restores its capacity for high-level performance.

Nutritional strategies also contribute to effective post-flow recovery, as flow states deplete specific neurochemical precursors that require replenishment. Prioritizing protein intake supports neurotransmitter production, while healthy fats assist in brain cell repair and provide stable energy. Hydration, particularly with electrolytes, is essential for maintaining cognitive function. Additionally, strategic micronutrients such as B vitamins, magnesium, and zinc help restore biochemical balance and optimize recovery.

Mindfulness practices play an important role in integrating insights from flow states while regulating the nervous system. Techniques like meditation, journaling, and breathing exercises create space for processing experiences and preparing for the next cycle of deep focus and high performance.

When this is not taken into account, we may experience the dreadful "flow hangover"—a period of temporary depletion that can include self-doubt, fatigue, or mild anxiety following an intense flow state. This is a normal physiological response to the neurochemical changes during flow, not a sign of failure or weakness. Understanding this pattern helps prevent misinterpreting these sensations as problematic when they're actually a natural part of the cycle.

One effective practice during recovery is post-flow visualization. By mentally revisiting the flow experience, focusing on the sensations and emotions it created, you strengthen the neural pathways associated with flow states. This mental rehearsal makes subsequent flow states more accessible, creating a positive feedback loop over time.

By now you might be tired of hearing this (and if you are, take that as a sign you need rest), but recovery isn't optional. Your brain, like an athlete after an intense performance, requires strategic renewal after flow states. This isn't laziness; it's sophisticated performance management

FLOW TRIGGERS: THE SCIENCE OF RELIABLE ACCESS

Now that we understand the flow cycle, how do we reliably trigger this remarkable state? Is flow something we can cultivate intentionally, or are we at the mercy of chance and circumstance?

The answer lies in understanding flow triggers—specific conditions and practices that significantly increase the likelihood of entering flow states. While individual triggers vary somewhat based on personality and context, decades of research have identified consistent patterns that apply across domains.

Before exploring specific triggers, it's worth acknowledging that some individuals appear naturally more prone to flow states than others. Research suggests genetic factors, particularly variations in dopamine receptor genes, may influence flow proneness.

Some people naturally have higher activity in D2 dopamine receptors, making them more inclined to seek out exciting and novel experiences. This natural inclination contributes to their ability to enter flow states more readily, as they're neurologically primed for the dopamine dynamics that facilitate flow.

Beyond genetics, psychologists have identified what Csikszentmihalyi called the "autotelic personality"—a constellation of traits that predispose individuals to flow experiences. These include:

- **Curiosity**: A natural interest in exploring and understanding new concepts or experiences.
- **Persistence**: The ability to maintain engagement with challenging activities over time.
- **Low Self-Centeredness**: Reduced preoccupation with self-image during activities.
- **High Autonomy**: Preference for independence and control in actions.
- **Collaborative Tendencies**: Ability to work effectively with others when needed.

While these traits may have genetic components, they can also be cultivated through intentional practice, creating "flow-prone characteristics" that enhance your ability to access flow states.

KOTLER'S FLOW TRIGGER FRAMEWORK

Flow researcher Steven Kotler has identified 22 reliable flow triggers—12 individual and 10 group-based—that significantly increase the likelihood of entering flow states. These triggers work by either driving focused attention (through norepinephrine and dopamine release) or reducing cognitive interference (through transient hypofrontality).

Individual Flow Triggers:

1. Curiosity and Passion: Engaging with subjects that naturally fascinate you triggers dopamine release and focused attention. The intrinsic motivation behind passionate engagement creates ideal neurochemical conditions for flow.

2. Autonomy: Having control over what you do, when you do it, and how you approach tasks significantly enhances flow potential. As the saying goes, "You always pay more attention when you're driving the car." This is why organizations like Toyota (with its Kaizen philosophy), 3M (with its 15%

approach), and Patagonia (with its "Let My People Go Surfing" policy) structure work to maximize employee autonomy.

3. Skill-Challenge Balance: Tasks that slightly exceed your current abilities—pushing you approximately 4% beyond your comfort zone—create the optimal tension for flow. This sweet spot prevents both boredom (challenges too low) and anxiety (challenges too high).

And yes, I know what you're thinking: "4%? How exactly am I supposed to measure that?" It's not like you can pull out a mental measuring tape and precisely calculate the gap between your abilities and the challenge. ("Hmm, this presentation feels about 3.7% beyond my comfort zone. Better ramp it up a notch!")

The point isn't mathematical precision; it's finding that Goldilocks zone where a task feels just challenging enough to demand your full attention without triggering the "I'm totally out of my depth" panic response. When you're stretching just beyond your current capabilities, but can still see the path forward, that's when flow comes knocking.

4. Clear Goals: Knowing precisely what success looks like for each task provides the direction and focus necessary for flow. Clear goals reduce cognitive load by eliminating uncertainty about what you're trying to achieve.

5. Immediate Feedback: Having rapid information about how well you're performing allows for micro-adjustments that maintain momentum. This doesn't require external feedback—it can come from the task itself or your own awareness of progress.

6. Deep Concentration: Creating uninterrupted blocks of time for single-tasking builds the cognitive momentum necessary for flow. Sustained attention serves as both a precondition and an amplifier for flow states.

7. Risk: Incorporating elements of physical, social, or emotional risk heightens focus and engagement. Risk is always personal—what feels risky to one person may be comfortable for another. This explains why activities with some element of risk (from public speaking to rock climbing) often trigger flow.

8. Novelty: Exposing yourself to new and unfamiliar experiences stimulates the brain's novelty-detection circuits, enhancing alertness and engagement. This is why companies like Facebook implement "Hackamonth" programs, where employees spend a month working on projects outside their normal responsibilities.

9. Unpredictability: Engaging with activities where the outcome is uncertain creates dopamine spikes that facilitate flow. Studies show that novelty combined with unpredictability can boost dopamine by up to 700%— comparable to certain stimulant drugs.

10. Complexity: Working with problems or environments that challenge multiple cognitive systems simultaneously often triggers flow. Complexity differs from difficulty—it's about richness and nuance rather than simple challenge level.

11. Pattern Recognition: Engaging in activities that require identifying meaningful patterns within information stimulates key brain regions associated with flow. This trigger explains why activities like chess, music composition, and scientific research frequently induce flow.

12. Deep Embodiment: Physical and sensory engagement with tasks enhances flow accessibility. This is why hands-on activities often feel more immersive than purely abstract mental work.

Group Flow Triggers:

For collaborative environments, additional triggers facilitate collective flow states:

- **Shared Goals**: Working toward common, clearly defined objectives.
- **Close Listening**: Active and empathetic attention to others' contributions.
- **Open Communication**: Free expression of ideas without fear of judgment.
- **Equal Participation**: Balanced contribution from all team members.
- **Familiarity**: Understanding team members' strengths and working styles.
- **Blending Egos**: Subordinating individual recognition to group success.
- **Sense of Control**: Maintaining autonomy within collaborative contexts.
- **"Yes, And..." Thinking**: Building on others' ideas rather than negating them.
- **Familiarity with Physical Environment**: Comfort and fluency in the workspace.
- **Shared Risk**: Collective investment in outcomes creates shared focus.

PRIMARY VS. SECONDARY FLOW ACTIVITIES

Not all flow experiences are created equal. Some activities naturally draw you into flow; others require more deliberate structuring to reach that state. This distinction is what Steven Kotler refers to as primary vs. secondary flow activities. Understanding this difference empowers you to engineer your environment, tasks, and schedule to maximize time spent in flow, rather than waiting for it to occur spontaneously.

Primary flow activities are your personal gateways to peak performance. With these tasks, you don't need to consciously "try" to reach flow—it happens naturally, pulling your attention effortlessly into immersive states. Examples include playing an instrument, engaging in extreme sports, creative writing, competitive gaming, performing on stage, or solving deep creative problems. The common thread? They're intrinsically motivating. People do them purely for enjoyment, without external incentives.

On the other end of the spectrum are **secondary flow activities**—tasks capable of producing flow, but only if intentionally structured. Unlike primary flow activities, these tasks don't naturally compel your full attention.

They typically involve necessary yet less intrinsically motivating work, such as writing reports, strategic planning, analyzing complex data, conducting negotiations, coding, or team management. At first glance, such tasks might seem inherently mundane or tedious.

The misconception many people hold is that these tasks simply can't generate flow. But that's a misunderstanding. The real obstacle isn't the tasks themselves, but how they're approached. By strategically applying flow triggers—breaking tasks into clear objectives, ensuring appropriate levels of challenge, minimizing distractions, and setting up real-time feedback loops—you can transform ordinary work into engaging flow experiences.

Recognizing this distinction highlights an important insight: the line between "work" and "play" is far more artificial than most realize. Yet, many professionals still mistakenly assume flow belongs exclusively in hobbies and creative pursuits, and that productive work must inherently feel difficult or tedious.

In reality, some of the world's most successful entrepreneurs, artists, and elite performers have designed their work specifically around flow principles, turning even routine tasks into immersive, rewarding experiences.

Understanding primary and secondary flow activities provides powerful leverage in your performance journey. You can optimize your schedule by allocating deep work blocks to tasks naturally aligned with flow. You can redesign your environment to eliminate distractions and friction points that disrupt your immersion. Perhaps most importantly, you can make intentional career choices aligned with your primary flow activities, maximizing the time spent in high-energy, peak-performance states.

If you've ever felt that work is a constant battle against distractions and boredom, the solution isn't more discipline—it's strategically applying flow triggers to transform mundane tasks into engaging, immersive experiences. The next section will dive deeper into advanced techniques for conditioning flow states, helping you move from sporadic experiences to consistent, repeatable access to peak performance.

ADVANCED FLOW TECHNIQUES

Once you understand the fundamental mechanisms of flow, you can implement advanced techniques that make flow states more accessible and sustainable. These approaches leverage neuroplasticity—your brain's ability to rewire itself through experience—to strengthen the neural pathways associated with flow.

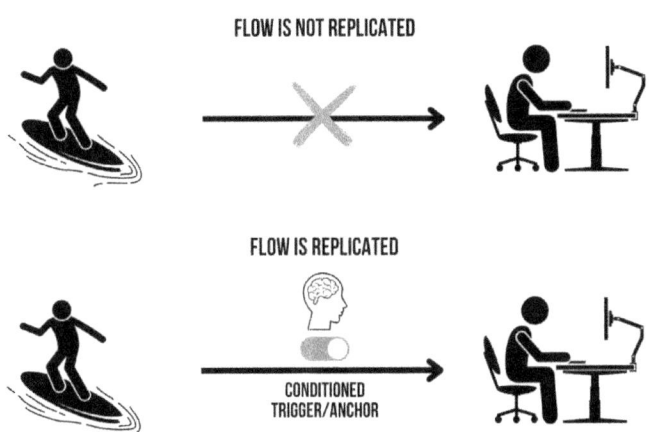

Flow Conditioning

Now that you've distinguished between primary and secondary flow activities, the next step is learning how to reliably enter flow states, even during tasks that aren't naturally immersive. This is where flow conditioning comes in. Its goal is straightforward: pair an external trigger consistently with flow experiences until that trigger becomes a reliable shortcut to the state.

The conditioning process involves four simple steps:

1. Identify Your Natural (Primary) Flow Activities

Start by pinpointing tasks where flow occurs effortlessly. Examples include:

- A sport you enjoy.
- A creative pursuit like writing, painting, or playing music.
- Intense problem-solving activities.
- Any task in which time seems to disappear and deep immersion is automatic.

2. Select a Trigger to Anchor Flow

Choose an external stimulus to associate with your flow states. Effective triggers typically engage the senses, such as:

- **Auditory:** A specific playlist, song, or background sound (e.g., white noise, binaural beats).
- **Visual:** A consistent workspace arrangement, particular lighting, or symbolic object.
- **Olfactory:** Essential oils, incense, or even your preferred brand of coffee.
- **Tactile:** Specific clothing (e.g., a favorite "work hoodie") or using a certain pen.
- **Gustatory:** A particular beverage, like green tea, black coffee, or a flavored supplement.

3. Pair the Trigger with Flow Repeatedly

Each time you engage in your primary flow activity, consistently use the chosen trigger. Repetition is crucial—you're training your brain to associate the external stimulus with deep immersion.

For example:

- Listening to the same playlist before entering flow trains your brain to recognize the music as a cue for deep concentration.
- Lighting the same scented candle or wearing a particular hoodie each time you write primes your brain for focused creativity.

4. Transfer the Trigger to Other Contexts

Once you've established a strong association, apply the trigger to facilitate flow in tasks where it's less automatic—such as deep work, presentations, or complex problem-solving.

Examples:

- A musician who easily enters flow when playing guitar might use the same pre-performance routine to prime creative brainstorming sessions.
- A surfer accustomed to peak concentration in the ocean might transfer the deep breathing exercises they use for surfing to tackle intense projects at work.

To further amplify this process, you can apply **anchor stacking**—engaging multiple senses simultaneously to strengthen your neural association with flow. The more sensory modalities you integrate, the deeper and more robust your conditioning becomes.

For example, rather than relying solely on music, you might simultaneously:

- Play a specific playlist (audio cue).
- Light a particular candle (olfactory cue).
- Wear a favorite hoodie (tactile cue).
- Sit in your designated workspace (visual cue).
- Drink matcha tea or coffee (gustatory cue).

Many elite performers intuitively develop these multi-sensory anchors. Stephen King famously begins writing at exactly 9 AM each day, sitting at the same desk with the same cup of tea, creating a powerful multi-sensory trigger for creative flow. Michael Jordan wore his University of North Carolina shorts beneath his NBA uniform and followed precise pre-game routines to trigger his performance state.

Done effectively, anchor stacking transforms flow from something elusive into a state you can reliably access, on-demand.

DISCOVERING HIDDEN FLOW TRIGGERS

While the techniques we've discussed help condition flow through conscious and deliberate anchors, some of the most powerful triggers are hidden— operating beneath conscious awareness. These triggers, unique to your personal experiences and biology, often hold the keys to reliably entering flow.

To uncover your hidden flow triggers, follow this archaeological three-step approach:

Step 1: Identify Peak Performance Phases

Recall periods of about 1–3 months in your life when you consistently performed at your highest level. Include any timeframe when productivity felt effortless, creativity flowed, or your effectiveness soared—not only in professional contexts but also during periods of notable personal performance.

Step 2: Inventory Your Conditions

List all contributing factors present during these peak times, even if they seem minor or irrelevant initially. Consider factors such as:

- Physical Environment: lighting, workspace setup, views, temperature.
- Daily Routines: morning practices, transitions, scheduling.
- Dietary Patterns: types of food, timing, fasting.
- Exercise Habits: intensity, timing, modalities.
- Social Dynamics: collaboration styles, isolation, interactions.
- Sleep Patterns: duration, consistency, quality.
- Challenge Levels: deadlines, competition, pressure.
- Tools and Technology: analog vs. digital, software used.

This comprehensive reflection often reveals surprising patterns. For example, one executive discovered that his peak performance periods consistently occurred when his desk was positioned near a window, offering subtle attentional resets through natural light and outside views. Another client noticed significant productivity boosts whenever she engaged in regular strength training before work, benefiting from the cognitive-enhancing neurochemistry triggered by intense exercise. A software developer I worked with found that listening to video game soundtracks from his youth greatly amplified his coding flow states by activating deeply ingrained neural pathways developed through years of focused gameplay.

Step 3: Systematic Experimentation

Reintroduce identified factors methodically into your current routine, carefully tracking their effects on your flow states. This isn't about exactly recreating past circumstances, but about understanding and leveraging the underlying conditions that boost your unique psychological and physiological systems.

The power of uncovering your hidden triggers lies in their personalization. While general flow triggers offer reliable starting points, these hidden triggers—finely tuned to your specific neurophysiology, life experiences, and psychological makeup—can provide a more potent and reliable route into flow states. They're your customized keys for accessing peak performance consistently and predictably.

By methodically excavating and leveraging these hidden triggers from past peak performances, you craft a personalized toolkit that empowers you to access flow in almost any context. The goal isn't dependence on specific circumstances, but rather deep understanding and optimization of your personal performance system.

THE PEAK EXIT STRATEGY

You've learned about ultradian rhythms and how respecting your biological productivity cycles optimizes performance. Building upon that insight, let's explore another powerful technique that dramatically enhances flow accessibility: the Peak Exit Strategy.

Many of us, despite knowing better, still unconsciously operate under a completion-based mindset—we feel compelled to finish tasks fully, tie up loose ends, and reach clear stopping points. Yet, this ingrained habit unintentionally suppresses a powerful psychological tool we can leverage: the Zeigarnik Effect.

Discovered in the 1920s, this psychological principle emerged from observations of restaurant servers who flawlessly remembered complex orders—until the meal was served, at which point the details faded from memory. Why? Because our brains naturally maintain active, unconscious processing loops for unfinished tasks. Rather than viewing incomplete work as failure, you can strategically leverage this mental phenomenon to sustain momentum between flow sessions.

When you deliberately step away from a task while you're still energized, clear on your direction, and deeply engaged—rather than pushing to the point of exhaustion—something remarkable happens. Your subconscious mind continues processing the task, maintaining neural activation patterns that dramatically ease your re-entry into flow in subsequent sessions.

Consider Julia, a software architect who struggled with inconsistent access to flow. After brilliant flow sessions, she'd often endure days of frustrating mental resistance. When she implemented the Peak Exit Strategy—stopping her coding sessions just after successfully completing a feature but before exhausting her mental resources—she found it remarkably easier to resume coding the following day. The cognitive barrier to re-entering flow dropped significantly.

The implications for mastering flow are profound. Recall that the "struggle phase," the initial friction before reaching flow, is often one of the greatest barriers to consistent peak performance. The Peak Exit Strategy creates a neurological bridge over this struggle, preserving neural activation patterns that prime your brain for rapid re-entry into flow.

This transforms your relationship with deep work. Rather than facing the full friction of a cold-start each session, you're returning to a task with a brain already primed for engagement. The resistance typically experienced at the onset of a work session is minimized, dramatically increasing your frequency and consistency of flow experiences.

By strategically exiting at moments of high energy and clarity, you're not just managing energy—you're actively engineering consistent, repeatable access to flow across multiple work sessions. Over time, your brain associates work more strongly with the positive experience of flow rather than the friction that precedes it, creating powerful neurological pathways that make peak performance increasingly accessible.

MENTAL REHEARSAL FOR FLOW

In Chapter 8, we explored mental rehearsal as a scientifically validated performance enhancement tool used widely by elite athletes, surgeons, and top performers. Visualization powerfully activates the same neural pathways involved in actual performance, priming your brain for skilled execution and tuning your Reticular Activating System to opportunities relevant to your goals.

But mental rehearsal also has a unique, powerful benefit specifically for accessing flow. Earlier in this chapter, we examined the struggle phase and introduced strategies like the Peak Exit Strategy to ease entry into flow. Mental rehearsal complements these strategies by neurologically priming your brain, further smoothing your transition into flow states.

When you vividly visualize yourself already immersed in flow before beginning your task, you're pre-activating the exact neural pathways associated with peak performance, reducing the cognitive effort needed to initiate deep concentration. Visualization also quiets the analytical, self-critical regions of your prefrontal cortex, which otherwise hinder effortless immersion. By rehearsing flow in advance, you establish clear mental models of what to expect, dramatically lowering cognitive uncertainty and friction.

Here's how to apply mental rehearsal specifically to prime flow:

Start with state visualization, spending 3–5 minutes vividly experiencing yourself fully absorbed in flow. Engage your senses and emotions—feel the ease, the quiet mind, and the satisfaction of peak immersion. Make this mental movie as vivid and multi-sensory as possible.

Next, briefly use process visualization to mentally rehearse the actual steps of your task. Imagine smoothly overcoming any potential obstacles, reinforcing neural patterns that support quick entry into flow.

What makes this technique particularly potent is how it combines psychological and physiological preparation. As you visualize flow states, your brain begins producing the neurochemicals associated with those states—dopamine increases in anticipation, norepinephrine levels adjust for optimal arousal, and stress hormones decrease to appropriate levels. You're essentially giving your brain a chemical head start toward the conditions that facilitate flow.

This mental priming creates what performance psychologists call "state-dependent memory"—when you begin the actual task, your brain recognizes the state you've rehearsed and more readily slips into that pattern of activation. Thus, mental rehearsal uniquely reduces resistance and makes consistent, repeatable access to flow states reliably achievable.

SONIC GATEWAYS TO PERFORMANCE

Earlier, we explored anchoring flow states through external triggers, including sensory cues like sound. Among these, music stands out as one of the most powerful and accessible neurological shortcuts for reliably shifting your brain state into flow.

The relationship between music and cognitive performance isn't just a matter of subjective preference; it's firmly rooted in neuroscience. Different musical structures elicit distinct neurological responses, either enhancing or disrupting your flow potential. When carefully selected, music leverages a phenomenon neuroscientists call predictive coding, where your brain unconsciously anticipates musical patterns just enough to sustain engagement without distracting conscious attention.

Classical and instrumental music is particularly effective since it doesn't engage your brain's language centers with lyrics. This leaves your cognitive resources fully available to focus deeply on your primary task. Movie scores, crafted explicitly to support emotional and cognitive engagement without distracting from visual storytelling, are prime examples of music ideally suited to facilitate flow.

For even more targeted neural entrainment, binaural beats offer a fascinating option. This technology involves playing slightly different frequencies in each ear, creating a third "phantom" frequency that corresponds to specific brainwave patterns. For example, playing 200 Hz in your left ear and 210 Hz in your right creates a 10 Hz differential that encourages alpha brainwaves—precisely the frequency associated with relaxed focus and creative flow states.

The effectiveness of these sonic tools depends heavily on matching them to your task demands and individual neurophysiology. Deep analytical work generally benefits from compositions with predictable structures and minimal emotional variation, while creative tasks might thrive on more complex, emotionally evocative pieces that stimulate novel connections.

Ultimately, finding your ideal sonic gateways to flow is deeply personal and relies on thoughtful experimentation. Create task-specific playlists, test different musical styles, and notice which consistently enhance your access to peak performance.

SUPPLEMENTS FOR FLOW

Having just explored the most foundational techniques for accessing flow states, it's important to acknowledge another useful tool: strategic supplementation. You might recall our detailed exploration of cognitive enhancers in Chapter 7, where we examined everything from basic compounds to advanced nootropics.

Rather than retreading that ground, let's examine specifically how these supplements relate to flow. The relationship between cognitive enhancement and flow isn't as straightforward as merely taking a pill—it presents a nuanced picture requiring careful integration within your overall performance strategy.

Flow states depend on a delicate neurochemical harmony—balancing dopamine and norepinephrine for focus, anandamide for creative insight, and serotonin and endorphins for mood stability. This complex orchestration explains why flow can't simply be "hacked" through isolated supplements or single-compound approaches.

Instead, supplements function best as targeted triggers within a comprehensive flow system. For example, your morning coffee isn't just providing caffeine; it becomes a consistent external cue, signaling your brain that it's time for deep, focused work. When combined intentionally with other flow triggers—like environment, routine, and optimal challenge—

supplements become powerful components of your holistic performance ecosystem.

Yet, effective integration requires discernment about when supplementation genuinely enhances flow versus when it creates harmful dependency. Too often, high performers fall into the "enhancement trap," needing increasingly potent compounds just to achieve baseline productivity. This cycle undermines the very neurochemical self-regulation essential for sustainable flow.

A healthier, more effective strategy views cognitive enhancers as occasional amplifiers, not daily necessities. Reserve the advanced compounds we explored in Chapter 7 for truly demanding cognitive challenges—significant creative endeavors, complex problem-solving sessions, or periods of extended cognitive load. This targeted approach preserves your brain's intrinsic capacities while providing meaningful support when genuinely required.

Ultimately, flow emerges most powerfully from harmonizing your brain's intrinsic capabilities with intentionally optimized environments and routines. While supplements can provide targeted boosts, they should never replace the foundational physiological and psychological optimization we've explored throughout this book.

PERSONALIZING YOUR FLOW JOURNEY

As we conclude our exploration of flow mastery—from triggers and mental rehearsal to sonic gateways and strategic supplementation—one truth becomes abundantly clear: flow isn't a one-size-fits-all phenomenon. Your unique neurophysiology, personal history, environmental conditions, and intrinsic motivations create a flow fingerprint as individual as you are.

Integrating flow into your life involves developing your personal flow profile—a clear understanding of the specific conditions, triggers, and practices that reliably lead you into your optimal states. This profile emerges from intentional experimentation and reflection, not from adopting generic solutions.

Begin by clearly identifying your primary flow activities—those tasks where you naturally experience flow. These could range from creative endeavors and strategic problem-solving to athletic or interactive experiences. Then, document patterns you notice, such as ideal challenge levels, effective feedback systems, optimal environmental conditions, and your internal mental states.

With this personalized inventory, strategically incorporate flow opportunities into your daily schedule. Rather than hoping for spontaneous moments of flow, deliberately design your days to ensure flow is not just possible, but likely. Treat these blocks of time with the rigor and priority you would reserve for your most important meetings or commitments.

Most importantly, approach flow cultivation as an evolving practice rather than a fixed endpoint. Regularly assess which strategies enhance or hinder your access to flow, remaining adaptable to new insights, changing circumstances, and deepening self-awareness. Recognize that what triggers flow today might shift as you gain new skills or encounter different challenges.

The journey toward flow mastery isn't about perfecting a rigid system; it's about developing an increasingly refined sensitivity to how your internal state, external environment, and current task interact. This dynamic calibration transforms flow from an occasional visitor into a reliable companion on your journey toward peak performance.

As we now shift toward understanding how motivation and clarity form the psychological foundations necessary for consistent flow, keep in mind that none of these elements exist in isolation. Each component—from the neurochemical foundations explored here to the motivational structures discussed next—operates as part of an integrated ecosystem, where progress in any area amplifies performance in all.

THE PSYCHOLOGICAL ARCHITECTURE OF FLOW

By now, you've explored the neurobiological foundations of flow and mastered several techniques to reliably access this state. But here's what many flow-seekers overlook: without the right psychological infrastructure, those techniques don't consistently work. Biology sets the stage, but psychology builds the foundation.

Remember our discussion of the flow cycle, especially the challenge of the struggle phase? When we examined why some people move through that friction while others abandon ship, we glimpsed something deeper: the psychological scaffolding that supports the entire flow experience.

You might wonder why we're addressing motivation and goals now, instead of waiting for the dedicated psychology chapters ahead. The reason is simple: these aren't just general performance enhancers; they're direct flow triggers. They prime your brain neurochemically and emotionally for the state of deep immersion. Without this internal architecture in place, no amount of environmental optimization or biological fine-tuning will reliably lead you into flow.

Think of it this way: all the flow triggers in the world won't help if your core motivations, goals, and sense of purpose are misaligned. It's like wiring your house with state-of-the-art tech, but skipping the foundation. Without psychological grounding, the whole system becomes unstable, no matter how optimized everything else may be.

This is why flow isn't just a neurochemical phenomenon. It's also a psychological one. The state arises at the intersection of biology and belief, physiology and purpose. You can't separate the two any more than you can separate the hardware and software of a high-performance system. They work in tandem or not at all.

Three psychological elements form the foundation of reliable flow experiences: motivation, clarity, and purposeful goals. When these align, they create the internal conditions that make flow not only possible, but probable. When they're weak or out of sync, flow becomes elusive—regardless of how well you've optimized your routines, workspace, or supplements.

This also explains something you've likely experienced: why the same task, under the same conditions, sometimes triggers flow, and other times doesn't. The difference often lies not in your external environment, but in these deeper psychological variables that determine your relationship with the task itself.

As we explore these elements more closely, keep in mind that this psychological architecture isn't something you build once and forget. It evolves with you shifting with your goals, your environment, and your sense of meaning. This evolving psychological architecture is why flow isn't a one-time breakthrough or a temporary hack; it's a lifelong practice. And it's this ongoing refinement that makes it not only sustainable but deeply rewarding.

THE SCIENCE OF MOTIVATION

Have you ever wondered why some activities effortlessly capture your complete attention while others, despite being equally important, require constant willpower to maintain focus? The answer lies in understanding the fundamental nature of motivation and its crucial role in accessing flow states.

Motivation isn't just about wanting something; it's about the psychological energy that drives sustained engagement with challenging activities. And when it comes to flow, the type of motivation matters far more than its intensity.

This distinction was illuminated through the groundbreaking work of psychologists Richard Ryan and Edward Deci, who developed the Self-Determination Theory. Their research revealed that motivation exists on a spectrum, with two primary categories at opposite ends:

Extrinsic motivation originates outside yourself—working for a paycheck, studying for a grade, exercising for appearance, or creating content for likes and followers. It's driven by external rewards or pressures rather than inherent satisfaction in the activity itself.

Intrinsic motivation, by contrast, comes from within—the natural desire to engage in activities for their inherent enjoyment, satisfaction, or alignment with your values. It's what drives people to pursue hobbies for hours without external rewards, lose themselves in creative projects, or voluntarily tackle challenging problems simply because they find them interesting.

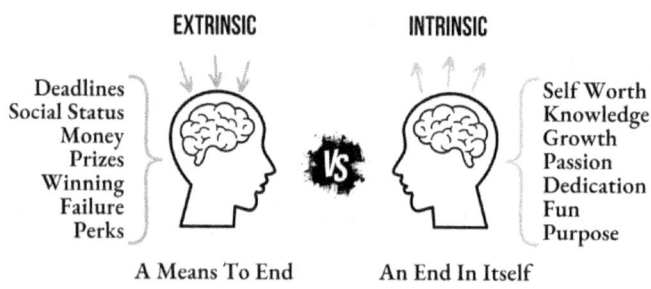

EXTRINSIC	INTRINSIC
Deadlines Social Status Money Prizes Winning Failure Perks	Self Worth Knowledge Growth Passion Dedication Fun Purpose
A Means To End	An End In Itself

Why does this distinction matter for flow? Research consistently shows that intrinsic motivation creates the psychological conditions necessary for flow, while purely extrinsic motivation often undermines them.

This principle was dramatically demonstrated in a classic study by psychologist Mark Lepper. He observed children who naturally enjoyed drawing and divided them into three groups: one received unexpected rewards for drawing, another expected rewards, and the third received no rewards. When researchers later measured their interest in drawing during free play, the children who expected rewards showed significantly decreased interest compared to the other groups.

This phenomenon, called the Overjustification Effect, reveals something profound about human psychology: introducing extrinsic rewards for intrinsically rewarding activities can actually diminish natural engagement. The expectation of external rewards shifts your focus from the inherent value of the activity to its instrumental value, fundamentally changing your relationship with the task.

For flow specifically, this creates a psychological barrier. When you're primarily motivated by external outcomes—recognition, status, financial reward—your attention naturally divides between the activity itself and its eventual payoff. This divided attention directly contradicts the complete absorption characteristic of flow states.

However, this doesn't mean all extrinsic motivation undermines flow potential. The relationship is more nuanced. Ryan and Deci identified several forms of extrinsic motivation that vary in their degree of autonomy and internalization:

1. **External regulation**—purely controlled by external rewards and punishments.
2. **Introjected regulation**—motivated by internal pressures like guilt or approval-seeking.
3. **Identified regulation**—recognizing and valuing the importance of a behavior.
4. **Integrated regulation**—fully assimilating behaviors into your sense of self and values.

As you move from external toward integrated regulation, extrinsic motivation becomes increasingly harmonious with intrinsic motivation rather than undermining it. This integration explains why some externally-rewarded work can still produce flow when you've fully internalized its worth and aligned it with your deeper values.

The practical implication is clear: to create psychological conditions conducive to flow, focus on cultivating and protecting intrinsic motivation. This doesn't mean abandoning all externally rewarded activities—modern life would make that impossible. Rather, it means finding ways to connect external requirements with internal motivations, transforming "have to" into "want to" whenever possible.

This motivational foundation creates the psychological receptivity necessary for flow triggers to work effectively. Without it, even perfect environmental conditions and masterful techniques will struggle to overcome the fundamental resistance created by misaligned motivation.

THE NEUROCHEMISTRY OF INTRINSIC MOTIVATION

The distinction between intrinsic and extrinsic motivation is deeply biological. Understanding the neurochemistry behind intrinsic motivation reveals why it creates such fertile ground for flow states and how you can deliberately cultivate it.

At its core, intrinsic motivation emerges from the activation of specific neurochemical systems that generate engagement, pleasure, and meaning. Five key intrinsic motivators serve as particularly powerful flow triggers, each with its unique neurochemical signature:

Passion acts as a natural focusing mechanism. It draws your attention toward activities that engage you without effort. Neurochemically, it triggers the release of both norepinephrine, which sharpens attention, and dopamine, which fuels reward and anticipation. This combination enhances focus while making the task inherently enjoyable—conditions that are ripe for flow.

Purpose connects your actions to something larger than yourself. It activates not only dopamine and norepinephrine but also oxytocin, the bonding hormone, and endorphins, which elevate mood. These systems overlap to create engagement that feels both meaningful and emotionally resonant—prime terrain for flow to emerge.

Autonomy, the sense of choice and control, stimulates acetylcholine pathways tied to attention and also boosts dopamine through the satisfaction of psychological needs. When you feel ownership over your actions, you're more likely to experience the sustained attention and deep immersion characteristic of flow.

Mastery taps into your brain's reward circuitry through progressive skill development. It triggers dopamine as you improve and may release anandamide—the so-called "bliss molecule"—during breakthrough moments. This creates a self-reinforcing loop where improvement itself becomes rewarding, pulling you deeper into the challenge.

Curiosity activates the brain's seeking system, powered by modest doses of dopamine and norepinephrine. It thrives on what neuroscientists call an "information gap"—the distance between what you know and what you want to know. That gap captures attention and drives exploration, both of which are prerequisites for flow.

This neurobiological understanding explains why forcing yourself to focus rarely produces flow, while pursuing activities aligned with these intrinsic motivators often leads effortlessly into flow states. You're not overriding your biology through willpower—you're working with it by engaging systems designed to create sustained attention and enjoyment.

The practical application is clear: rather than treating motivation as something you need to generate through discipline or external pressure, focus on aligning your activities with these intrinsic motivators. When passion, purpose, autonomy, mastery, and curiosity converge, your brain naturally produces the engagement necessary for flow—no forcing required.

CREATING SUSTAINABLE DRIVE

When you understand how intrinsic motivators work individually, something even more powerful emerges—the opportunity to align and stack these motivators to create compound effects. This is what I call the "Motivational Stack," and it's where motivation transforms from fleeting inspiration into sustainable, self-perpetuating drive.

Think of each motivator—passion, purpose, autonomy, mastery, and curiosity—as its own energy source. On their own, each one offers momentum. But when they align—when your passion fuels a meaningful purpose, develops your mastery, satisfies genuine curiosity, and reflects your autonomy—their impact doesn't just add up. It multiplies.

This compounding effect activates a broader range of engagement and reward systems in the brain, creating what neuroscientists call cross-domain reinforcement. Success in one domain amplifies motivation in others. Instead of needing to generate drive, you create a system where motivation fuels itself.

I've observed this phenomenon countless times with clients who discover the "Kid at Christmas Effect." Remember that childhood feeling of Christmas Eve anticipation? When you couldn't sleep because tomorrow held something so exciting? That same neurological pattern—driven by anticipatory dopamine release—becomes available when your motivational stack fully aligns. You actually become excited about tomorrow's work rather than dreading it.

This changes everything about how you experience the struggle phase of flow. What used to feel like resistance becomes part of the excitement. The challenge becomes the hook, not the hurdle.

When your motivational architecture is aligned like this, something remarkable happens. Progress feels inevitable. Distractions lose their grip. Tasks that used to require willpower start pulling you forward. Cognitive function improves. Creativity expands. Learning accelerates. Your brain isn't just more focused—it's more capable.

Even effort itself feels different. What once required grinding determination now feels like play—not because it's easier, but because your relationship with challenge has changed. Motivation becomes less like fuel you burn and more like a current you tap into.

And most importantly, it becomes self-perpetuating. You're no longer dependent on pep talks, deadlines, or external incentives. The work itself fuels the drive to keep going. One win creates momentum for the next.

This is why some people seem to operate with inexhaustible energy while others burn out, even under similar conditions. The difference isn't discipline—it's alignment.

At the peak of this alignment is what Peter Diamandis calls a Massively Transformative Purpose (MTP)—a goal so resonant it integrates all your motivators around a central, meaningful pursuit. It doesn't have to be world-changing. What matters is that it speaks to your core values while serving something beyond yourself.

When this kind of alignment is in place, flow moves beyond productivity into something deeper. What Mihaly Csikszentmihalyi called vital engagement—a life filled with absorbing, meaningful work that contributes to something bigger than you. Flow becomes not just a tool for performance, but a pathway to fulfillment.

THE COGNITIVE FOUNDATION FOR FLOW

Our brains are constantly processing an overwhelming amount of information, automatically prioritizing what triggers our alarm systems or activates our desire. This evolutionary programming served us well when survival required immediate threat detection and resource acquisition. But in today's complex world, this default programming often misaligns with our deeper objectives and optimal performance states.

Goal clarity serves as the cognitive override that redirects your brain's natural attention patterns toward what matters most. Without this clarity, your neurological default settings remain in control, bouncing your focus between perceived threats and immediate gratifications rather than meaningful progress on important work.

The biological cost of ambiguity is substantial. When your objectives are unclear or internally conflicted, your brain splits its processing power across multiple possible outcomes. This triggers a state neuroscientists call prediction error—where your brain can't effectively anticipate what's coming next. That uncertainty drains energy, increases cognitive load, and activates low-grade stress responses that directly block access to flow.

It's why people often feel exhausted after days filled with vague, directionless tasks—despite getting very little done. Clarity doesn't just improve productivity. It rewires how your brain allocates attention and conserves energy, reducing the metabolic cost of decision-making and helping your system stabilize.

The distinction between hope and strategic clarity illustrates this principle perfectly. Hope-based thinking—the vague wish that things will somehow work out—keeps your brain in a state of uncertainty. This uncertainty triggers persistent vigilance circuits, as your brain continually scans for potential threats and opportunities without clear direction.

In contrast, strategic clarity—what I call the "reverse engineering mindset"—provides your brain with precise coordinates for attention allocation. By working backward from clear outcomes to specific actions, you create the cognitive certainty that allows your brain to fully engage with present tasks rather than continually evaluating possibilities.

This kind of clarity matters tremendously for flow because it fundamentally shapes how your brain engages with your work. First, it sharpens focus. Clear goals tell your brain exactly where to direct attention—and just as importantly, what to ignore. Without that filtering mechanism, your attention naturally fractures, making the sustained concentration required for flow neurologically impossible.

Clarity also eliminates decision fatigue. When your goals are well-defined, the major choices are already made, reducing the constant stream of micro-decisions that drain cognitive energy. Instead of spending mental resources on navigational thinking—what to do next, whether you're on track—you preserve that energy for the actual work.

Equally important, clarity helps calibrate challenge. Specific, well-scoped goals allow you to operate within that sweet spot between ease and overwhelm. Psychologists call these "proximal goals"—targets that are close enough to feel achievable, but just far enough to stretch your current skill level. This delicate calibration is essential for keeping flow active without triggering stress or boredom.

Finally, clear goals create built-in feedback. When objectives are vague, your brain lacks reference points for measuring progress, which creates uncertainty and disrupts immersion. But when goals are concrete and measurable, your brain receives real-time feedback on effectiveness. That feedback loop reinforces engagement and helps sustain the seamless progression characteristic of flow.

Beyond performance, the psychological toll of ambiguity is immense. As we explored in Chapter 8, when your brain can't predict outcomes or determine the right course of action, it defaults to hypervigilance. That sustained stress activation blocks the very neurophysiology required for flow.

This is why even highly skilled, deeply motivated people can't enter flow when their objectives are unclear. It's not a matter of effort or willpower. Without clarity, your brain can't do what it's built to do.

ENGINEERING FLOW-FRIENDLY OBJECTIVES

Once clarity is in place, the next step is designing goals that do more than guide—they actively trigger flow. This is where strategic goal architecture becomes essential: the deliberate design of objectives to facilitate optimal performance states.

One of the most powerful distinctions in goal setting is between **end goals** and **means goals**. End goals represent the final outcomes you want to achieve—the "what" you're aiming for. Means goals are the specific actions, steps, and strategies that move you toward those outcomes—the "how" of your approach.

Both matter, but their impact on flow is very different. End goals offer meaning and direction, but they often sit too far in the future to provide the immediate feedback and clarity required to trigger flow. Without well-structured means goals, the path becomes too ambiguous. You can be deeply inspired by the destination and still feel stuck on the journey.

The solution lies in breaking down end goals into flow-optimized means goals—a process that unfolds in three key steps.

First, define your end goal with precision. Vague aspirations like "build a successful business" or "improve my health" don't provide the specificity needed for reverse engineering. Clearer formulations like "build a $5M revenue business delivering specific value to specific customers" or "achieve specific biometric targets while enjoying sustainable fitness practices" offer concrete, navigable endpoints.

Second, break that goal down into smaller parts using a process cognitive scientists call "chunking." This turns overwhelming objectives into manageable components—each one maintaining enough challenge to stay engaging, but not so much as to trigger avoidance.

Think of your goals as a stairway. At the top sits your Massively Transformative Purpose—the big, compelling reason behind it all. Beneath that, long-term goals (three to ten years) guide your direction, followed by annual and quarterly targets that bring it into the near future. Monthly and weekly goals form your operational path. And finally, at the base, daily objectives and specific tasks become the immediate steps beneath your feet. Each layer narrows your focus while preserving a direct link to your larger vision.

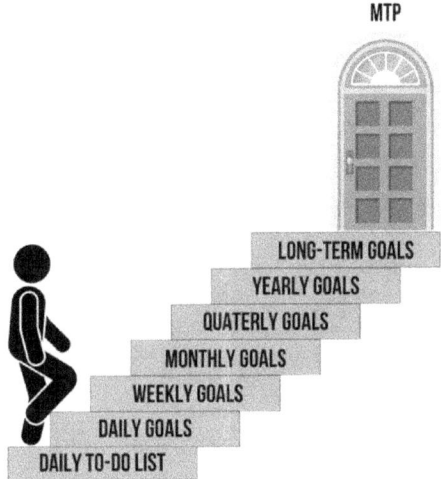

This progressive breakdown transforms abstract aspirations into concrete actions while maintaining clear visibility of how each step connects to your larger purpose.

The goal stairway concept addresses a common paradox in goal setting: the tension between ambition and achievability. Set goals too high, and they trigger anxiety rather than flow. Set them too low, and boredom prevents flow. The ideal goal architecture resolves this tension through progressive challenge calibration.

This approach acknowledges the "shoot for the stars" paradox—the observation that while ambitious targets can inspire extraordinary effort, goals perceived as impossible can actually reduce performance by triggering defensive psychological responses. The solution isn't lowering your ultimate aspirations but rather creating intermediate targets that maintain motivation while remaining perceivable as achievable.

The 4% rule we discussed in the flow cycle provides the perfect calibration mechanism for these intermediate targets. By designing each step to be just beyond your current capabilities, you create the optimal challenge/believability level for triggering flow.

As your capabilities grow, the challenge must evolve with them. What once required intense concentration becomes automatic, freeing you to take on more complex tasks while maintaining the same optimal challenge-skill ratio. This adaptive scaffolding creates a sustainable growth trajectory where flow remains accessible, even as the terrain becomes steeper.

The ultimate goal architecture for flow isn't static—it adapts with you, recalibrating challenge, focus, and feedback to keep you immersed as you level up and your world changes.

FLOW-OPTIMIZED GOAL SETTING SYSTEM

Structuring goals to support flow begins with architecture—clear end goals, progressive steps, and challenge calibration. But even within that scaffolding, the way individual goals are designed plays a critical role. To consistently trigger flow, a goal needs to do more than organize your actions or mark your progress—it must align with how the brain actually enters and sustains peak states.

The classic SMART framework (Specific, Measurable, Achievable, Relevant, Time-bound) offers a strong starting point. But optimal performance demands more than general motivation principles. Flow states require a specific kind of goal design—one that integrates the neuropsychological conditions for deep focus, immediate feedback, and intrinsic drive.

That's where the **Modified SMARTER framework** comes in: a flow-optimized evolution designed to transform your goals into reliable gateways to peak performance.

Specific: Flow-optimized goals eliminate ambiguity not just about the outcome, but about the path. This precision reduces the brain's need to constantly recalculate direction, minimizing cognitive load and freeing attention for deep immersion.

Measurable: Measurement isn't just about endpoints; it's about constant feedback. Like a climber adjusting grip with every move, or a writer watching the word count grow, real-time feedback helps your brain self-correct in motion, keeping flow uninterrupted.

Action-oriented: Flow emerges from doing, not thinking about doing. Goals that focus on specific actions—not just outcomes—support the merging of action and awareness that defines the flow state.

Relevant: As you know, intrinsic motivation is a prerequisite for flow. Goals that resonate with your personal values and interests pull attention naturally, making deep focus feel less like effort and more like gravity.

Time-bound: Deadlines matter—but not for pressure. In flow-optimized goals, timeframes create rhythmic structure, like musical timing that enables improvisation. Proper timing enhances engagement without tipping into anxiety.

Exciting: Flow requires neurochemical readiness. Goals that genuinely excite you trigger the dopamine and norepinephrine response that primes your brain for deep focus—not because of external rewards, but because of the challenge itself.

Revised: Static goals become stale. Flow-optimized goals evolve alongside your capabilities, preserving the challenge-skill balance and ensuring the task stays immersive rather than overwhelming or underwhelming.

This Modified SMARTER framework offers the structure. But even the best-structured goal will misfire if it's pointed in the wrong direction. Having a perfectly tuned Formula 1 car doesn't help much if you're trying to drive up a mountain.

So before optimizing how you pursue your goals, we need to clarify which goals are actually worth optimizing. That's where we go next.

PRACTICAL GOAL IDENTIFICATION PROCESS

Structuring goals for flow is one thing—choosing the right ones is another. It's easy to get trapped pursuing objectives that sound impressive but lack personal resonance. Real flow comes not just from how goals are built, but from whether they actually reflect the life you want to live. That's where most people get off track.

Most of my clients already have specific objectives in mind when we begin this process—and that's perfect. However, as we discussed in Chapter 6 with the Wheel of Life concept, true high performance requires balance across multiple life domains. Unfortunately, this balance is what most tend to neglect.

This is where the PRW framework becomes valuable, ensuring we don't overlook important aspects of a fulfilling life. This acronym stands for:

Play Goals: Adventures, fun, material acquisitions, travel, and hobbies that make life vibrant and engaging.

Rest Goals: Self-development, health, friends, family, and the relationships that provide foundation and meaning.

World Goals: Your contribution to society, community impact, service to others, and the legacy you want to create.

Considering these aspects of life helps you craft holistic goals that enhance your entire life experience, not just your career.

The Dream 100 Exercise

To uncover these deeper aspirations—especially the ones hiding beneath professional performance goals—I often recommend the Dream 100 exercise. The name can be misleading. The goal isn't to write 100 items for the sake of volume, and it's not about building a bucket list. It's about what happens when you go deep enough to move past the obvious.

In the first 20 or 30 entries, most people list what they think they're supposed to want: revenue milestones, titles, travel destinations, maybe a six-pack or a sabbatical. But something interesting happens when you keep going. You start to run out of surface-level answers. And that's where the real material lives—goals you didn't even realize you had, values you hadn't yet named, or desires that had been quietly buried under obligation and expectation.

The process is simple: take 30 to 45 minutes, grab pen and paper, and list every dream, goal, or aspiration that comes to mind across the different domains of life (Career & PRW). Don't edit yourself. Don't judge. Just get it all down. Then, let the list sit for a day.

When you return, go through it slowly. Cross off anything that no longer sparks energy. Circle what still feels alive. The real insight often isn't in the number of items you keep—but in the patterns that emerge when you see your inner priorities laid bare. Sometimes, even goals you thought were settled take on new meaning.

Andreia, our now "famous" clinic owner, had always assumed her next move was expansion—more locations, more staff, more scale. But when she worked through this exercise, the goal that kept resurfacing wasn't about building bigger. It was about building better. What truly energized her was the idea of creating a specialized treatment methodology that could change her field. That insight completely redirected her focus—from what she thought she should pursue to what actually lit her up.

Focusing Your Goal Priorities

After generating your list of potential goals, particularly if you've completed the Dream 100 Exercise, you might face an interesting challenge—too many compelling possibilities. While having multiple aspirations isn't inherently problematic, trying to pursue everything simultaneously often leads to scattered focus and diminished results.

Think of it like a garden—pruning isn't about eliminating healthy plants, but rather about creating space for the most important ones to thrive. Similarly, we need systematic approaches to identify which goals deserve our immediate attention and which might better serve us in future seasons.

The Goal Tournament Strategy

One effective approach for prioritizing multiple goals involves what I call the Goal Tournament—inspired by elimination brackets in sports competitions like March Madness or the World Cup knockout stages. This strategy transforms the overwhelming task of comparing many goals into a series of simpler, head-to-head decisions.

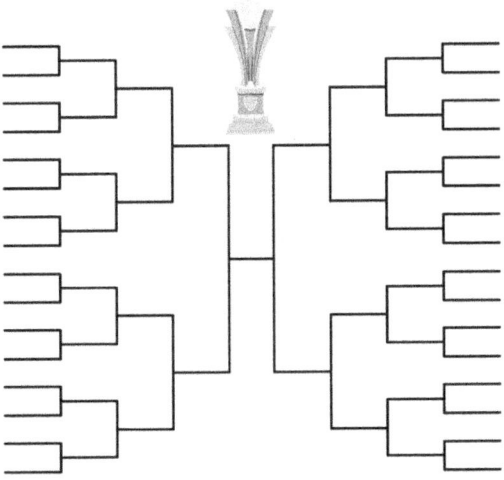

Here's how it works:

1. Group similar goals into categories (career, health, relationships, etc.)
2. Within each category, pair goals against each other.
3. For each pairing, ask: "If I could only pursue one of these in the next year, which would create more meaningful engagement?"
4. Continue through the brackets until you've identified the "champions" in each life domain.

This process often reveals surprising clarity about what truly matters—sometimes by affirming what you already knew, and other times by highlighting something you'd overlooked. Take Marcus, a product manager juggling half a dozen promising ideas. He was convinced he needed to develop them all in parallel. But by the final round of the tournament, one clear winner emerged: writing a book on systems thinking. It wasn't the most lucrative option, but it was the one that made him lose track of time. That clarity gave him permission to go all-in—without the lingering guilt of the goals he temporarily set aside.

The Three-Year Focus Exercise

Sometimes, even after tournament-style elimination, we still struggle to identify our most meaningful objectives. This is where a powerful perspective shift can help cut through the noise.

Imagine you've just been told you have three years left to live. The diagnosis is certain, and the timeline is fixed. How would you spend that time? What would suddenly become urgent? What would instantly lose importance?

This thought experiment isn't meant to be morbid—it's about clarity. When we remove the illusion of infinite time, priorities often become crystal clear. The goals that emerge from this exercise typically align naturally with flow states because they connect deeply with your intrinsic motivations.

Consider Ryan, the entrepreneur we met earlier. When he applied this exercise, here's what surfaced: "I realized I was chasing growth for growth's sake. When I really thought about meaningful impact in a limited timeframe, I completely shifted my focus to developing a mentorship program for underprivileged youth interested in tech. That clarity changed everything—suddenly work felt purposeful rather than just profitable."

All of these tools—the Dream 100, the Goal Tournament, the Three-Year filter—serve one central purpose: focus. Not to shrink your life, but to carve out space for what truly matters now. Flow can't emerge in a state of constant divided attention. It needs direction, intensity, and meaning. You're not cutting off possibilities—you're choosing which seeds to plant this season. The rest can wait their turn.

Turning SMARTER Goals Into Action

By now, you've identified high-leverage goals and learned how to frame them using the SMARTER framework. But that's just the first half of the equation. A clearly structured goal doesn't create flow on its own—it needs to be translated into action. The following steps will show you exactly how to do that.

Step 1: Apply the SMARTER Framework

Take one of your top goals and run it through the SMARTER lens to transform it from a vague intention into a crystal-clear objective. For each goal:

1. Clarify the specific outcome and process with precise detail.
2. Establish measurement mechanisms that provide immediate feedback.
3. Define the actions that will generate daily engagement.
4. Connect the goal explicitly to intrinsic motivators.
5. Set appropriate timeframes that create productive tension.
6. Ensure the goal genuinely excites you.
7. Build revision mechanisms to maintain the optimal challenge.

Let's look at this in practice. Jen, our real estate executive, started with a familiar ambition: "Expand my business." After applying the SMARTER framework, her goal became:

"Launch a neighborhood-specific marketing system for our three target communities by creating one complete neighborhood guide per month for the next quarter—each featuring 10 insider tips from local residents—eventually generating 15 qualified leads per neighborhood monthly, while establishing myself as the go-to neighborhood specialist in areas I personally love exploring."

This revised goal:
- Specifies exactly what she's creating and when.
- Defines performance benchmarks (guides per month, tips per guide, leads per neighborhood).
- Connects clearly to her intrinsic interests.
- Creates measurable outcomes and real-time feedback loops.
- Builds tension and focus with defined time constraints.
- Leaves room for revision based on outcomes.

Sure, this goal is a mouthful. But that's intentional. You don't need to memorize the goal. You just need to know exactly where you're going. Once established, this clarity makes daily decision-making feel effortless—like navigating with a high-resolution map instead of guessing directions at every fork in the road.

Step 2: Break It Down into Strategic Milestones

Earlier, we introduced the Goal Staircase—a tool for mapping your ambitions across time horizons, from your Massively Transformative Purpose down to today's tasks. But even once you've landed on a specific step—say, a quarterly or monthly SMARTER goal—you still need to break it down into clear, strategic checkpoints that make execution visible and actionable.

Once you've defined your SMARTER goal at the quarterly or monthly level, the next step is to identify a series of strategy milestones—trackable progress points that allow you to maintain momentum, spot bottlenecks early, and keep your effort aligned with the outcome.

Let's return to Jen's example. In Step 1, she refined her vague goal of "expanding the business" into a SMARTER objective centered on launching a neighborhood-specific marketing system across three communities.

Here's how she broke that quarterly goal into strategic milestones:

Outcome
Launch one neighborhood guide per month for the next quarter, each with 10 insider tips from local residents—building toward a system that generates 15 qualified leads per neighborhood monthly.

Strategy Milestones
- Complete research on the first target neighborhood by end of week 2.
- Secure 5 resident interviews by end of week 4.
- Publish the first guide by end of month 1.
- Establish a distribution system reaching 500 local residents by week 6.

This level of breakdown transforms a quarterly goal into something you can actually track and navigate. You're no longer working toward a distant aspiration—you're climbing a visible path with concrete footholds. But turning these milestones into daily traction requires one more layer of structure—one that builds momentum and minimizes friction at the point of execution.

Step 3: Build Momentum With Micro-Deadlines
Once you've broken your goal into strategic milestones, the next challenge is turning intention into action. This is where many people stall—not because the goal is unclear, but because they haven't structured their effort in a way that sustains momentum.

That's where micro-deadlines come in.

Think of these as short-term checkpoints that convert a long-term objective into a steady rhythm of progress. Depending on the nature of your goal, you might create deliverables for the next:
- 24 hours
- 48 hours
- 72 hours
- 7 days
- 14 days
- 28 days

You don't need to use every interval every time—the key is to create just enough structure to keep attention anchored in the present while maintaining visibility into what's coming next. This structure is especially powerful when paired with complex, multi-week initiatives.

Let's return to Jen. After defining her quarterly outcome and weekly milestones, she used micro-deadlines to stay in motion without feeling overwhelmed.

Her first 72-hour window looked like this:

- **Day 1:** Finalize list of three target neighborhoods.
- **Day 2:** Begin demographic and competitor research on the first neighborhood.
- **Day 3:** Draft interview questions and send outreach emails to five residents.

Each of these actions was bite-sized enough to avoid resistance, but meaningful enough to generate momentum. With every completed task, her brain received a small dopamine reward, reinforcing her drive to stay engaged and lowering the activation energy for the next task.

This is how micro-deadlines support flow. They transform ambiguity into traction—providing just enough structure to reduce cognitive friction without creating rigidity. You're no longer staring at a quarterly goal wondering where to begin. You know exactly what needs to happen next, and when.

Applied consistently, this technique removes one of the biggest obstacles to flow: decision fatigue. When your path is already mapped in digestible increments, your brain stops expending energy on navigation and starts focusing entirely on execution.

Social Synchronization

While not suitable for every objective, shared goals can significantly amplify flow potential through what neuroscientists call "group flow." When we align our goals with others, we tap into additional flow triggers like collective chemistry and shared risk.

Look for opportunities to transform individual goals into collaborative pursuits. This might mean:

- Finding accountability partners pursuing similar objectives.
- Creating mastermind groups for goal sharing and support.
- Building teams around shared missions.
- Contributing to larger community initiatives.

Group flow isn't always available—but when it is, it creates access to a deeper tier of motivation and momentum that's difficult to replicate alone.

FROM INTERNAL ARCHITECTURE TO ENVIRONMENT AMPLIFIERS

By now, you've done the hard work of clarifying what matters. You've chosen meaningful goals, filtered for what truly resonates, and structured them to activate your best psychological and biological systems. You've mapped your objectives through SMARTER goal design, broken them down into strategic milestones, and embedded them into a rhythm of micro-deadlines that generates steady traction.

This entire process isn't just about getting more done; it's about shifting how you experience what you do.

You're not approaching goals as external obligations or performance checklists. You're engaging with them as vehicles for meaning, momentum, and mastery. You've created a structure that supports autonomy, rewards curiosity, and calibrates challenge to your growing skillset. You've removed ambiguity, minimized decision fatigue, and brought intentionality into your workflow—setting the stage for consistent, repeatable access to flow states.

And because your system will evolve as you do, don't forget to recalibrate the challenge. What once stretched you may soon feel automatic. Flow thrives when your ambition levels up with your ability.

Now, there's one more layer to amplify everything you've created: the environment you operate in. Because even the most optimized internal architecture can be undermined by an environment that distracts, depletes, or derails your attention. The next section explores exactly how to design physical and digital surroundings that reinforce—not resist—your flow-ready physiology and psychology.

ENVIRONMENTAL ARCHITECTURE OF FLOW

Even the most finely tuned biology and psychology can be short-circuited by one invisible force: your environment.

By now, you've explored what it takes to build flow from the inside out—from understanding your neurobiology and brainwave rhythms to architecting your goals, routines, and motivational structures for consistent immersion. You've optimized both the *hardware* and *software* of peak performance. But unless your environment reinforces that architecture, friction remains inevitable.

Distraction, mental fatigue, and procrastination aren't always the result of poor discipline or lack of willpower. More often, they're symptoms of an environment that conflicts with your neurobiology. If your space constantly tugs at your attention, triggers subtle stress responses, or interrupts deep concentration with shallow cues, even the best systems will struggle to take root.

This isn't just theory—it's observable science.

In the early 1970s, behavioral scientist Leah Robbins conducted one of the most illuminating studies on environmental influence. She tracked Vietnam War veterans who had become addicted to heroin during deployment. Approximately 20% were addicted overseas, and nearly 40% had used the drug. But once they returned home? Only about 5% remained addicted. Compare that to the relapse rates of traditional rehab programs, which hover around 90%, and you get a startling insight. Their recovery wasn't driven by therapy or willpower; it was driven by context. When removed from the environment that had shaped their behavior—its routines, stress cues, and emotional associations—the addiction lost its grip. They didn't need to fight the habit because they no longer lived in the architecture that created it.

The same principle applies to more subtle behaviors as well. In a hospital study focused on beverage selection, researchers simply made water more visible and accessible while placing soda in less convenient locations. The result? Water sales rose by 26%, while soda purchases dropped 11%—without a single change in pricing or education. The environment did the heavy lifting.

Your environment isn't just a backdrop for performance; it's an active participant in creating or blocking flow states. When it's aligned with your biology and your goals, it becomes a quiet collaborator—amplifying focus, reducing resistance, and reinforcing the very systems you've worked hard to build. When it's misaligned, even your best habits will require constant energy to maintain.

This is why the saying "productivity is the child of your environment" resonates so deeply with high performers. It's not about working harder; it's about removing invisible barriers that make working easier.

In the pages ahead, we'll explore exactly how to shape your surroundings—physical and digital alike—to become amplifiers for flow. Because once your environment works for you, rather than against you, consistency in peak performance stops being aspirational. It becomes inevitable.

THE ERGONOMIC FOUNDATION

Before we can consistently access high-performance mental states, we need to address a simple biological truth: physical discomfort hijacks attention. Flow demands immersion, but discomfort—whether from an aching back, strained neck, or poor posture—anchors awareness in the body, not the task.

Think back to our discussion of transient hypofrontality, that beneficial deactivation of the brain's analytical center during flow. Physical strain reverses that process. It brings your prefrontal cortex back online, forcing you into micro-surveillance of your discomfort rather than staying absorbed in the work.

Sustained comfort, then, isn't a luxury. It's a non-negotiable for cognitive clarity.

Start with your chair. An ergonomic design that supports your spine's natural curvature reduces muscular tension and eliminates the need for constant positional adjustment. That frees up subtle but significant amounts of mental energy. Some high performers even switch to saddle chairs or kneeling stools to maintain an upright posture with less effort.

Next, check your screen position. A monitor at eye level and roughly an arm's length away minimizes strain on your neck and optimizes your visual processing. Poor alignment might not feel like a problem at first. But over time, it subtly pulls you out of focus and into fidget mode.

Integrating a standing desk adds flexibility. Instead of locking your body into one position for hours, you gain the ability to shift based on task type or energy level. That physical dynamism helps regulate arousal and maintain engagement, especially during longer work blocks.

ENGINEERING THE SENSORY ENVIRONMENT

Just as we discussed the importance of trigger stacking for flow induction, your workspace's sensory elements create a compound effect on your flow potential.

As you already know, natural light exposure isn't just about visibility—it regulates your circadian rhythms and enhances cognitive function through specific photoreceptor pathways we explored in Chapter 7. Thus, it's crucial to position your workspace to maximize natural light while avoiding the common pitfall of facing directly into bright windows or streets that create visual distraction.

Sound is another major player. Total silence might seem ideal, but for many, it makes minor interruptions even more jarring. On the other hand, unpredictable noise can wreck immersion. The sweet spot? A stable auditory backdrop—whether that's soft ambient sound, instrumental music, or strategically placed sound-dampening materials to control what reaches your ears.

Temperature matters more than most realize. It isn't just about working in your favorite T-shirt or avoiding the need to layer up like you're prepping for a ski trip. It directly influences the neurochemical balance required for focus, fluid attention, and deep cognitive processing. Research shows that performance tends to peak between 70–73°F (21–23°C)—a narrow band where your physiology can fully support the demands of high-focus work.

You don't need to micromanage your thermostat, but it's worth keeping in mind. If your workspace constantly leaves you shivering or sweating, you're creating biological resistance to flow. Slight adjustments here can make a noticeable difference in how long and how easily you stay locked in.

Then there's air quality—often invisible, yet critical. Poor airflow reduces oxygenation and increases cognitive strain. Something as simple as opening a window, adding an air purifier, or incorporating plants can create a noticeable boost in mental clarity and energy.

You don't need a perfect setup to benefit from environmental design. You just need to identify friction points and nudge them toward support. Small adjustments to light, sound, air, and temperature don't just make your space more pleasant—they create the conditions where deep work becomes your default.

DISTRACTION ELIMINATION ARCHITECTURE

Flow may be your brain's highest-performance state, but it's also one of its most delicate. Each interruption triggers stress hormones, resets attention circuits, and increases the time it takes to regain deep focus.

And the most potent source of distraction? Other people.

While collaboration is essential, unstructured social interruptions can quietly destroy your ability to enter sustained focus. The solution isn't isolation but intentional interaction design. If possible, position your workspace so you're not facing foot traffic or directly visible to others. This reduces unconscious eye contact, which often invites conversation without either person realizing it.

Next, establish clear focus signals. Just as we used sensory anchors to trigger flow, we can create environmental cues that signal "do not disturb." Headphones, visual markers like desk flags or status lights, or even working in designated focus zones can train others to recognize your flow mode without explanation. The key is consistency. These signals should become part of the social fabric of your workspace.

But human interaction is just one layer. The physical layout of your space carries just as much influence—because your visual field is also a cognitive battleground.

Every item you can see while working competes for attention. That unopened mail, stack of books, or half-finished snack? Your brain notices all of it, even when you think it doesn't. Neuroscientists call this "cognitive overhead"—the subtle mental tax your environment imposes on your working memory. Over time, it adds up, quietly pulling energy away from deep concentration.

This doesn't mean you need to become Marie Kondo's next case study. The goal isn't aesthetic minimalism—it's cognitive clarity. Purposeful workspaces reduce friction, lower mental load, and help your brain engage fully with what matters. Think of your deep work zone like a chef's prep station: everything you need within arm's reach, everything else tucked away but easily accessible. That's functional design for high-performance thinking.

Now, about that phone.

A device sitting face-up on your desk is more than just a minor temptation. One study found that even when your phone is off, simply having it visible reduces available mental bandwidth and impairs performance on tasks requiring sustained attention. That's how powerful its pull is. And when it's on, every buzz, ping, or banner stokes craving loops that simmer in the background, even if you don't consciously react.

If it's imperative that your phone stays in view—say, for urgent messages or coordination—at least take control of the stimulus. Turn it face-down. Disable nonessential notifications. Use focus modes or app timers. Position the screen so alerts don't flicker at the edge of your vision. But if you can? Remove it entirely during deep work blocks. Out of sight, out of system strain.

When you design your space this way, you're not just reducing distractions. You're creating a flow runway—a clear, intentional path into your best cognitive states. Each unnecessary object removed or strategically placed frees up processing power. And in that clarity, flow becomes not just possible, but natural.

> **Creating Strategic Friction**
>
> Think of friction like nature's behavioral speed bump. Just as water follows the path of least resistance, our brains naturally gravitate toward the easiest available actions. The trick isn't fighting this tendency but rather using it to our advantage.
>
> Instead of relying on heroic self-control to resist distractions, create environmental barriers that make unwanted behaviors more difficult. That might mean putting your phone in a different room during deep work, storing the TV remote in a drawer, or—if you're really serious—setting up a timed lock box for particularly tempting distractions.
>
> The same principle works in reverse for behaviors you want to encourage. Want to read more? Leave that book right where your phone usually sits. Looking to exercise in the morning? Sleep in your workout clothes. The goal is to make flow-supporting behaviors the path of least resistance.

SOCIAL ENVIRONMENT ENGINEERING

In our digital age, the greatest threat to flow isn't necessarily a cluttered desk or poor lighting—it's the constant expectation of availability. We've somehow evolved from "I'll get back to you when I can" to "Why haven't you responded to my message from three minutes ago?!" This shift hasn't just changed our communication patterns; it's fundamentally altered our capacity for deep engagement.

Resurrecting Strategic Unavailability

Remember how we discussed the importance of protecting our cognitive resources? Well, here's a radical idea: you don't actually need to be available every moment of every day. In fact, the most successful performers often achieve their results precisely because they master the art of strategic unavailability.

Think of your attention like a premium streaming service. Just as Netflix doesn't make every show available all the time (creating artificial scarcity that actually increases value), your availability should be thoughtfully managed.

This isn't about becoming a hermit; it's about creating structured systems for engagement that protect your flow potential.

Start by implementing communication batching. Rather than letting your inbox become an all-day anxiety generator, treat it like a scheduled meeting with clear boundaries. The world probably won't end if you check emails twice a day instead of every two minutes. (Spoiler alert: it hasn't yet.)

The Art of Boundary Conversations

Here's where many flow protection systems fall apart: the moment someone challenges our boundaries. But rather than viewing these conversations as confrontational, think of them as opportunities to enhance collective performance.

For work environments, try this approach: "I've noticed something interesting in my productivity patterns. When I maintain focused blocks from 9-11 AM and 2-4 PM, I'm actually able to deliver better results for our team. Would you be open to trying a system where we concentrate our collaborative work outside these times?"

For personal relationships, the conversation might sound like: "I'm working on being more present in all areas of my life. That means when I'm working, I'm fully focused, and when I'm with you, you have my complete attention. Can we discuss how to make this work for both of us?"

The key isn't just establishing boundaries; it's helping others understand how these boundaries ultimately serve them too. When you're more focused and productive, everyone benefits from your enhanced performance and presence.

Meeting the Meeting Monster

If there's one thing that devours flow states more voraciously than constant digital connectivity, it's the modern meeting culture. But rather than accepting every calendar invitation as inevitable, consider this framework for evaluation:

- Is this meeting actually moving something important forward?
- Could the same information be handled more efficiently in a well-crafted email or brief video update?
- Is live discussion adding real value, or is it just organizational habit masquerading as collaboration?

Unplanned, lengthy, or unnecessary meetings don't just consume time; they fracture the periods of deep work essential for meaningful outcomes.

One effective solution gaining traction is adopting **asynchronous meetings**. Instead of forcing real-time attendance, asynchronous meetings let participants engage at a time aligned with their workflow and cognitive rhythm. The benefits are substantial:

Flexibility: Team members respond when it suits their schedules, protecting their peak performance windows for focused, uninterrupted work.

Inclusivity: Participants in different time zones or with varying responsibilities have equal opportunities to contribute thoughtfully without the disruption of inconvenient meeting times.

Efficiency: Responses crafted in thoughtful, distraction-free settings can significantly elevate the quality of input. Often, this approach reduces the need for lengthy synchronous sessions entirely, freeing up more time for deep, productive engagement.

Documentation: Written or recorded exchanges automatically create valuable records, enhancing clarity, alignment, and accountability, and providing easily accessible references for future decision-making.

By thoughtfully questioning the assumptions around traditional meetings and strategically adopting asynchronous communication methods, you can reclaim significant blocks of high-value time. The shift from habitual meeting culture to intentional interaction is about creating an environment where flow can naturally thrive, amplifying both individual and team performance.

REMOTE WORK ENVIRONMENT STRATEGIES

The rise of remote work has created a strange paradox in our pursuit of flow. On the one hand, working from home eliminates office distractions—no more surprise desk visits or ambient office chatter. On the other, it introduces an entirely new set of challenges. Your sanctuary can quickly become your saboteur if it's not thoughtfully engineered.

This starts with your workspace. Earlier, we explored how consistent physical anchors can serve as psychological triggers. That principle becomes even more important when working from home. Without clear boundaries, the line between performance and relaxation blurs. One minute you're writing a proposal; the next, you're reheating leftovers or answering the door.

The fix isn't building a luxury office—it's definition. Even a dedicated corner can become your flow command center if it's deliberately designed. Think of it like a cockpit: everything within reach, nothing extraneous, and a clearly defined purpose. When you enter that space, your brain should know it's time for focused execution, not casual browsing or background noise.

Then there's the visibility paradox. In the absence of physical presence, many remote workers feel compelled to prove they're "on" at all times—the digital equivalent of looking busy when the boss walks by. But that impulse directly undermines deep work. Flow doesn't emerge under surveillance pressure; it needs psychological safety and uninterrupted blocks of time.

Instead of playing digital peekaboo, establish systems that communicate your rhythms. Shared calendars, status indicators, and clearly defined focus windows can all reduce the need for constant check-ins. You're not hiding, you're creating transparent structures that maintain both trust and productivity.

But let's not ignore the social equation. Isolation has its own costs. The brain is wired for connection, and too much solitude dulls creative energy. The goal is to integrate social interaction in ways that support—rather than sabotage—your mental performance.

Start by building clean transitions between deep work and collaboration. Just as planes follow strict takeoff and landing protocols, your day needs clear entry and exit points between focus and communication. These transitions could be scheduled team check-ins or personal rituals that help reset attention between modes.

Beyond your immediate team, tap into professional communities that stimulate challenge and creativity. Look at this not as just networking but as intellectual cross-pollination. Virtual masterminds, online groups, or structured knowledge-sharing sessions can reintroduce novelty and stimulation without the ping-ping chaos of constant messaging.

And when it comes to your life outside work, design connection as intentionally as you plan your deadlines. Treat your post-work social time like a micro-deadline: specific, energizing, and time-bounded. A virtual coffee catch-up, a shared game session, or even a scheduled evening walk with a friend—a planned connection avoids bleeding into the kind of endless digital noise that sabotages tomorrow's focus.

The goal isn't to become a hermit or a hyper-scheduled robot. It's to reclaim your space, time, and energy from the forces that fracture it—and create an ecosystem where deep work, creativity, and meaningful connection can actually coexist.

CREATING FLOW-FRIENDLY ORGANIZATIONAL CULTURES

Some workplaces feel like cognitive greenhouses—nurturing focus, energy, and momentum. Others? More like running through mud with ankle weights. It's not just vibes. It's design, psychology, and feedback culture working in concert—or against it.

The Personalization Principle

The most flow-conducive organizations understand a crucial truth: sustainable high performance isn't about rigid uniformity, but about designing environments flexible enough to support individual flow patterns. Think of it like a well-designed city—you need both highways for momentum and quiet neighborhoods for deep thought.

It goes far beyond just having good coffee in the break room (though let's be honest, that doesn't hurt).

This flips a lot of conventional office wisdom. Those open-plan offices that were supposed to supercharge collaboration? Research shows they often do the opposite, turning into environments of quiet avoidance where people slap on headphones just to survive the noise.

Instead, progressive organizations create what could be called *flow ecosystems*—spaces that adapt to support different cognitive needs throughout the day.

These don't need to be elaborate. Even small options can offer real leverage:

- Quiet zones for deep work.
- Spaces designed to invite collaboration.
- Flexible areas that shift with team needs.
- Private nooks that minimize noise and distractions.

The key isn't covering every configuration. Instead, it's providing a few intentional ones that let people match their environment to their current mental demands.

The Feedback Loop

Here's something high-performing cultures get right: they treat their workspaces like living laboratories. Instead of guessing what their people need, they build simple, fast ways to gather and act on feedback. Not once a year—continuously.

Forget the dusty suggestion box in the break room. The best systems install *rapid feedback loops*—fast cycles of trial, reflection, and revision that evolve with their team's needs.

Take one tech company I worked with. Rather than revamp the whole office overnight, they launched a series of small "flow experiments"—targeted tweaks to certain zones, like lighting changes or adjustable seating. Teams could book these test spaces, try them out, and share what helped or hindered performance. Patterns emerged, and over time, they optimized spaces specifically for different types of cognitive work.

Supporting Individual Flow Within Organizational Constraints

Not every organization can gut its floor plan or redesign from scratch—and that's okay. Even within constraints, it's possible to create what we might call *flow microclimates*—small, intentional spaces that reduce friction and support deep engagement.

This might look like:

- Clear signal systems for focus time.
- Team norms around interruption management.
- Assigned zones or hours for different types of work.
- Communication agreements that reduce unnecessary noise.

As always, the goal isn't perfection but traction. Small shifts compound over time, building conditions that make flow more likely and more sustainable.

Because in the end, culture isn't what's written in policy docs—it's what we reinforce every day. And when we build cultures that support clarity, autonomy, and intentional performance rhythms, we stop waiting for flow to show up and start engineering it.

CREATING YOUR COMPLETE FLOW ENVIRONMENT

Now that we've explored the various dimensions of environmental design, let's talk about turning all this knowledge into actual changes in your workspace. After all, theory without application is about as useful as a Ferrari without an engine—impressive to look at, but not taking you anywhere.

Step One: Diagnose, Don't Redesign (Yet)

Before rushing to redesign your entire workspace (or ordering that standing desk you've been eyeing), take a step back and observe. Flow thrives on precision, not impulse. Think of this phase as performance reconnaissance: you're looking for the specific environmental factors that support or sabotage your attention.

Over a few days, pay close attention to when you feel most focused versus when your concentration slips. What's in your field of view? What's the noise level? Are you physically comfortable? Who's around you?

You're not judging—just collecting data like a behavioral scientist. Focus on:

- Times of day when you're most locked in.
- Environmental patterns linked to distraction.
- Physical elements that pull or preserve energy.
- Social interactions that either elevate or erode your momentum.

Step Two: Start with High-Leverage, Low-Friction Fixes

This is where most people go wrong. They try to change everything at once and end up creating "environment shock"—a complete overhaul that collapses under its own complexity. Instead, start small.

Target simple, high-leverage upgrades:

- Reposition your desk to avoid visual clutter.
- Put your phone in another room during focus blocks.
- Add a desk signal or wearable cue to indicate deep work mode.
- Declutter the immediate field of vision around your primary workspace.

These changes require minimal effort, don't rely on others, and create noticeable improvements in how your brain engages.

Step Three: Expand Gradually, Layer by Layer

Once the first improvements have settled in and your brain starts trusting the new setup, move on to larger or more nuanced upgrades. Think of this like environmental strength training—you increase the load as your system adapts.

This might include:

- Introducing more sophisticated sensory anchors.
- Negotiating shared space boundaries with your team or household.
- Rearranging furniture to better support work rhythms.

Each change builds on the last, gradually creating a space that feels tailored for flow—because it is.

None of this requires perfection. What matters is that you're evolving your space to support—not sabotage—your focus. Every friction point you remove, every intentional cue you add, is a vote for your future high-performance self.

MANAGING DOPAMINE FOR FLOW (AN ESSENTIAL BONUS)

Initially, our deep dive into flow environment optimization was meant to conclude this chapter. We mapped out how to architect your surroundings—both physical and social—to reliably trigger your optimal performance states. But as we finished discussing how to eliminate distractions from your workspace, I realized we hadn't fully explored the deeper neurobiological reason why distractions wreak such havoc on your ability to access flow.

We've briefly touched on dopamine before. It's woven into the fabric of the ASCENDO framework, underpinning motivation, reward, and sustained performance. However, dopamine's unique vulnerability to our modern environment deserves special attention—not because it's inherently more important than other neurotransmitters, but because it's the one most profoundly disrupted by today's constant distractions.

Think about it: most neurochemical systems still operate largely as nature intended. Endorphins respond predictably to exercise. Serotonin aligns reliably with sunlight exposure. Dopamine, however, faces pressures it never evolved to handle—endless digital notifications, instant gratification entertainment, and engineered artificial rewards. It's like trying to navigate with a compass thrown into a magnetic storm. Instead of providing clear guidance, your dopamine system becomes erratic, pulling you off course and jeopardizing the flow states you've carefully cultivated.

This final segment addresses exactly that: recalibrating dopamine in a world designed to hijack it, ensuring your flow isn't just achievable, but sustainable.

THE MODERN DOPAMINE ECOSYSTEM

Think back to early human environments—a landscape of scarcity where finding food, securing shelter, or making a new tool represented significant rewards. Our dopamine system evolved to motivate these essential behaviors, creating anticipation and satisfaction that helped ensure survival.

Today's dopamine landscape is drastically different—our ancient reward circuitry faces near-constant artificial stimulation. Your ancestor might have experienced a dopamine spike from discovering a fruit tree after hours of searching. Today, you get similar neurochemical hits from a single social media notification, and you encounter hundreds of these daily.

This isn't random. Tech companies deploy teams of behavioral scientists specifically to exploit these ancient reward pathways. Each platform feature—infinite scrolls, autoplay functions, notifications—is meticulously engineered to trigger dopamine releases that mimic and often surpass natural rewards. Studies show these artificial triggers can spike dopamine by up to 700%, generating the type of intense neurochemical response historically reserved for survival-critical discoveries.

The implications for flow are profound. Remember our earlier analogy of dopamine as a compass thrown off by modern distractions? That disruption doesn't just confuse your sense of reward; it actively blocks your ability to detect the subtle neurochemical shifts essential for flow.

The distinction between natural and artificial dopamine triggers becomes crucial here. Natural triggers—like completing a challenging task, learning something new, or achieving a meaningful goal—activate what neuroscientists call "earned reward circuits," where effort and reward remain balanced.

Artificial triggers, however, create "supernormal stimuli"—rewards artificially detached from any real effort. It's like injecting pure sugar directly into your bloodstream instead of eating fruit—you bypass all natural limiting factors, leading to inevitable overconsumption.

Ultimately, this mismatch makes it harder to find satisfaction in meaningful, challenging activities—exactly the activities where flow emerges.

DOPAMINE RESISTANCE: YOUR FLOW'S HIDDEN BARRIER

Just as antibiotics can inadvertently create resistant bacteria, constant dopamine stimulation breeds a neurological resistance that quietly erodes your ability to access flow states. This goes beyond mere distraction; it fundamentally alters how your brain processes rewards and sustains focus.

The mechanics here are subtle yet powerful. Every dopamine spike from notifications or endless scrolling activates your nucleus accumbens—the brain's reward center. The hippocampus remembers what caused that pleasure, while the amygdala conditions you to chase after it again, reinforcing a self-perpetuating loop.

As discussed previously, natural dopamine rewards—like solving challenging problems or achieving meaningful goals—produce moderate, sustainable neurochemical responses. Yet these subtle signals become increasingly difficult for your brain to recognize amid the constant flood of intense artificial stimulation.

This leads directly to what neuroscientists call "delay discounting": your brain begins favoring instant artificial rewards over more valuable yet delayed ones. Suddenly, writing that important report (high reward but delayed) feels far less appealing compared to the immediate hit of checking your phone (small reward but immediate). Even when you consciously know what matters most, your recalibrated reward system quietly tugs you toward quick gratification.

Further complicating matters is the opponent-process theory, which explains why artificial dopamine hits grow progressively problematic. Each artificial high is swiftly followed by a corresponding low as your brain struggles to restore equilibrium. Over time, you require increasingly frequent stimulation simply to feel normal, making the subtle satisfaction inherent in deep work or creative engagement progressively harder to experience.

This resistance places your dopamine system in a paradoxical role: the very mechanism evolved to motivate and sustain flow becomes its biggest obstacle. It's like trying to savor subtle flavors after scorching your taste buds with excessively spicy food—your sensitivity, at least temporarily, has been compromised.

The Attention Crisis

In our hyper-connected world, attention has become our scarcest resource. Not just for productivity, but for our fundamental capacity to access sustained focus and flow.

Research shows our attention spans are declining rapidly. Many professionals now operate in what writer Linda Stone calls "continuous partial attention"—constantly scanning for new inputs but rarely fully absorbing anything. This state of perpetual mental fragmentation directly opposes flow's core requirement: complete immersion.

This fragmentation contributes to **Attention Deficit Trait (ADT)**, an environmentally induced condition distinct from genetic ADHD. ADT arises when our brain's executive center, the frontal lobe, is chronically overstimulated by constant inputs. Overloaded, it delegates control to primitive brain regions, triggering stress responses that neurologically block the deep focus flow demands.

ADT creates a perfect storm of flow barriers:
- **Constant rushing** prevents careful challenge calibration.
- **Frequent task-switching** disrupts sustained engagement.
- **Overcommitment** eliminates the mental space necessary for flow.
- **Chronic distraction** makes deep immersion nearly impossible.

Together, these factors form what's called the "overwhelm equation": when demands consistently exceed cognitive resources, our brains defensively restrict access to their highest-performing states, trapping us outside the flow zone.

THE NEUROCHEMISTRY OF SELF-SABOTAGE

While we typically associate dopamine with pleasure, its true role is more nuanced. Dopamine primarily drives motivation by creating anticipation—not by rewarding us during pleasurable experiences, but by spiking just before they happen.

Intriguingly, dopamine doesn't discriminate between pleasure and pain. Risky or even harmful behaviors can trigger dopamine release, not merely despite their discomfort, but often precisely because of it. Specifically, dopamine surges in anticipation of the relief or reward that follows pain's cessation, making pain itself paradoxically motivating.

In a dopamine-resistant world, this creates a troubling dynamic. As routine pleasures lose their potency through overstimulation, our brains might unconsciously seek pain or chaos as alternate stimulation. This isn't conscious masochism; rather, it's our desensitized reward circuitry desperately pursuing more intense experiences—whether healthy or harmful—to achieve that elusive dopamine spike.

We see this play out in our personal lives through repeated self-destructive behaviors. Unhealthy relationships, harmful habits, or self-defeating decisions can become strangely attractive. The discomfort itself becomes rewarding—offering either the excitement of unpredictability or the distorted validation of negative self-beliefs.

Professionally, this same neurological pattern leads to unconscious sabotage. Missed deadlines, neglected responsibilities, unnecessary conflicts—these aren't merely lapses in discipline. Often, they're our brains manufacturing stress and chaos as alternative dopamine triggers, subconsciously compensating for diminished reward sensitivity.

For flow, this pattern is particularly destructive. Not only does dopamine resistance dull our engagement with meaningful activities, but it may actively drive us toward conditions that make flow impossible. Ironically, our overstimulated reward system learns to find motivation in turmoil, directly undermining the clarity, calm, and deep engagement that flow requires.

YOUR HIDDEN COMPETITIVE ADVANTAGE

Here's the fascinating upside to what initially seems like a dire situation: as sustained attention becomes increasingly rare, its value skyrockets. Cal Newport captures this perfectly when he observes, "The ability to perform deep work is becoming increasingly rare at exactly the same time it is becoming increasingly valuable in our economy."

Today's average performers spend their days trapped in cycles of dopamine-driven distraction—constantly overwhelmed, chasing notifications, and confusing urgency for importance. Meanwhile, high performers operate differently. They've learned to optimize their dopamine systems, effortlessly accessing flow states and fiercely guarding their attention. Their decisions consistently reflect meaningful engagement over mere reaction to external stimuli.

The result isn't simply heightened productivity; it's an extraordinary competitive advantage in any field demanding creativity, complex problem-solving, or sustained excellence. By understanding and strategically working with your dopamine biology, you create conditions where flow shifts from possible to probable—becoming your cognitive default rather than an elusive state.

Imagine the advantage this grants you. While others remain stuck in superficial cycles of stimulation, you're developing a deep, resilient capacity for meaningful work. This isn't just a minor edge. It's a fundamental shift that, to outside observers, can appear almost superhuman. Not because of superior talent or intelligence, but because you've learned to align with your biology rather than fight it.

DOPAMINE OPTIMIZATION PROTOCOL FOR FLOW

By now, you've recognized that sustained high performance isn't achieved through isolated tactics, but by strategically integrating multiple layers—from physiological optimization and environmental design to psychological triggers and attention management. Some recommendations that follow may resonate from earlier chapters; think of this section not as mere repetition, but as a synthesis—an opportunity to connect these strategies through the lens of dopamine optimization. As we recalibrate your reward system, you'll deepen your understanding of how dopamine fits into the broader puzzle of holistic performance, restoring its natural role as a motivator for meaningful, flow-driven engagement.

Step 1: Sensory Management

We've talked extensively about optimizing your environment; now, let's specifically address the high-dopamine triggers sabotaging your flow. Think of this phase as resetting overstimulated senses, akin to taking a caffeine break to restore natural energy levels.

Begin by identifying your primary dopamine triggers. Which apps, devices, or environmental cues consistently draw you into cycles of constant stimulation? Your goal isn't outright elimination, but strategic friction to help your brain return to its natural reward patterns.

Start small but precise. If your smartphone is the top offender, create deliberate physical separation during focus periods—place it out of sight or in another room entirely.

Step 2: Single-Context Engagement

Dopamine functions optimally when your brain engages fully in one context at a time. Yet most of us have trained our brains to crave constant task-switching, disrupting deep focus in all areas of life.

Implement single-context engagement. When you're eating, just eat. When exercising, simply exercise. During conversations, stay fully present. This retrains your dopamine system to value sustained attention over fleeting novelty.

Apply this same principle to task management. Group similar tasks together rather than bouncing among projects. Process emails in designated blocks, and schedule phone calls to prevent fragmentation throughout your day.

Step 3: Intentional Boredom Training

Here's a counterintuitive insight: embracing boredom strategically can enhance your capacity for flow. Just as physical endurance develops through progressive overload, your attention system grows stronger through controlled exposure to low-stimulation periods.

Build your "boredom threshold"—your ability to stay engaged without external stimulation. Small steps make this manageable:

- Arrive early for events without reaching for your phone.
- Stand in line without seeking distraction.
- Drive without music or podcasts.
- Engage in simple tasks without background entertainment.

Think of these as deliberate "recovery sessions" for your overstimulated dopamine pathways. Just as we've emphasized physical recovery's role in sustaining peak performance, these quiet moments recalibrate your reward system for deeper engagement.

Step 4: Strategic Dopamine Fasting

Although "dopamine fasting" is a trendy term, research from experts like Dr. Anna Lembke demonstrates its genuine neurobiological benefits. The key insight? Dopamine spikes arise from more than just digital sources. They also emerge from everyday activities like caffeine, intense workouts, and even continuous learning.

Think of dopamine fasting as a spectrum rather than a strict regimen. Start with short digital detoxes—perhaps an afternoon without screens. Gradually expand your fasts to other areas as you become attuned to subtler dopamine triggers:

- Begin with scheduled, tech-free periods.
- Introduce temporary reductions in caffeine or alcohol.
- Eventually, experiment with reducing background music, casual conversation, or even intense learning sessions.

Some practitioners pursue silent retreats or extended low-stimulation experiences. Though extreme, their logic is sound: these deeper resets can profoundly recalibrate your dopamine sensitivity. Remember, the goal isn't permanent abstinence; it's strategically restoring your sensitivity to natural rewards—including the subtle satisfactions essential to flow states.

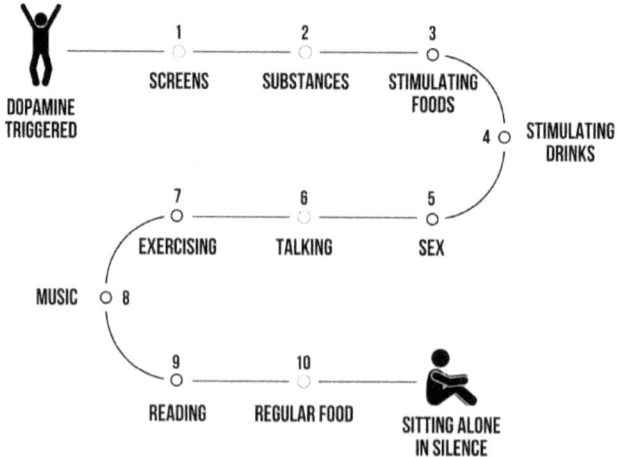

Step 5: Building Sustainable Patterns

Long-term dopamine optimization isn't about intermittent detoxes but embedding sustainable patterns into your daily life. Consider this your baseline operating system for sustained high performance.

First, manage cognitive load deliberately. We often succumb to "information FOMO," consuming countless books, podcasts, and courses simultaneously. Ironically, this pursuit can become a dopamine-driven distraction, undermining true learning.

Instead, embrace deep engagement. Choose one book and read it fully rather than skimming multiple ones. Master one expert's approach deeply instead of bouncing among influencers. This isn't restricting knowledge; it's enhancing genuine understanding and skill acquisition.

Expand this deliberate focus across all areas of your attention. Like training for a mental marathon, progressively challenge your sustained concentration through manageable increments: reading physical books without interruption, engaging deeply in single-topic projects, or completing tasks without yielding to distraction impulses.

Cultivate metacognitive awareness—the ability to observe your attention patterns without judgment. When you notice an impulse to seek stimulation, pause for ten breaths. Create space to reflect on whether this impulse aligns with your deeper objectives. Consider keeping a simple attention log to document these impulses. Awareness is your first step toward transformation.

Above all, approach this process as skill development rather than limitation. You're not restricting your experiences; you're expanding your capacity for meaningful, fulfilling engagement. By managing dopamine strategically, you're making flow not merely possible, but increasingly natural—an integral part of how you experience the world.

THE FLOW INTEGRATION PROTOCOL

You've now explored the science of flow states from multiple dimensions: neurobiological foundations, psychological prerequisites, environmental design, and sophisticated dopamine management techniques necessary for reliable access. Yet understanding these elements individually isn't enough. True mastery emerges from thoughtfully integrating them into your daily life.

Think of what we've covered as ingredients in a master chef's kitchen. High-quality components matter, but the extraordinary emerges from their precise combination and timing. Your flow practice demands similar orchestration—aligning the right elements at exactly the right moments to consistently achieve optimal performance states.

After navigating these advanced elements, you might feel both inspired and slightly overwhelmed. That's natural; this is the largest chapter of the book, and we've explored substantial territory. But remember the paradox of performance: sometimes less truly is more. Rather than attempting to implement every strategy simultaneously, start by identifying where you most consistently encounter resistance to flow.

Is your environment frequently breaking your concentration? Does your physiology consistently pull you away from deep work? Are your objectives unclear or uninspiring? Or perhaps your dopamine system feels overstimulated and needs recalibration. Identifying your primary barrier provides a practical, effective entry point.

Select just one area to optimize first. If your workspace distracts you, start there. If your energy fluctuations disrupt deep work, prioritize physiological alignment. If ambiguous goals dampen your engagement, clarify them first. This approach isn't about ignoring other factors but achieving manageable, progressive improvement that compounds over time.

Think of this process as mastering any sophisticated skill: you begin with foundational practices, gradually develop proficiency, and progressively integrate more nuanced techniques as your capabilities grow. Your flow practice will evolve in a similar way, becoming increasingly refined as you develop deeper insight into how these elements synergize uniquely for you.

MOVING FORWARD: FROM PHYSIOLOGY TO PSYCHOLOGY

As we conclude our comprehensive exploration of physiology—the second pillar of holistic performance—we're now positioned to delve deeper into the sophisticated terrain of psychological mastery. Throughout these chapters—from nutritional optimization and stress regulation to environmental flow strategies—you've discovered how your biology provides a solid foundation for exceptional achievement.

Yet you've probably noticed an interesting dynamic: even while examining biological principles, we frequently crossed into psychological territory. This overlap isn't accidental. Human performance defies neat boundaries. Your mental state influences biology just as powerfully as your physical condition shapes your cognitive capacity.

This interplay beautifully exemplifies our holistic approach. While our focus will now shift more explicitly toward psychology, always remember that each pillar reinforces and enriches the others. The biological optimization you've already implemented establishes an ideal platform for the psychological insights ahead—just as the psychological skills you're about to acquire will help sustain and elevate your physiological practices.

Let's now build upon this strong foundation, beginning with the psychological architecture essential for sustained high performance.

RESEARCH & RESOURCES

As always, please visit the Holistic Performance Resource Hub to access the research and additional materials mentioned in this chapter.

To do so, go to hplink.org/resourcehub or scan the QR code below.

CHAPTER 11
BUILDING UNBREAKABLE PERFORMANCE

"A hero is an ordinary individual who finds the strength to persevere and endure in spite of overwhelming obstacles."

– Christopher Reeve

What allows some people to thrive under pressure while others collapse at the first sign of adversity? What allows certain individuals to push through setbacks, failures, and seemingly impossible odds while others, equally talented and intelligent, quietly bow out?

For centuries, the answer was assumed to be talent. Some people were just born for it, while others weren't. But that's a myth. The truth is far more practical and empowering.

Grit, the ability to sustain long-term effort despite obstacles, is what separates extraordinary achievers from those who almost make it. But here's where many people misunderstand grit: it's not purely about raw determination. More importantly, it's not something you simply have or don't.

Grit is a skill. And like any skill, it can be systematically developed.

Psychologist Angela Duckworth made this clear when she conducted her now-famous studies on high-performance fields. One of her most revealing experiments took place at West Point, the elite U.S. military academy known for its brutal first-year program called "Beast Barracks." Every summer, thousands of incoming cadets—many of whom were top students and athletes—arrived on campus prepared to endure some of the most intense physical and mental training in the world. West Point had always assumed that IQ, leadership scores, or physical fitness would determine success in the program. However, when Duckworth analyzed the data, none of those factors predicted who would make it through and who would quit. The best predictor? Grit.

Duckworth also studied contestants in the National Spelling Bee, where conventional wisdom suggested that raw intelligence would separate the best from the rest. Yet the kids who made it to the final rounds weren't necessarily the smartest. Instead, they were the ones who practiced the longest, who persisted through failures, and who refused to quit after an early loss.

She expanded her research into the business world, tracking high-stakes salespeople who either thrived under relentless rejection or broke under pressure. Once again, the same factor determined success: not talent, not intelligence—grit.

At first glance, this might seem like another call to "just push harder," but that's precisely where most people misunderstand grit. It's not about sheer willpower or constantly muscling through exhaustion. That kind of thinking is exactly what *leads* to burnout.

Because here's the thing: grit is more nuanced and more sustainable because it's biological as much as psychological.

Sustained effort doesn't come from motivation alone; it relies on effective energy management—regulating stress, optimizing recovery, and structuring habits so resilience becomes automatic.

If you've followed the book so far, you've already laid a foundation for this. You've optimized tasks and habits to eliminate overwhelm, dialed in your biology for sustained energy, learned to master stress, and experienced effortless engagement through flow states.

But what happens when life doesn't cooperate?

What do you do when your routine collapses, external pressures spike, setbacks pile up, and everything in you wants to quit?

True resilience emerges here—not just in moments of peak performance, but in the capacity to sustain it amid chaos.

This chapter will guide you through that process. Together, we'll uncover:

- The science of grit and why it's much more than mere perseverance.
- How biological factors underpin resilience, with energy rather than willpower fueling sustained effort.
- Methods to catch burnout before it takes hold, by recognizing its early warning signs.
- Why procrastination often emerges from burnout and how clarity, energy management, and realistic expectations help mitigate it.
- Ways to build contingency systems, ensuring that even when life derails your plans, you stay on track.

Because here's the reality: unbreakable performance isn't about blindly pushing forward. It's about designing systems that make quitting unnecessary.

Let's build it.

THE FOUNDATION OF SUSTAINED EXCELLENCE

At its core, grit is the intersection of passion and perseverance over time. It's what separates those who merely start from those who stay the course—not for days or weeks, but for years.

If talent determines your starting point, grit determines how far you actually go.

It's easy to assume that the most naturally gifted people dominate every field, but time and again, research shows that talent alone isn't enough. Some of the world's most accomplished individuals weren't the most "gifted" starting out—they were simply the ones who kept showing up.

Angela Duckworth's research consistently finds that grittier individuals outperform their more naturally gifted peers across domains, from academia to military training to business. But this idea isn't new.

History is filled with examples of people who started as "unremarkable" but outlasted those with early advantages. The difference wasn't just their motivation but the compounding effect of their persistence.

Small, consistent investments of effort accumulate into extraordinary results over time. But most people focus on the end goal—the equivalent of staring at their desired bank balance—rather than on the process that actually creates the outcome.

The grittiest individuals? They focus on the system, not the result.

They don't obsess over where they "should" be. They build habits and structures that ensure they make progress every single day, no matter how small the step. Over time, that consistency builds an advantage that raw talent alone never could.

This systematic approach to grit rests on the following four foundational pillars.

Interest: Cultivating the Engine of Effort

Conventional wisdom tells us to "follow our passion," as if it's something we're born knowing. But research suggests something far more counterintuitive: passion isn't just discovered; it's developed.

Highly gritty individuals don't necessarily start off knowing what they love. Instead, they nurture their interests deliberately.

Consider how master chefs develop their palates over time. The best sommeliers don't wake up one day with an instinctive ability to detect subtle wine notes. They train their senses through exposure and study. What begins as a vague interest becomes expertise through strategic immersion.

The same applies to high performance. Grit isn't just about sticking with something; it's about strategically deepening engagement so that what once felt like effort becomes part of who you are.

If you haven't yet found what excites you, don't wait for passion to appear. Start by following your curiosity. Passion isn't a lightning strike. It's a slow burn, fed by deliberate exposure, learning, and refinement.

Practice: The Architecture of Mastery

Interest alone isn't enough. True grit demands deliberate practice.

Many assume that simply logging hours guarantees mastery. But repetition alone isn't enough—the quality of your practice matters more than its quantity.

Elite performers across fields structure their practice precisely. They set increasingly challenging goals, engage in rigorous feedback loops, and objectively measure progress. They don't rely on motivation; they build conditions where improvement becomes inevitable.

For you, growth must be structured, measurable, and intelligently designed. The difference between progress and stagnation isn't just effort—it's the strategic framework surrounding your effort.

Purpose: Beyond Personal Achievement

The grittiest individuals don't just work hard for themselves. They connect their work to a larger mission.

Research shows that individuals who tie their efforts to something bigger than themselves demonstrate significantly higher resilience and perseverance. It's one thing to work for personal gain. It's another to feel like your work contributes to something meaningful.

This is why finding your purpose is so powerful. It doesn't mean you need some grand mission to "change the world." It simply means understanding why your effort matters—whether it's for your team, your family, your industry, or even just your future self.

When setbacks arise, people with a strong purpose push through, while those with only self-interest often burn out. Purpose acts as a psychological shock absorber, giving you a reason to keep going even when progress feels slow.

If you feel stuck, ask yourself:

"If I persist through this challenge, who benefits beyond just me?"

The answer might just be the fuel you need.

Hope: Practical Belief in the Process

Hope is more than blind optimism. It's a pragmatic belief in the process. Unlike simple positivity, hope implies faith in your actions, even when results aren't immediately visible.

Many people quit prematurely. They mistake delayed results for failure, when in reality, grit is about outlasting the delay.

Having clear evidence of progress is critical. When the road ahead is uncertain, your brain needs tangible proof that your actions are working.

This is where proper systems become crucial. Whether it's tracking small wins, reviewing past progress, or reinforcing habits, gritty individuals don't just believe; they build structures that keep them engaged even when motivation fluctuates.

Ultimately, grit isn't about pushing harder; it's about strategically designing your life so that stopping becomes impossible.

THE ENERGY-RESILIENCE CONNECTION

When elite athletes stumble in crucial moments, commentators often talk about "cracking under pressure." But what if the real issue isn't mental strength or motivation? What if the difference between breaking and bouncing back comes down to something simpler, yet more fundamental—your energy reserves?

Your capacity to persevere—your ability to push through obstacles, maintain focus, and recover from setbacks—is directly tied to your physiological energy systems. When your body is depleted, even the strongest mindset will eventually break down.

This explains why most burnout cases don't start with a lack of discipline or motivation. They begin with chronic energy depletion.

Nicole, a senior executive we met earlier, learned this the hard way. She had always prided herself on being mentally tough, pushing through long hours and high-pressure decisions. But after months of overloading her schedule, she noticed something unsettling. Small problems that she would have easily handled before started feeling overwhelming. She found herself second-guessing decisions, snapping at her team, and struggling to focus in meetings.

"I thought I was losing motivation," she admitted. "But once I started tracking my health, I realized I was running on empty."

Nicole's story reveals a pattern we've seen time and again—not a failure of motivation, but a failure of physiological capacity. One of the most potent biological markers we have for this is Heart Rate Variability (HRV), which, as we explored in Chapter 8, reflects how well your nervous system adapts to stress. Research from the HeartMath Institute shows that individuals with high HRV transition smoothly between states of effort and recovery, allowing them to maintain high performance without crashing. But when HRV is low, the body gets stuck in a chronic stress loop—making even minor obstacles feel insurmountable.

This is exactly what Nicole experienced. Her body simply couldn't keep up with the demands placed on it.

Likewise, as we learned from Roy Baumeister's research in Chapter 5, self-control is finite—it drains with repeated use. Relying solely on willpower eventually leads to exhaustion. True resilience isn't about pushing harder but about managing energy so your cognitive and emotional reserves remain intact.

This brings together everything we've explored in previous chapters. Optimizing your sleep, nutrition, movement, and recovery isn't just about feeling better—it's about sustaining peak performance without burnout.

If you're running low on energy, every challenge feels monumental. But when your body is biologically prepared, resilience becomes second nature.

This brings us to a critical question: How do you prevent energy depletion before it undermines your performance?

THE PHYSIOLOGY OF BURNOUT

Burnout doesn't explode onto the scene—it seeps in. You don't wake up one morning unable to function. It starts as a slow leak, a subtle dulling of motivation, a creeping emotional detachment. But make no mistake: burnout isn't just tiredness. It's a neurological shift that rewires your brain and fundamentally alters how you experience work, stress, and even grit itself.

In the early stages, most people assume burnout is just a slump—something a long weekend or a tighter schedule can fix. But by then, changes are already underway in the brain. Studies from the Karolinska Institutet in Sweden show that chronic stress enlarges the amygdala, the part of the brain responsible for emotional reactivity and fear. Small frustrations that used to roll off your back now feel like personal threats. Simultaneously, burnout weakens the link between the amygdala and the prefrontal cortex—the region governing executive function and emotional regulation. This breakdown makes it harder to think clearly, control impulses, or stay motivated.

Cognitive function takes a hit, too. Activity drops in the anterior cingulate cortex, the brain region responsible for error detection and sustained attention. The result? Foggy thinking, disengagement, and a sharp decline in the ability to focus. This explains why even seasoned top performers suddenly feel like they're falling apart under pressure. Burnout doesn't just exhaust you; it breaks your brain's capacity to recover from stress.

The external conditions that drive burnout are also widely misunderstood. Most people blame long hours or intense workloads. And yes, overwork plays a role. But research from Dr. Christina Maslach—a pioneering psychologist from UC Berkeley and one of the world's leading experts on occupational burnout—tells a more nuanced story: burnout isn't just about how much you work, but how your work is structured.

According to her, six key factors predict whether burnout will take hold:

1. **Work Overload**: When demands consistently exceed your ability to recover, your brain shifts into survival mode.
2. **Lack of Control**: Jobs with little autonomy create psychological stress. Micromanagement erodes resilience.
3. **Insufficient Reward**: When effort isn't met with recognition, the dopamine system registers the work as meaningless.
4. **Breakdown of Community**: Lack of social support weakens emotional regulation. We're wired to co-regulate stress through connection.
5. **Absence of Fairness**: Unequal treatment or recognition leads to resentment, cynicism, and detachment.
6. **Value Conflict**: When your job clashes with your core values, it creates internal friction that quietly drains your energy.

Despite the seriousness of burnout, most people don't recognize it until it's entrenched. The early warning signs are subtle: trouble concentrating, minor memory lapses, creeping decision fatigue. Then come the emotional symptoms—mood swings, irritability, disengagement from work or relationships. Finally, the body joins the rebellion: disrupted sleep, energy crashes, weakened immunity. By the time physical symptoms show up, recovery is no longer a quick reset—it's a whole system reboot.

And that's the mistake most professionals make. They think as long as they're still functional, they're fine. But burnout doesn't wait for collapse to start causing damage. The real key isn't just knowing how to recover but knowing when to intervene.

In Chapter 7, we explored how recovery builds biological resilience. However, theory isn't enough. In practice, what matters most is catching the slide before it becomes a crash.

Brian, an operations manager I worked with, figured this out the hard way. He used to burn out every few months—until he started paying attention. "Now," he told me, "I watch for the signs. If I catch myself snapping at people over nothing or just staring at my screen without doing anything, that's my signal. I step away and reset."

What Brian discovered matches what the research shows: you need internal tripwires. Predefined triggers and simple protocols remove the need for decision-making when your cognitive bandwidth is already tapped. Think of them like circuit breakers. They don't just stop you from frying the system; instead, they prevent the overload in the first place.

Your signals might be different: procrastinating on tasks that used to excite you, doom-scrolling between emails, overreacting to something trivial. The key is to notice the shift—then act. Sometimes, all it takes is a ten-minute walk or one of the physiological resets from Chapter 7 to get back on track.

This isn't just about energy. It's about protecting the clarity and composure grit depends on.

Grit isn't about pushing until you break; instead, it's about knowing how to manage effort so you don't have to.

Which brings us to one of burnout's sneakiest consequences: procrastination.

At first glance, burnout and procrastination seem unrelated. One looks like overwork, the other like avoidance. But they're often two sides of the same coin. When chronic stress and mental fatigue take hold, your brain begins to perceive effort itself as a threat. Not because you're lazy but because it's trying to conserve what little energy remains.

That's why burnout so often masquerades as procrastination. Even meaningful tasks start to feel overwhelming. Avoidance becomes a coping mechanism, which only adds more pressure, which leads to more avoidance. It's a loop.

And that loop doesn't mean you're weak. It means your system needs a reset.

If grit is about showing up and staying in the game, procrastination is the warning light saying you're about to get benched.

Ignore it, and you burn out. Respond to it, and you stay resilient.

WHY WE DELAY WHAT MATTERS

For most high performers, procrastination is one of the most frustrating and counterintuitive obstacles they face. It's tempting to chalk it up to laziness or lack of discipline, but as we explored in the last chapter, that's a shallow take.

Procrastination isn't a failure of willpower. It's neurobiological, emotional, and structural. And more importantly, it's one of the most persistent killers of sustained effort.

At the chemical level, dopamine is often the prime suspect. When the brain becomes conditioned to quick, low-effort rewards—like social media, inbox checks, or busywork—it starts avoiding tasks that require deeper, more sustained engagement. You want to focus, but your brain is craving a fast hit.

But procrastination isn't just about distractions. If it were, gritty individuals wouldn't struggle with it. Yet they do. This happens because procrastination isn't just a dopamine issue but a friction issue.

One of the biggest hidden drivers? Cognitive overload. When your brain sees a task as ambiguous or too complex, it hesitates. That hesitation is a protective mechanism. Vague, undefined tasks feel like walking into a fog. And when the direction isn't obvious, your brain defaults to avoidance.

This is why clarity is such a powerful antidote. As we explored earlier, breaking work into clearly defined steps eliminates cognitive drag. Your brain no longer has to burn energy figuring out where to begin—it just starts.

But even when the steps are clear, avoidance can persist. Why? Because many tasks aren't hard in a technical sense—they're hard in an emotional one. Challenging conversations, high-stakes presentations, creative work that opens you up to criticism... These don't just require effort. They require vulnerability.

In those moments, the brain isn't dodging work. It's dodging discomfort.

That's what makes procrastination the quiet opposite of grit. Grit sustains effort despite the challenge. Procrastination sidesteps effort when uncertainty or emotional risk is involved. And it doesn't always show up with flashing lights. Sometimes, it's subtle—a browser tab, a busy task, a sudden urge to reorganize your desk... A micro-escape.

This is why understanding procrastination is critical to building real resilience.

If you can't see avoidance for what it is, you'll mislabel it as a motivation issue. And that's dangerous. Because every "I'll do it later" moment chips away at grit. Not because you're undisciplined but because your engagement strategy is broken.

The fix isn't to push harder. It's to pull smarter.

This is where gamification and strength-based engagement become so powerful. They make progress feel rewarding. They turn the work itself into a feedback loop. You're no longer forcing effort—you're inviting it.

If procrastination is what happens in the absence of structure, then the solution isn't just eliminating distractions. It's designing systems that make forward motion feel frictionless even on the hard days.

STRENGTH ACTIVATION & PERFORMANCE LEVERAGE

If procrastination is the silent momentum killer, leveraging strengths is the ultimate amplifier. Unbreakable performance isn't just about persistence but about deploying your natural advantages with precision. Think of it like a military campaign: while overall resilience matters, strategic use of your strongest assets is what drives breakthrough results.

Research from the Gallup Organization flips conventional wisdom on its head. While most people assume success comes from fixing weaknesses, Gallup's study of over two million professionals found the opposite: those who focused on their strengths were six times more likely to be engaged at work and three times more likely to report an excellent quality of life.

Why? Because working against your natural tendencies requires more cognitive effort, more energy, and more motivation. It's like swimming upstream. But when you structure your workflow to align with what comes naturally, you reduce friction. Momentum builds on its own.

The problem? Most people don't know what their strengths are.

According to researcher Alex Linley, only about one-third of people can accurately identify their core strengths. And, if you think about it, it makes sense. When something comes easily, we often assume it's easy for everyone. It's like being a fish unaware of water. This blind spot creates a performance drag: we obsess over weaknesses while ignoring our biggest levers for growth.

That's why systematic strength discovery is essential. Not just a loose list of things you're "good at," but a structured assessment of your natural advantage across three categories:

1. Innate Talents: Your instinctive patterns of thought, feeling, or behavior.
2. Developed Skills: Competencies you've built through focused repetition.
3. Knowledge Areas: Subject matter where you've accumulated deep insight.

Each of these fuels your performance differently. But when stacked together, they create an exponential effect.

Take Josh, a coach who couldn't seem to gain traction. "I was trying to become a charismatic speaker because I thought that's what success looked like," he told me. However, through structured reflection, he uncovered that his real edge came from deep analytical thinking and strategic advising. "Once I started designing my work around those strengths, everything shifted. I stopped fighting my nature."

The lesson? Strengths aren't just what you're good at. They're what energize you. They're the activities that feel effortless, make time disappear, and leave you sharper rather than drained.

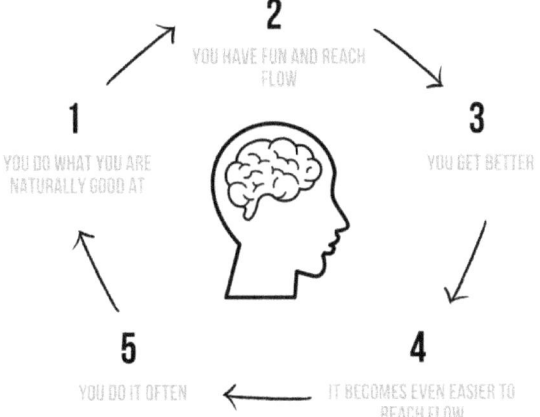

One of the simplest ways to uncover these strengths is through reflection exercises.

Marcus Buckingham's Strengths Finder method suggests asking yourself: *"What activities do I excel at that also bring me excitement?"*

This is an important distinction. Many people are good at things they don't enjoy, often because they've been forced into them through repetition. But true strengths are different. They create a sense of *effortless effort*, where engagement feels natural rather than forced.

Another approach comes from Alex Linley's Strengths Spotting Protocol. Instead of focusing on what you struggle with, it asks you to reflect on moments when you felt the most authentic, energized, and naturally skilled. Think back to your childhood: what activities pulled you in without external motivation? What do you do now that makes hours feel like minutes? Where do others come to you for advice or help?

For those who prefer a structured approach, personality assessments like the Big 5, VIA, Enneagram, and StrengthsFinder can provide deeper insights.

Regardless of the method, the key is to look for patterns, not just single traits. Your performance edge comes from how your strengths work together, not in isolation.

And here's where the magic happens: when you deliberately stack strengths, you begin building meta-skills.

A meta-skill is a high-leverage, transferable capability. Develop your creative talent in design? You're not just becoming a better designer. You're training strategic thinking and innovative problem-solving. Hone your resilience through crisis leadership? You're not just surviving pressure. You're building composure, adaptability, and tactical decision-making.

Strengths aren't static—they're scalable. The more you refine and stack them, the more surface area you create for growth.

That's why strength activation isn't just about feeling good. When work aligns with your natural wiring, you eliminate internal resistance. Flow becomes accessible. Progress feels organic. And what used to require force becomes something closer to flight.

ENGINEERING EFFORTLESS ENGAGEMENT

One of the most powerful ways to make grit effortless is through gamification—the process of applying game mechanics to real-world tasks to enhance engagement and motivation. At its core, gamification works because it taps directly into your brain's natural reward circuitry, turning effort into something self-reinforcing rather than something you have to will yourself into.

That's why apps like Duolingo make language learning addictive, why fitness trackers sustain consistent movement habits, and why video games can hold attention for hours without a drop of discipline. Properly applied, gamification not only makes work more fun but also builds resilience by transforming progress into its own reward system.

We've already explored how feedback loops, progress tracking, and flow states fuel engagement. Gamification simply systematizes these elements, embedding them into your daily process. It's not about making things easier; it's about turning effort into something your brain actively wants to return to.

Games don't depend on willpower. They work because of structure: clear goals, rapid feedback, escalating difficulty, and regular rewards. Top performers often adopt the same framework—breaking complex goals into levels, tracking visible progress, and celebrating meaningful milestones.

One of the simplest ways to do this is by framing work as a challenge.

Instead of seeing a major project as an overwhelming obligation, break it down into levels, each representing a milestone toward completion. Many organizations already apply this concept without realizing it. Sales teams set targets that function as "missions," rewarding those who close the most deals within a timeframe. A team member who levels up the fastest might be named *Sales Champion of the Week*, creating a sense of progression and achievement rather than just hitting quotas.

Rewards also play a major role in reinforcing effort. While we've discussed intrinsic motivation, there's no denying that well-structured incentives drive consistent performance. Innovative organizations understand this and use tangible rewards like bonuses, extra time off, or professional development opportunities to reinforce high performance.

Even in personal development, this principle applies. After completing a month-long fitness challenge, you might reward yourself with a gift card, a new experience, or even just a day off to recharge. The point isn't the size of the reward but the reinforcement of effort leading to tangible benefits.

Social dynamics deepen the impact. Leaderboards, shared challenges, or collaborative sprints activate the brain's social reward pathways. Whether it's a personal challenge with a friend or a shared learning goal with colleagues, the sense of mutual progress strengthens accountability and drive.

But here's where it really clicks: gamification becomes a force multiplier when aligned with your strengths.

A natural analyst might turn strategic milestones into scoreboards. A high-empathy communicator might build momentum through collaborative mini-wins. The point isn't to make everything a game but to make your unique performance profile more rewarding to express. You're not hacking discipline; you're designing traction.

There's also an often-overlooked benefit: gamification increases tolerance for imperfection. Games are built on retries, learning curves, and bouncing back from failure. That same mechanic protects your grit. One off-day doesn't derail the system. Instead, it becomes a normal part of the process.

Gamification helps you show up more consistently—but consistency alone doesn't make a system resilient. The real test comes when routines break, motivation dips, or chaos hits. That's where most people fall off. Not because they lack discipline but because they lack backup plans.

CONTINGENCY ARCHITECTURE

No matter how well you structure engagement, setbacks will happen. Workloads shift, priorities change, unexpected disruptions appear—and they never ask for permission.

At this point in the book, one pattern should be clear: top performers don't just rely on grit to push through—they design for recovery. They don't depend on perfect conditions. They build systems that stay operational even when life doesn't cooperate.

That's the real performance advantage. Not just willpower but architecture.

While most people build routines for when things go right, high performers build for when things go wrong. And that's the essence of *contingency architecture*: designing strategic fail-safes so that a single disruption doesn't derail your entire system.

Always remember that grit is about staying adaptive when the plan breaks. Habits help, sure. But what separates fragile effort from sustainable performance is *preloaded adaptability*—the skill to switch tracks without losing momentum.

One of the most powerful tools for this is scenario planning. Resilient performers don't wait to react; they stress-test their workflow in advance. They ask:

- What's most likely to derail my progress?
- Where am I fragile?
- If my plan breaks, do I have a fallback that activates automatically?

Once those pressure points are mapped, they build *If/Then protocols*—simple, executable scripts that remove hesitation in the moment:

- If I miss my morning deep work session, then I will block off 90 minutes later in the day and eliminate nonessential tasks.
- If an unexpected priority disrupts my workflow, then I will shift my top task to the next available deep focus block.
- If I start feeling decision fatigue by mid-afternoon, then I will switch to low-effort tasks and avoid making critical choices.

These aren't productivity hacks. They're structural responses to stress, removing friction precisely when decision fatigue is highest. You're not improvising. You're executing a protocol.

But this kind of contingency thinking can't stop at the daily level. True resilience is architectural. It's built into the bones of your system.

That's where *modular planning* comes in.

High performers don't rely on single points of failure. For example, instead of relying on one fixed time block for deep work, they create multiple entry points throughout the day so that productivity isn't lost if their first attempt is disrupted. Instead of structuring their week around one static priority list, they create adaptive priority hierarchies that allow them to shift tasks dynamically based on circumstances.

This adaptability ensures that performance remains consistent rather than being entirely dependent on conditions staying ideal.

In short, they don't build systems that work on perfect days. They build for the imperfect ones.

The most resilient performers don't try to avoid chaos. They just make sure it never stops them from moving forward.

INTEGRATING YOUR UNBREAKABLE PERFORMANCE

By now, you know the truth: unbreakable performance isn't about endless grit or blind persistence. It's about engineering effort to be sustainable. The most brilliant performers aren't more motivated—they've just built systems that make consistency feel like a natural byproduct, not a daily uphill battle.

Forget perfection. The real win is keeping the wheels on when life swerves off-course. You don't need twenty strategies to start. You just need one point of leverage.

So here's your move: pick the weakest link in your current system and build around it. That might mean crafting a backup plan for when your deep work block gets hijacked, gamifying a task that always drags, or reinforcing a recovery practice that tends to get skipped when things get busy (which, let's be honest, is all the time).

Then, test it. Watch what shifts. Iterate like a scientist.

Because the real game here isn't about working harder but about setting the rules so that progress compounds even on the hard days.

And if something still feels off, dig deeper. Maybe it's not the structure—it's the fit. You're not here to mold yourself into a generic routine. You're here to build a performance system that reflects how *you* operate at your best.

If you haven't already, revisit the strength-identification frameworks we covered. Take a personality test, review past wins, or scan for recurring patterns. The better you understand what energizes you, the easier it is to build a system that runs on self-reinforcing effort instead of constant willpower.

This chapter gave you the architecture. Next, we dive inward—into the mental tools that keep performance intact when the outside world starts to unravel.

Because there will be pressure. There will be chaos. But with the right psychological tools, you'll be the one who thrives despite it.

RESEARCH & RESOURCES

To take this further, you'll find a few supporting tools in the Holistic Performance Resource Hub—including the Maslach Burnout Inventory, the Grit Scale, and a curated set of personality tests to help you better identify and leverage your strengths.

As always, the hub also includes the complete list of studies, books, and articles referenced throughout the chapter.

Visit hplink.org/resourcehub or scan the QR code below.

CHAPTER 12
MINDSET UNLEASHED

"Antifragility is about more than resilience or robustness. The resilient resists shocks and stays the same, the antifragile gets better."

– Nassim Nicholas Taleb

Grit gets you through the storm. Antifragility makes you stronger *because* of it.

For years, resilience has been seen as the gold standard of mental toughness—the ability to endure, recover, and keep moving forward despite adversity. And while resilience is critical, it has one major flaw: it assumes that the best we can do is *withstand* stress. But what if we could do more than survive difficulty? What if we could actually become *stronger because of it*?

That's the fundamental difference between resilience and antifragility.

Coined by financial theorist and best-selling author Nassim Nicholas Taleb, *antifragility* describes systems that don't just endure stress—they improve from it. Unlike fragile systems that break under pressure, or resilient systems that merely withstand it, antifragile systems grow stronger precisely because of volatility, uncertainty, and challenge. Think of how muscles rebuild after intense training or how the immune system strengthens after controlled exposure to viruses. Antifragility isn't about surviving hardship but about using stress as fuel for transformation.

A key concept we need to understand is that resilience has its limits. A resilient performer bounces back from setbacks. An antifragile performer evolves from them. Traditional resilience relies on maintaining a strong baseline, but antifragility is about turning stress into an advantage.

Most people unknowingly operate in a fragile psychological state, avoiding stress, failure, and discomfort because they believe these experiences weaken them. This is why setbacks derail so many people. They spend years building their identity around success, but the moment they face a real challenge—

whether it's failure, uncertainty, or external pressure—their confidence crumbles.

Antifragility rewires that equation. It changes how we interpret pressure, reframes failure as fuel, and turns uncertainty into a necessary catalyst for growth. Instead of treating stress as something to survive, antifragile individuals use it to level up.

In the last chapter, we built grit-based systems—reinforcing strengths, structuring engagement, and designing contingency plans to sustain effort over time. But structure alone isn't enough. Systems can break. Routines can falter. And no matter how well-designed your workflow is, life will introduce volatility.

This chapter takes the mental game of performance to the next level. It's not just about staying strong under stress; it's about engineering a mindset that thrives on it.

We'll explore:

- How belief systems and mindset dictate whether stress becomes fuel or friction.
- The hidden saboteurs that quietly cap your performance ceiling.
- How identity engineering reshapes how you respond under pressure.
- The paradox of peak states—and how high performance can break you if mismanaged.
- How to convert adversity into an actual psychological advantage.

Because this isn't about gritting your teeth through hardship; it's about building a mind that turns hardship into an asset.

THE PSYCHOLOGY OF PEAK PERFORMANCE

As we've discussed, antifragility fundamentally transforms how we understand performance. By now, you know that the conventional wisdom about top performers—that they succeed because of superior talent, better habits, or superhuman discipline—misses a critical layer. Research consistently shows that their real edge doesn't just come from what they do, but also from how they think.

Performance isn't just about skill or effort. It's about how your mind interprets challenge, failure, and possibility.

Two people can experience the same setback—one breaks, the other gets stronger. The difference? The mental frameworks they've built.

This section dives deeper into constructing those frameworks.

There's a reason why *Growth* vs. *Fixed Mindset* has become one of the most studied concepts in performance psychology. In her research, psychologist Dr. Carol Dweck found that individuals with a fixed mindset see their abilities as static—something they either have or don't. They interpret failure as a statement of their limitations rather than an opportunity to improve.

A growth mindset, on the other hand, sees failure as data—feedback that informs the next step rather than a verdict on ability. People with this mindset don't just recover from setbacks better; they actually seek out challenges, knowing that discomfort is where skill expansion happens.

But here's the problem: most people don't realize that their mindset isn't a conscious choice but an unconscious default.

We don't wake up one morning and decide, "You know what? I think I'll have a fixed mindset today." Instead, it's shaped by years of experiences, conditioning, and the narratives we internalize about success and failure.

This brings us to the real work of rewiring how we see ourselves under pressure. Because your mindset in those moments determines whether stress sharpens you or shatters you.

SUBCONSCIOUS PERFORMANCE BARRIERS

Every high performer carries an invisible ceiling—a self-imposed limit, often inherited from past failures or unchallenged assumptions. Maybe it's the memory of bombing a speech that cements the belief, *"I'm just not a public speaker."* Or maybe it's those arbitrary societal expectations—what some have rightly called *Brules* (bullshit rules we've blindly accepted as truth).

Ever hear someone say, *"I'm just not a creative person,"* or *"I'm too old to learn something new,"* or *"I'm not the kind of person who does X"*? These aren't facts. They're L.I.E.s—Limited Ideas Entertained. Mental ceilings we install and reinforce simply because we've never tested them.

The reality? Most of the hard limits you think exist are actually just reinforced beliefs.

This is where performance psychology takes a turn. Instead of just fixing weaknesses or training harder, the real leverage is in breaking the mental ceilings that limit growth.

Think of your mind like a flashlight in a dark room. What you focus on determines what's visible. Most people go through life with a narrow beam, only seeing the possibilities that align with their existing beliefs.

If you believe you're "bad at numbers," your brain filters out any success that contradicts that belief. If you see yourself as a mid-level performer, you subconsciously sandbag any opportunity that threatens that label. If you've always avoided leadership roles, your mind rejects anything that contradicts that self-image—even if you're ready.

Expanding the *belief spotlight* means hunting for counter-evidence. You're not trying to convince yourself with affirmations—you're looking for real-world proof that your story might be wrong.

Maybe you think you "can't focus for long"—until deep work protocols reveal you can, just under the right conditions. Perhaps you believe you are "not a writer"—until one idea you post online resonates with thousands. Maybe you've told yourself you're "bad at sales"—until you start seeing it as authentic storytelling and realize it fits you perfectly.

This isn't about irrational positivity. It's about *data*. Gathering proof that challenges your limitations—until they're not limitations anymore.

Because at the end of the day, it's not talent or discipline that caps your performance.

It's the model you use to define what's possible.

Change the model, and the ceiling disappears.

IDENTITY ENGINEERING

If beliefs set the boundaries of performance, identity determines how consistently you operate within them. We often think of identity as something fixed—as if we're simply "wired" a certain way from birth. But neuroscience tells a far more empowering story.

Identity isn't something you *have*; it's something you *do*. It's a sophisticated neural network constructed through countless experiences, self-talk, and repeated behaviors. This network goes beyond just influencing your decisions. It often makes them for you before you're even consciously aware.

Your identity fundamentally dictates your response under pressure. Identifying as a peak performer causes your brain to filter challenges through that lens, making resilience and adaptability your default state. When you view yourself as someone who struggles under stress, each encounter with adversity neurologically reinforces that limiting reality. Consider how this manifests in real situations. Someone with a history of public speaking difficulties carries more than nervousness before presentations. Their brain has constructed a framework automatically categorizing them as "not a natural speaker," filtering every future opportunity through this lens and triggering familiar physiological responses that strengthen the pattern. Those who consistently succeed under pressure develop entirely different neural pathways. They associate high-stakes situations with optimal performance, preparing their bodies for excellence rather than mere survival. This creates a fundamentally different experience of identical external circumstances. The relationship flows bidirectionally: actions reinforce identity just as identity drives actions. A business owner with early failures might unconsciously develop an identity centered on "I'm bad at making money." Once established, this neural pattern leads the brain to seek confirming evidence, potentially undermining opportunities that contradict this narrative. Self-concept represents one of the most overlooked performance drivers. While many focus solely on changing habits, building skills, or optimizing environments, genuine transformation requires shifting who you believe yourself to be. Beyond asking "What do I need to do?" lies the more transformative question: "Who do I need to become?" Most people never recognize their current identity programming. They mistake their self-perception for objective reality when it actually represents a constructed narrative awaiting rewiring. Operating on unconscious programming installed decades ago, they build their self-concept on limited experiences or misinterpreted feedback. The power of this understanding comes from recognizing these neural patterns remain malleable. Through strategic experiences, focused attention, and deliberate practice, we can reshape the networks defining our response to challenges. Neuroplasticity—our brain's capacity to form new connections—means your identity functions as a dynamic system rather than a fixed trait. Awareness forms the first step toward reconfiguration. You cannot reprogram what you haven't acknowledged. By bringing unconscious patterns into light, you establish the foundation for transformation through strategic neural architecture redesign.

THE THREE LEVERS OF IDENTITY TRANSFORMATION

According to globally renowned coach Tony Robbins, there are three primary mechanisms through which identity operates and can be transformed: our actions, our mental-emotional state, and our language. Let's explore each of these levers and how they can be strategically deployed to reshape who you believe yourself to be.

Actions: The Physical Pathway to Identity Shift

Identity forms most fundamentally through consistent behavior. What defines us isn't occasional action but repeated patterns that strengthen specific neural pathways and their associated identity constructs.

As entrepreneur Alex Hormozi puts it: "You don't become confident by shouting affirmations in the mirror, but by having a stack of undeniable proof that you are who you say you are. Outwork your self-doubt."

This insight reveals a crucial truth: while mindset work matters, transformation requires action. Confidence emerges not from positive thinking alone but from tangible evidence accumulated through consistent behavior.

Consider Kevin, who struggled with public speaking despite years of preparation. His transformation came not through additional mental rehearsal but by volunteering to speak at every company meeting for three months. "The first few presentations were terrifying," he admits, "but by the tenth, something had fundamentally shifted. I wasn't acting more confident—I had become a confident speaker."

Such evidence doesn't require perfect performance. Even small, consistent steps create neural architecture supporting new identities. Each aligned action rewires your brain, making that identity increasingly accessible and automatic.

Mental-Emotional State: The Biochemical Foundation

Our state—the combined mental and emotional condition we operate from— profoundly shapes how we interpret experiences and how these experiences influence our identity. As we explored in Chapter 8, identical events can either reinforce or undermine your desired identity depending entirely on your state while experiencing them.

Consider a roller coaster ride—the same physical experience generates either euphoria or terror based on the rider's mental-emotional condition. This goes beyond subjective difference; it represents fundamentally different neurochemical processes that strengthen or weaken neural pathways related to your identity.

Your state significantly impacts your actions as well. A resourceful, positive state naturally leads to bold, confident behaviors that reinforce a strong identity. Negative states typically produce hesitation, procrastination, or avoidance—behaviors that cement limitation rather than capability.

The way you manage your state both reflects and reinforces your self-concept. Those who view themselves as resilient maintain resourceful states even during challenges. This creates a self-reinforcing cycle where state and identity continuously strengthen each other.

Understanding the indirect triggers affecting your state becomes essential for identity management. Emotions often stem not only from immediate circumstances but from deeper factors. Anger might arise not directly from a frustrating situation but from underlying exhaustion. Recognizing these more profound influences allows more effective state regulation. This connects directly to the interoception skills we developed in Chapter 8.

By developing awareness of what triggers negative states and creating protocols to shift into more resourceful ones, you establish the biochemical foundation for identity transformation. This awareness doesn't require denying negative emotions but rather recognizing when they undermine your optimal identity and having the tools to recalibrate.

Language: The Architecture of Self-Perception

Perhaps the most powerful yet overlooked lever in identity transformation lies in language—both spoken words and internal dialogue. As philosopher Ludwig Wittgenstein observed, "The limits of my language mean the limits of my world." This represents not philosophical abstraction but neurological reality.

Words literally create our reality by shaping thought patterns that become actions. The English language contains approximately 3,000 terms for describing emotions, with two-thirds skewed toward negative feelings. This linguistic abundance of negative terminology both reflects and reinforces our brain's negativity bias—our tendency to prioritize and remember negative experiences.

This bias operates at the neural level. Our brains allocate more resources to processing negative events as a survival mechanism. While this adaptation helped our ancestors remain vigilant against threats, in modern life, it manifests as an internal critic undermining our ideal identity.

Self-awareness becomes crucial here. By monitoring our internal dialogues and external communication, we uncover the narratives defining our perception of self and world. These patterns often operate below conscious awareness, silently reinforcing limiting identities through seemingly innocent phrases:

- "There's never enough time" reinforces an identity of someone perpetually behind and overwhelmed.
- "I'm just unfocused" strengthens neural pathways, making distraction more likely.
- "I always hire the wrong people" cements an identity of poor judgment in personnel decisions.

These statements function as self-fulfilling prophecies, rewiring your brain to make the stated limitation more persistent.

Transforming these language patterns involves three steps:

First, awareness and identification. Document your frequent negative phrases, particularly noting self-talk patterns during challenges or opportunities. Common examples include "There's no way I can stick to my schedule" or "I'm bad at marketing."

Second, conscious reframing. For each negative phrase, craft a positive counterpart reflecting capability and potential. "There's never enough time" becomes "I prioritize my key tasks." "I'm such a slow writer" transforms into "Each day, my writing improves." This isn't about denying reality but framing it to reinforce your desired identity.

Third, consistent repetition. The power of new phrases emerges through reinforcement. The more you use them, the more they become ingrained, gradually reshaping your self-perception and actions. As neuroscience confirms, "Neurons that fire together, wire together." With repeated activation, these neural connections become more durable and integrated.

STRATEGIC LANGUAGE OPTIMIZATION

Beyond basic reframing, specific language patterns provide potent leverage for identity transformation. These linguistic tools offer specific pathways to reshape your self-concept.

The Power of "Don't" vs. "Can't"

Research by consumer psychology pioneer Dr. Vanessa Patrick reveals that how we frame our self-imposed rules significantly impacts our ability to follow through. The key finding: using "don't" rather than "can't" creates a profound shift in how we perceive limitations.

"Don't" emphasizes personal choice and agency, focusing on what you've decided against rather than what you're unable to do. This transforms perceived limitations into conscious decisions, reinforcing an identity of someone making deliberate choices rather than facing external constraints.

"Can't" implies an external force limiting your options, fostering a victim mentality that undermines agency. "Don't" eliminates this blame dynamic, encouraging ownership and responsibility.

Most importantly, "can't" requires constant willpower, while "don't" registers as a decision already made. This subtle distinction reduces the cognitive load associated with maintaining boundaries.

In practice, transform "I can't eat sweets" into "I don't eat sweets." Each reframing reinforces an identity built on choice rather than limitation.

Transforming "Have To" Into "Get To"

Another decisive linguistic shift replaces "I have to" with "I get to." This simple change transforms perceived obligations into opportunities, altering both your emotional relationship with tasks and the identity reinforced through them.

Compare "I have to go to the gym" with "I get to go to the gym." The first frames exercise as an external obligation, reinforcing an identity of someone requiring external pressure for self-care. The second reframes the same activity as a growth opportunity, supporting an identity of someone who values personal well-being.

This shift doesn't ignore genuine responsibilities—it recognizes the privilege within many "obligations." Having deadlines means meaningful work. Family commitments mean people who care about you. Financial responsibilities mean resources to manage.

By choosing "get to" language, you create a neurological shift toward gratitude and agency, both strengthening an empowered identity.

The "Because" Trap and Excuse Architecture

The word "because" functions as a justification machine. Research shows that simply using this term triggers our brains to accept excuses, even illogical ones. In a study on line-skipping behavior, researchers found people significantly more likely to allow someone to cut ahead if they used "because"—even when the justification made no sense.

This automatic acceptance mechanism becomes a silent identity saboteur when turned inward. Whenever you use "because" to explain performance gaps, missed goals, or procrastination, you reinforce neural pathways supporting limitation rather than capability:

- "I didn't finish the project because I'm just not good with deadlines."
- "I didn't make those calls because I'm not a natural salesperson."
- "I didn't exercise because I was tired."

Each statement seems innocuous—a simple explanation of circumstance— but neurologically, they function as identity reinforcers, making similar outcomes more likely.

Breaking free from this cycle requires recognizing your justifications and actively challenging them. When catching yourself using "because" to explain shortfalls, ask: "Is this reason truly valid, or am I using it as an escape?" Then reframe with action: "How can I ensure a different outcome next time?" This shifts your language from justification to solution, supporting an identity of capability rather than limitation.

BEYOND SELF-TALK

While internal dialogue forms the foundation of identity, external communication creates social reinforcement that either supports or undermines your desired self-concept. Your words, when interacting with others, don't merely express thoughts—they shape how others perceive and respond to you, creating feedback loops that strengthen or weaken your identity.

The Complaint Contagion

According to organizational anthropologist Dr. Judith Glaser's Emotional Language Theory, our words don't just express emotions; they literally shape them through neurochemical responses.

Negative language triggers the amygdala, leading to heightened stress and fear responses that overpower the brain's rational center. The prefrontal cortex—responsible for reasoning and emotional regulation—becomes less effective when flooded with stress hormones released through negative communication.

This neural response affects more than mood—it directly impacts identity. Each complaint-focused conversation strengthens neural pathways supporting a victim's identity rather than an empowered one. You literally train your brain to focus on problems instead of solutions, on limitations instead of possibilities.

The antidote isn't forced positivity but strategic appreciation. Research by social psychologist Dr. Barbara Fredrickson demonstrates that focusing on gratitude broadens perspective, fosters resilience, and strengthens relationships—all essential components of a strong identity. This shift can be as simple as reframing "This traffic is awful" to "I'm grateful for this time to listen to music and relax."

The Power of "I Am" Statements

No linguistic pattern impacts identity more directly than "I am" statements. These declarations don't merely describe your current state—they program your future by reinforcing specific neural pathways.

Dr. Carol Dweck's Growth Mindset Theory highlights the profound difference between fixed statements like "I am bad at public speaking" and growth-oriented ones like "I am learning to become a confident speaker." The first creates a permanent identity limitation, while the second establishes an identity of growth and development.

Every "I am" statement makes a declaration to both your brain and the world about who you are. These statements become self-fulfilling prophecies through neurological reinforcement.

This doesn't mean avoiding honest self-assessment but being strategic about identity implications. Even when acknowledging current limitations, framing them as temporary states rather than permanent traits creates space for growth and transformation.

THE ULTIMATE IDENTITY LEVER

Throughout our exploration of identity engineering, one theme emerges clearly: ownership serves as the meta-skill unlocking transformation. Taking complete responsibility for your thoughts, language, state, and, ultimately, your actions becomes the key that unlocks an empowered self.

When blaming external factors or relying on chance, you remain a passive observer, allowing circumstances to dictate your identity. By taking ownership, you step onto the path of active identity creation, becoming the architect rather than the inhabitant of your self-concept.

This doesn't require ignoring external influences or denying hardships. It means acknowledging them while recognizing your power to choose your response. This ownership extends to keeping promises to yourself. Consider a friend who constantly cancels plans. The first cancellation might be forgiven, but repeated flakiness erodes trust. This scenario mirrors your relationship with yourself. When failing to follow through on personal commitments, from skipped workouts to overindulging, you chip away at your self-confidence and internal integrity.

Each broken promise diminishes self-confidence, fuels negative self-talk, and creates growing dissatisfaction. Conversely, each kept promise strengthens your identity as someone reliable, disciplined, and worthy of trust—even from yourself.

To enhance this self-trust, start with small, achievable daily commitments. Establish non-negotiable actions you complete regardless of mood or circumstance. Regularly reflect on your commitments, adjusting them to remain challenging but attainable. Celebrate each kept promise, reinforcing neural pathways supporting your desired identity.

Harnessing The Alter Ego Effect

While reshaping your authentic identity forms our primary focus, another powerful approach can accelerate transformation: strategically adopting an alter ego. This method, popularized by performance coach Todd Herman, challenges you to embody personas encapsulating your most desired behaviors and traits.

The Alter Ego Effect leverages identity-based habits. Rather than focusing on what you need to do differently, you shift attention to becoming the kind of person who naturally performs those behaviors. It's about embodying characteristics of your ideal self, making your actions an authentic expression of your desired identity.

This approach isn't about pretending—it creates a bridge between your current and desired identities. By temporarily stepping into a carefully crafted persona, you access capabilities just beyond your current self-concept. Over time, these experiences integrate into your core identity, making previously challenging behaviors feel natural.

Creating an effective alter ego begins with envisioning your "Perfect Life Character"—a version of you living your dream life, embodying qualities you aspire to. Through reflection, identify habits ready for shedding, behaviors needing less space, positive actions to maintain, and new challenges to embrace.

Next, confront what's holding you back—challenges like imposter syndrome, lack of intentionality, societal pressures, self-doubt, and emotional barriers. This honest assessment allows the creation of a persona specifically designed to overcome these obstacles.

The power often comes from giving your alter ego a distinct name and identity, like Beyoncé's "Sasha Fierce" or Kobe Bryant's "Black Mamba." This naming gives presence and power, making it easier to summon when needed. Many high achievers use specific rituals to activate their alter egos—whether symbols, mantras, or physical items triggering the transition.

As you master this art, you can create distinct alter egos for various life dimensions: an assertive professional persona for work, a patient presence for family interactions, or a disciplined "fitness beast" for health pursuits. Each alter ego calls forth your full potential in different contexts.

This isn't role-playing for its own sake—it's strategic identity management, allowing access to your optimal self across life domains. Eventually, the strongest aspects of these alter egos integrate into your authentic identity, creating lasting transformation through temporary embodiment.

Taking ownership of your identity isn't a one-time event but a continual process of self-discovery and intentional growth. It requires ongoing commitment, but the rewards prove immense. By consciously reshaping your neural architecture through strategic action, state management, and language optimization, you unlock your true potential and pave the way for a life filled with purpose, meaning, and fulfillment. Remember: you author your story. Take ownership of the pen, and write a masterpiece worthy of your potential.

THE SELF-SABOTAGE TRAP

We've explored how dopamine dysregulation can lead to self-sabotage—pushing us toward quick hits of pleasure while making sustained effort feel exhausting. Looking deeper, it becomes clear that self-sabotage isn't merely neurochemical. It's psychological, emotional, and deeply tied to identity.

Most people assume that when they fail to follow through on goals, it stems from a lack of discipline or motivation. Yet repeatedly, we see high performers—people with strong habits, systems, and discipline—still hitting invisible walls blocking their next level. They procrastinate on opportunities that could change everything. They withdraw just as success comes within reach. They create unnecessary chaos when things finally flow smoothly.

These behaviors appear irrational. Why would someone desiring success actively undermine it? Beneath this contradiction lies a powerful mechanism few recognize: an internal thermostat governing how much success, happiness, and growth we subconsciously permit ourselves to experience.

Psychologist Gay Hendricks identified this as the Upper Limit Problem—the concept that we all maintain a subconscious comfort zone for success. When life begins exceeding that threshold, we instinctively pull back. Not because we consciously want failure, but because part of our neural architecture isn't calibrated for that achievement level yet.

Think of your mind as a sophisticated climate control system. If your internal thermostat for success is set at 72°F, all your mental and behavioral systems work to maintain that range. When an opportunity arises that could elevate your life to 85°F—greater recognition, increased income, expanded influence—your system automatically triggers cooling mechanisms to return to your established "normal," even when that normal no longer serves your highest aspirations.

The real challenge: most people never realize this thermostat exists. They attribute struggles to external obstacles or temporary motivational lapses, utterly unaware that their own subconscious programming actively maintains the status quo.

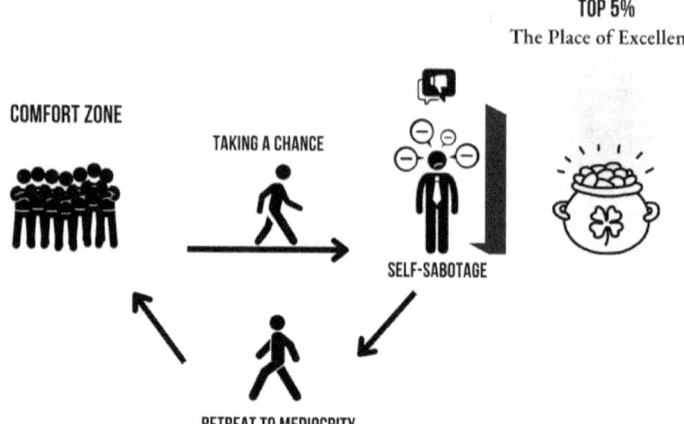

This self-imposed ceiling isn't monolithic—it manifests through several distinct patterns, each playing a unique role in keeping you within familiar boundaries.

THE SEVEN PSYCHOLOGICAL SABOTEURS

Over decades of research, psychologists have attempted to categorize self-sabotage through various frameworks—from Freudian defense mechanisms to contemporary behavioral models. Drawing from these sources and patterns observed in high performers, we can identify eight distinct saboteurs that repeatedly derail peak performers from reaching their full potential.

Each saboteur operates through unique mechanisms, but they share a common purpose: maintaining psychological equilibrium by keeping you within what feels "normal," regardless of whether those boundaries support your highest aspirations.

The Overwhelmer

The Overwhelmer thrives on the chaotic symphony of overwork and insufficient recovery, masquerading as dedication while quietly leading toward burnout and diminished productivity.

This saboteur emerges from a culture glorifying busyness and undervaluing strategic rest. Entrepreneurs, executives, and ambitious professionals often fall into this trap, believing more hours inevitably lead to greater success.

The sabotage operates through several mechanisms: constant overwork impairs decision-making abilities in the prefrontal cortex; fatigue erodes self-control, leading to impulsivity; physical and mental health deteriorate; creativity diminishes; and eventually, complete burnout follows.

Combating the Overwhelmer requires developing awareness of these patterns, implementing strict work boundaries, prioritizing tasks based on impact rather than urgency, scheduling regular recovery periods, and adopting a holistic approach that values quality over quantity. Additionally, challenge conventional wisdom about productivity by staying open to innovative approaches that break traditional work patterns.

The Quick-Fix Seeker

This saboteur relentlessly pursues immediate results while dismissing gradual progress. It thrives in our instant-gratification culture, prioritizing speed over quality and short-term wins over sustainable growth.

The Quick-Fix Seeker sabotages through short-term thinking, impatience with natural learning curves, missed opportunities for depth, and eventual burnout from constant pressure for immediate results.

The most telling sign: giving up right before exponential growth would occur—abandoning projects just before the compound effect of consistent effort would yield significant results.

Overcoming this saboteur requires setting realistic expectations, embracing a growth mindset, valuing learning over immediate perfection, practicing patience, and implementing reflective practices that help recognize incremental progress. Be cautious of falling into repetitive patterns of solution-seeking that prevent true innovation and deep learning.

The Distortionist

The Distortionist warps perception, bending interpretations to fit distorted narratives. This saboteur thrives on cognitive biases—systematic deviations from rational judgment.

It operates through selective abstraction (focusing on single negative details while ignoring positive context), personalization (attributing external events to yourself without logical connection), and magnification/minimization (catastrophizing problems while undervaluing achievements).

These distortions impair decision-making, reduce resilience, and stifle growth by attributing outcomes to fixed traits rather than effort and strategy. The Distortionist can also manifest as an over-reliance on past experiences or conventional wisdom, limiting your ability to see novel solutions and adapt to changing circumstances.

Combating the Distortionist requires cultivating mindfulness, seeking objective feedback, employing cognitive reframing techniques, and developing a growth mindset—viewing abilities as developable rather than fixed. Actively challenge your existing mental models and seek diverse perspectives to break free from restrictive thinking patterns.

The Comfort Seeker

The Comfort Seeker resists stepping beyond the familiar—preferring known territories over uncertain potential. While providing temporary security, this saboteur ultimately hampers growth, innovation, and achievement of full potential.

It limits personal development by preventing new skill acquisition, causes missed opportunities, and reinforces limiting beliefs. This saboteur proves particularly deceptive because comfort feels good momentarily, making long-term costs less obvious.

Strategies for overcoming include embracing eustress (positive stress driving growth), understanding neuroplasticity to reduce change-related anxiety, taking incremental steps toward discomfort, seeking manageable challenges, and expanding your comfort zone through strategic learning experiences. Be intentional about challenging your existing approaches and seeking out environments that push you beyond familiar boundaries.

The Misinterpreter

The Misinterpreter thrives on misunderstandings, leading to incorrect conclusions from ambiguous information. This cognitive distortion results from biases, insufficient data, or over-reliance on intuition without adequate evidence.

It manifests through misattributed causality (incorrectly identifying reasons behind successes or failures) and arbitrary inference (drawing definitive conclusions from insufficient information).

This saboteur impairs decision-making through resource misallocation, erodes trust in team settings, and stunts growth by preventing an accurate assessment of performance and feedback.

Countering the Misinterpreter requires seeking diverse perspectives before drawing conclusions, emphasizing data-driven decisions, fostering environments where questions and curiosity flourish, and establishing regular review processes to identify potential misinterpretations. Continuously challenge your initial assumptions and seek comprehensive understanding.

The Light Fearer

This subtle but powerful saboteur manifests as fear of outshining others or believing success might bring negative consequences like isolation, heightened expectations, or overwhelming responsibilities.

The Light Fearer plays on deep concerns about how achievement might change relationships, personal identity, and life demands. It's particularly prevalent in environments that value conformity over individual excellence.

It operates through self-limiting behaviors, avoiding opportunities showcasing talents, and impaired growth from reluctance to embrace challenges that could elevate performance.

Strategies for overcoming include reframing success as collective achievement rather than zero-sum, cultivating supportive networks celebrating excellence, directly addressing fears through conscious examination, and embracing growth mindset viewing achievement as development rather than final destination.

The Self-Doubter

While many attribute self-sabotage to fear of success, psychologist Ellen Hendrickson offers a deeper perspective: true self-sabotage often stems not from fearing ambition itself but from dreading potential failure and public humiliation.

The Self-Doubter erodes confidence and fosters deep-seated unworthiness—not just occasional insecurity but fundamental belief in personal inadequacy. It manifests as impostor syndrome, where external evidence of competence does nothing to overcome the internal conviction of being undeserving.

This saboteur leads to analysis paralysis, risk avoidance, diminished performance through constant internal criticism, and limited growth due to excessive caution.

Combating the Self-Doubter involves cultivating self-compassion, challenging negative self-talk with objective evidence, seeking support and feedback, and celebrating achievements to build success records, gradually shifting self-perception.

EXPANDING YOUR THERMOSTAT FOR SUCCESS

The moment you recognize these patterns operating in your life, you gain leverage to disrupt them. The key isn't fighting against your subconscious thermostat—it's systematically recalibrating it so your next level of success, confidence, and growth feels normal rather than threatening.

This recalibration begins with strategic exposure. The fastest way to reset your success threshold is immersing yourself in environments where higher performance is standard. If you believe earning $100,000 annually represents your ceiling, regularly interacting with seven-figure earners challenges that belief not through abstract theory but through direct experience. Your subconscious gradually adjusts, perceiving that achievement level as normal rather than exceptional.

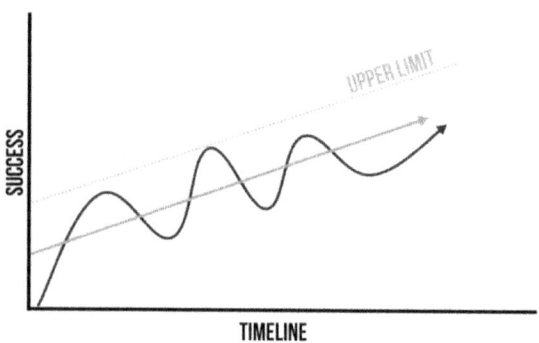

Language calibration provides another powerful lever. As we explored in our discussion of identity, self-sabotage thrives in subtle phrasing patterns:

- "I don't deserve this."
- "This is happening too fast."
- "What if this doesn't last?"

Each reinforces your current thermostat setting. The solution? Deliberate reframing—training yourself to say:

- "I'm learning to operate at this new level."
- "Success at this scale is becoming my new normal."
- "I grow stronger every time I step into the next level."

Finally, you must develop comfort with discomfort. Your next growth stage will naturally feel unnatural—it represents a new setpoint. Rather than interpreting that discomfort as evidence that you're "not ready," recognize it as confirmation that you're expanding. The discomfort isn't a sign of failure—it's evidence of your evolution.

Self-sabotage isn't about insufficient willpower or motivation. It's an unconscious defense mechanism designed to maintain psychological consistency by preventing you from becoming a version of yourself that feels unfamiliar.

The work isn't pushing harder or implementing more productivity hacks. It's expanding your capacity to receive success without triggering the internal resistance that pulls you backward to familiar territory.

Because true high performance isn't just about working harder—it's about making your next level of achievement feel not just possible but inevitable.

FROM SELF-SABOTAGE TO PSYCHOLOGICAL ANTIFRAGILITY

Self-sabotage keeps us stuck in predictable loops—ones designed not to serve our highest potential but to maintain psychological stability. And as we explored in the last section, the subconscious works relentlessly to protect us from perceived threats, even when those threats are actually opportunities for expansion.

But what if we didn't just avoid self-sabotage? What if we went beyond resilience and rewired our minds to actively thrive under pressure, uncertainty, and setbacks?

That's what this section is about.

Antifragility isn't about enduring stress—it's about leveraging it. It's about crafting a mental framework that grows stronger under pressure rather than merely withstanding it. Most importantly, it's about building a system where uncertainty and volatility become fuel for expansion rather than sources of fear.

People who thrive in high-stakes environments don't have less fear, less stress, or fewer setbacks. They've simply trained their minds to process adversity differently. To them, pressure isn't a warning sign—it's evidence of expansion.

Let's start with one of antifragility's most misunderstood aspects: balancing risk and stability without becoming fragile in either direction.

1. Balancing Stability with Strategic Volatility

When people think about becoming mentally stronger, they typically fall into one of two traps:

Some play it too safe, avoiding stress, risk, and uncertainty, believing that staying within their comfort zone ensures security. Over time, this approach makes them remarkably fragile. The moment reality forces them into unpredictable situations, they collapse under pressure.

Others chase extreme risk without safety nets. They take massive, reckless leaps without structure or backup plans. When high-risk bets don't pay off, they suffer catastrophic failure.

Neither approach leads to antifragility. True antifragility isn't about blind exposure to chaos—it's about structuring your life to benefit from volatility without being destroyed by it.

This is where the **_Barbell Strategy_** comes in.

Coined by Nassim Taleb, this strategy suggests that building antifragility requires simultaneously balancing extreme security with extreme adaptability—while avoiding the fragile middle ground where people take risks that harm them without helping them grow.

Imagine holding a barbell. On one end lies stability—a foundation ensuring you're never completely wiped out. On the other, volatility—calculated exposure to stressors forcing growth and adaptation. The mistake most people make? Staying in the fragile middle—taking just enough risk to get hurt but not enough to benefit from uncertainty.

BARBELL STRATEGY

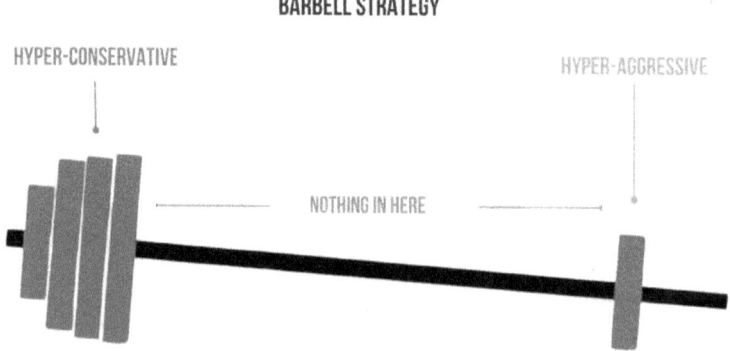

Consider the example of the employee who avoids taking on new challenges to stay comfortable—only to be blindsided when they're suddenly let go and have no alternative career options. Or the entrepreneur who bets everything on a single business model and thrives for a while, right up until a market shift wipes out their entire foundation. Or the athlete who trains the same way for years, believing in the safety of routine, only to watch their performance quietly decline from a lack of adaptation.

The antifragile approach splits effort between extreme security and extreme adaptability:

- In business: Maintain stable income while allocating resources to high-risk, high-reward experiments.
- In personal growth: Maintain strong routines and core competencies while regularly pushing yourself into discomfort and new experiences.
- In mental resilience: Establish grounding rituals while periodically exposing yourself to unpredictable situations.

This structure ensures failure in one area won't break you, while success in another can elevate you dramatically. The key is asymmetry—limiting the downside while keeping the upside uncapped.

2. Embracing Time-Tested Wisdom

How do you determine what belongs on the "stability" side of your barbell? How can you ensure your foundational systems are strong enough to support risk-taking?

This is where the **Lindy Effect** comes in—a principle suggesting that the longer something has been around, the more likely it is to persist into the future. Things that have survived time and adversity are often more antifragile than short-lived trends.

Most people chase what's new—the latest self-help framework, newest business hack, or cutting-edge productivity system. In doing so, they often ignore foundational principles that have withstood time's test.

Antifragile thinkers balance innovation with proven, time-tested strategies:

- Stoic philosophy has guided high performers for over 2,000 years—not because it's trendy, but because it has repeatedly proven itself in war, politics, business, and personal adversity.
- Fundamental strength training principles haven't changed for decades, even as fitness fads come and go.

- Timeless negotiation, persuasion, and strategic warfare tactics—rooted in human psychology—remain the backbone of business and leadership.

When applying the Lindy Effect to the Barbell Strategy, you ensure your stability foundation is built on principles that have already survived countless stressors rather than trendy, unproven methods.

3. Expanding Mental Flexibility

If the Barbell Strategy teaches us how to balance risk and stability, **Psychological Optionality** teaches us how to stay adaptive under uncertainty. It's the difference between someone who collapses when their only strategy fails and someone who effortlessly shifts gears, finding new ways to succeed.

Fragile thinkers operate with a single model of the world—a rigid, linear system that works until it doesn't. They define themselves by one skill, one approach, one strategy. When circumstances change, they're left scrambling.

The most adaptable individuals cultivate multiple paths to success, developing the ability to switch perspectives, adjust strategies, and reinvent themselves when necessary. This is psychological optionality: thinking in multiple dimensions, pivoting when needed, and operating from abundance rather than limitation.

To develop this flexibility:

1. Break free from fixed interpretations of problems by forcing yourself to see situations through multiple lenses before reacting.
2. Ask yourself: "What am I not seeing? What's another way to frame this problem? If I were forced to find three different solutions, what would they be?"
3. Expose yourself to diverse ways of thinking by engaging with ideas, disciplines, and philosophies outside your immediate field.

The best thinkers aren't specialists viewing the world through single lenses. They're generalists with deep expertise in multiple areas, allowing effortless gear-shifting. They think like artists when creativity is needed, like scientists when precision matters, and like strategists when navigating uncertainty.

True optionality extends to identity as well. The more rigidly you define yourself, the harder adaptation becomes when circumstances change. If your entire sense of self ties to one role, career, or achievement, then when that role shifts, you face an identity crisis. By cultivating a flexible self-concept, seeing yourself as an evolving system rather than a fixed entity, you remain adaptable through change.

4. Training the Mind Through Voluntary Hardship

There's a reason the world's toughest people don't panic when things go wrong. It's not that they're immune to stress or fear but that they've trained themselves to be comfortable with discomfort.

Most people treat hardship as an unfortunate, unexpected event—something to be avoided at all costs. But antifragile individuals see hardship differently. To them, hardship isn't just something that happens; it's something they actively seek out and train for.

Growing up in Portugal, I would often hear an expression from the older generation: "A vida é mole para quem é duro, e dura para quem é mole."

Roughly translated, it means: Life is easy for those who are tough, and hard for those who are soft.

At the time, I laughed it off as just another saying grandparents use while shaking their heads at younger generations. But as I experienced more of life, I realized the profound truth in those simple words.

The more fragile you are, the harder life becomes. The less discomfort you can handle, the more suffering you experience. It's a paradox that most people miss—avoiding discomfort doesn't make life easier; it makes you less capable of handling life's inevitable challenges.

This is why, back when we discussed morning routines in Chapter 6, I mentioned including a resilience booster. Some people incorporate cold exposure, plunging into ice-cold showers first thing in the morning. Others wake at challenging hours, deliberately resisting the snooze button's siren call. Some push through workouts they don't feel like doing, training their minds to act despite resistance.

But here's what most people miss: true voluntary hardship isn't just physical—it spans three dimensions, with the psychological aspects being the most powerful for building antifragility.

Physical challenges—like cold exposure, uncomfortable workouts, etc—train your nervous system to remain calm under stress. When you can control your breath and mind in freezing water, you're building the physiological foundation for composure in any stressful situation.

But the mental dimension is where things get interesting. In our distraction-engineered world, training yourself to endure cognitive discomfort becomes a superpower. Most people are mentally fragile—unable to sit still, focus deeply, or persist through boredom. They seek constant stimulation, jumping between tasks, losing themselves in mindless scrolling.

Try this experiment: sit in silence for ten minutes—no phone, no stimulation, no distractions—just you and your thoughts. For most people, this simple challenge feels almost unbearable. Their minds race, seeking escape. Yet this ability to be alone with your thoughts without distraction might be the most critical skill for navigating our hyper-connected world.

Even more powerful is training emotional hardship—deliberately placing yourself in situations of potential rejection, failure, or social discomfort. This doesn't mean being reckless, but it does mean recognizing that your emotional comfort zone is likely too small.

I've watched countless clients transform when they started actively seeking rejection rather than avoiding it. One business owner made it a personal challenge to ask for something outrageous once a week—a massive discount, an impossible deadline, access to someone far above his pay grade. He was shocked to discover how often these "impossible" requests were granted. But more importantly, he found that the rejections stopped feeling devastating—they became data points, nothing more.

This emotional resilience translates directly into antifragility. When you've trained yourself to handle social discomfort, rejection, and failure, you develop the capacity to take calculated risks that others avoid. You can pursue opportunities that might not work out, knowing you'll survive either way. The psychological freedom this creates is extraordinary.

Antifragile individuals don't wait around hoping they'll magically develop resilience when life gets tough. Instead, they ensure their mental toughness through deliberate practice sessions that build psychological calluses before they're needed. Developing resilience only when life forces it upon you means forever playing defense, always reacting to what happens. The proactive approach flips this script entirely, turning voluntary hardship into a genuine competitive advantage in every area of life.

This isn't about seeking unnecessary suffering. It's about strategic exposure to stressors that force adaptation. It's about preparing for chaos, while others merely hope it never arrives. By systematically expanding your comfort with discomfort—physically, mentally, and emotionally—you create a mind that doesn't just resist pressure but actively transforms it into growth.

Remember: the strongest person isn't the one who never falls—it's the one who has fallen enough times to know exactly how to get back up.

TAKING CONTINGENCY FURTHER

Consider this ancient wisdom: "It's better to be a warrior in a garden than a gardener in a war." The warrior in peaceful times might look unnecessarily prepared, but when chaos erupts, their training makes all the difference.

This is the essence of contingency thinking—not constantly living in fear but acknowledging reality: challenges will come, often when least expected. The difference between those who crumble and those who thrive isn't luck or innate toughness—it's preparation.

In Chapter 10, we discussed the importance of "If-This/Then-That" planning—having pre-set responses for common obstacles so that when distractions or setbacks happen, you already know how to handle them without hesitation.

That's an essential first step. But there's a world of difference between having a plan for one disruption and being prepared for real-world chaos. Think of it like a fire drill for your brain. The best time to discover you panic under pressure isn't during an actual emergency but when you still have time to adjust your responses.

Antifragile systems don't just handle one problem at a time. They absorb multiple shocks simultaneously and somehow come out stronger. This is why real contingency planning goes beyond simple if-then scenarios.

A soldier doesn't train in perfect conditions. They simulate battlefield chaos, testing their ability to adapt when plans shatter, communications fail, and unexpected threats emerge. A pilot doesn't just memorize emergency procedures for engine failure. They train for scenarios where multiple critical systems fail at once, forcing them to prioritize under extreme pressure.

This approach transforms how you handle life's inevitable complications. Most people's breaking point isn't a single challenge but the overwhelming feeling when several things go wrong at once. Your car breaks down the same day you lose a client and your child gets sick. Your project deadline moves up while your key team member quits and your supply chain collapses.

Life rarely throws one problem at a time. It launches simultaneous challenges, each amplifying the others.

The solution isn't creating more contingency plans. It's developing a contingency mindset.

Start by running mental "worst-case scenarios"—actively imagining how you'd react if multiple systems failed simultaneously. What if your most important project collapsed the same day a personal crisis hit? How would you pivot if you lost your primary income source tomorrow? What happens if your identity-defining skill suddenly becomes irrelevant?

The goal isn't dwelling on catastrophe. It's eliminating blind spots and forcing your brain to develop adaptive pathways before you need them. When you mentally rehearse complex failure scenarios, you're literally building neural networks that support calm, effective responses rather than panic.

You'll notice something fascinating happens when you regularly practice these mental scenarios: your brain gets better at improvisational problem-solving. Real-world challenges that would have overwhelmed you before suddenly feel manageable—not because they're easier, but because you've expanded your capacity to handle complexity.

This approach transforms how you handle life's inevitable complications. By mentally rehearsing complex failure scenarios, you build neural pathways that support adaptive thinking when real challenges arise. The result isn't just better preparation—it's a fundamentally different relationship with uncertainty.

While most people hope difficulties never arrive, you'll develop the capacity to extract opportunities from them. That's the essence of antifragility—not just surviving chaos but leveraging it as fuel for growth.

Nature's Redundancy Principle

Ever notice how your body doesn't just have one kidney when you technically only need one to survive? Or how your brain can reroute neural connections after injury? This isn't random; it's brilliant biological engineering for contingency.

Nature never builds systems with zero redundancy. Your DNA contains error-correction mechanisms. Your immune system maintains multiple defense layers. Your brain creates backup pathways for critical functions.

The most antifragile individuals apply this same principle across many life domains. Here are a few examples:

Financial redundancy: Beyond emergency funds, they develop multiple income streams that operate independently. When one revenue source faces disruption, others continue flowing.

Skill redundancy: Rather than developing a single expertise, they build complementary capabilities that create multiple paths to value. The designer who also codes. The scientist who communicates complex ideas to the public. These intersections become valuable when environments change.

Emotional redundancy: They cultivate diverse support connections—mentors for guidance, peers for understanding, and friends for lightness. This network ensures no single relationship bears the entire weight of their emotional needs.

Just as your two kidneys aren't inefficient "backup" (they're intelligent redundancy), these buffers aren't paranoid over-preparation. They're sophisticated architecture that converts volatility from a threat into an advantage.

FROM SETBACK TO STRENGTH

When adversity strikes - whether from a planned challenge or an unexpected crisis - your brain doesn't just passively experience it. Your neurological system processes the event through distinct phases that determine whether this experience becomes a source of lasting damage or remarkable growth.

This processing happens whether you're conscious of it or not. But by understanding and deliberately guiding this natural sequence, you can transform almost any setback into a foundation for greater capability.

Let's explore the four distinct phases of this process—Deal, Feel, Heal, and Seal—and how mastering each one transforms your relationship with adversity.

Phase 1: Deal — The Prefrontal Override

The moment adversity hits, your amygdala fires up, triggering a cascade of stress hormones. This is where most people get stuck in an extended fight-or-flight response that clouds judgment and burns mental energy.

The antifragile approach involves what neuroscientists call a "prefrontal override"—deliberately activating your prefrontal cortex to assess reality without emotional distortion:

"Here's what actually happened. These are the concrete facts. These are the immediate implications."

This isn't cold detachment but strategic clarity. By engaging your prefrontal cortex first, you prevent the amygdala from hijacking your cognitive resources, allowing you to direct energy toward solutions rather than resistance.

I watched this play out with Manuel, one of my clients who faced a catastrophic data loss in his business. While his team panicked, he immediately focused on the objective reality: which data was affected, what recovery options existed, and what immediate steps would minimize damage. This prefrontal engagement didn't eliminate the challenge, but it prevented the emotional spiral that would have made it worse.

Phase 2: Feel — The Emotional Integration Circuit

Here's where antifragile psychology diverges most dramatically from toxic positivity. While some approaches encourage suppressing negative emotions, research shows this actually prolongs their neurological impact and prevents processing.

When you allow yourself to feel the emotional weight of setbacks—without being consumed by them—something incredible happens in your brain. The ventral striatum and anterior cingulate cortex activate in a pattern neuroscientists call "emotional integration," essentially metabolizing difficult emotions rather than storing them.

The key distinction is between *experiencing* emotions and *identifying* with them. When you say "I am devastated" instead of "I feel devastation," you're neurologically encoding that state as part of your identity rather than a temporary experience.

People often make the mistake of bypassing this phase, creating "emotional residue"—unprocessed neural patterns that resurface later as anxiety, burnout, or decision paralysis. When you allow yourself to feel without judgment, you're completing a necessary neurobiological cycle.

Phase 3: Heal — The Neuroplastic Learning Loop

Once you've faced reality and processed the emotional impact, your brain enters its most extraordinary phase—what researchers call "post-traumatic growth potential." This is where your neural architecture becomes remarkably adaptable, actively scanning for lessons and restructuring connections based on new information.

This heightened neuroplasticity represents a temporary window where adversity can literally rewire your brain for greater capability. However, only if you direct it properly. Most people miss this opportunity, allowing random associations to form instead of intentionally extracting the lessons that would prevent similar failures.

The antifragile approach involves three specific questions that activate different regions of the prefrontal cortex:

1. "What systems failed under pressure?" (activating analytical processing).
2. "What unexpected vulnerabilities were revealed?" (engaging pattern recognition).
3. "What specific changes would prevent this in the future?" (stimulating solution-focused networks).

This isn't just reflection; it's strategic neural reorganization. You're building new synaptic connections that transform the failure from a setback into a structural advantage.

Phase 4: Seal — Identity Reconsolidation

The final phase is where temporary adaptation becomes permanent transformation. Neuroscientists call this "reconsolidation"—the process where existing neural networks are opened, modified, and then stabilized in their new configuration.

This is where you transition from "I experienced a failure" to "I am someone who has evolved beyond this type of failure."

The most powerful way to facilitate this phase is through strategic narrative construction—literally telling yourself the story of what happened in a way that emphasizes growth, learning, and evolution rather than victimhood or shame. This isn't denial or toxic positivity; it's selective attention to the aspects of experience that build rather than diminish your capabilities.

This four-phase process—Deal, Feel, Heal, Seal—isn't just a cute framework. It's a neurobiologically sound approach to transforming adversity from something that breaks you down into something that builds you up.

The remarkable thing? This process can be learned, practiced, and mastered—turning life's inevitable challenges from sources of suffering into catalysts for evolution.

THE PSYCHOLOGY OF SUSTAINABLE SUCCESS

If mental toughness alone guaranteed lasting success, every stubborn person would be thriving. Yet, in reality, the path to sustainable excellence requires more than just the ability to withstand pressure.

In my work with high performers, I see a consistent pattern. They build incredible resilience, push through any obstacle, and accumulate impressive achievements. However, somehow, fulfillment remains elusive. It's like climbing a mountain only to discover it was just the foothill of an even larger peak.

Despite mastering antifragility and achieving their goals, many remain perpetually dissatisfied, always grinding, constantly chasing the next milestone without ever feeling like they've truly arrived.

The problem isn't their capacity for hard work or ability to handle pressure. They've mastered half the equation, but something critical is missing.

Think of it like training yourself to run a marathon—building the endurance and strength to push through every mile. But if you never look around, never enjoy the race, never feel proud of how far you've come, you're left endlessly chasing finish lines without ever truly experiencing the joy of running.

This is why we need to integrate Positive Psychology with the antifragility we've built so far. Not as a replacement, but as the essential complement that transforms mere survival into genuine thriving.

While antifragility teaches you how to grow from adversity, Positive Psychology shows you how to generate the mental resources that make sustained performance enjoyable. It's about engineering a system that delivers both toughness and happiness.

LEARNED OPTIMISM

Dr. Martin Seligman, often called the father of Positive Psychology, didn't start his career studying happiness. Ironically, he began by investigating why people give up.

In his groundbreaking research on learned helplessness, Seligman discovered something remarkable about how the brain processes setbacks. When dogs in his experiments were subjected to unavoidable shocks, they eventually stopped trying to escape, even when escape later became possible. They had literally learned to be helpless.

The implications for human performance were profound. When people repeatedly face situations where they feel powerless, their brains don't just register disappointment—they undergo neurological adaptation. The motivation centers literally recalibrate, reducing effort output because they've "learned" that effort doesn't make a difference.

What transformed Seligman's work, however, came from an unexpected source—his five-year-old daughter. As the story goes, Seligman was irritably weeding his garden when his daughter began playfully throwing weeds into the air. After he snapped at her, instead of retreating, she stood tall and delivered unexpected wisdom:

"Daddy, do you remember when I used to whine all the time? One day, I decided to stop, and I did. If I can stop whining, you can stop being so grumpy."

This seemingly simple moment triggered a profound insight: If helplessness could be learned, couldn't optimism be learned through the same neurological pathways?

This question led to decades of research confirming that our response to challenges isn't fixed—it's programmable. The key discovery was that it's not events themselves that determine our resilience but the explanatory style we use to interpret them.

Seligman identified two distinct explanatory styles that people use when facing setbacks:

The **pessimistic style** frames challenges through what he calls the three Ps:
- Permanence: "This will always be this way."
- Pervasiveness: "This ruins everything."
- Personalization: "This is entirely my fault."

The **optimistic style** takes the opposite approach to each P:
- Permanence: "This is temporary and will pass."
- Pervasiveness: "This affects one specific area, not my entire life."
- Personalization: "Many factors contributed to this, not just me."

This isn't about positive thinking or denying reality. It's about taking control of your interpretations. Remember how your explanations and language patterns directly shape your neural architecture? This is that principle in action.

When you consistently interpret setbacks through the lens of temporary, specific circumstances rather than permanent, pervasive failures, you maintain agency over your response. Each time you choose the optimistic explanatory style, you're reinforcing those neural pathways we discussed earlier—the same pathways that determine whether you persist or surrender when facing obstacles.

In essence, learned optimism is taking ownership applied specifically to how you process setbacks. It's another powerful lever in transforming your relationship with adversity.

BEYOND OPTIMISM

When most people hear "positive psychology," they imagine reciting affirmations in the mirror or forcing a smile despite difficulties. This superficial understanding misses the science-based depth that makes this field so powerful for building antifragility.

Positive psychology isn't about fake positivity or denying life's challenges. It's about deliberately cultivating psychological resources that enhance resilience and performance. Dr. Martin Seligman, after decades researching how people overcome adversity, developed the PERMA framework, identifying five core elements of psychological flourishing:

- Positive emotion: Experiencing feelings like joy, gratitude, and contentment.
- Engagement: Becoming fully absorbed in activities (similar to flow states).
- Relationships: Building and maintaining positive connections with others.
- Meaning: Belonging to and serving something beyond yourself.
- Accomplishment: Pursuing achievement, competence, and mastery.

Throughout this book, we've already explored several of these elements. Our deep dive into flow states in Chapter 10 covered engagement. Our exploration of social connections in Chapter 8 addressed relationships. Our work with purpose-driven goals touched on meaning.

However, to create a complete psychological architecture for antifragility, we need a systematic approach to cultivating the remaining elements, particularly positive emotion and accomplishment. This is where a daily practice becomes essential.

I've developed a simple yet powerful framework called GPSx3 that targets these psychological resources through three daily reflections:

- G – Gratitude: Three specific things you're grateful for today.
- P – Pride: Three things you're proud of accomplishing or handling well.
- S – Success: Three wins, however small, that represent progress.

Let's explore how each component builds antifragility through different aspects of the PERMA model:

Gratitude activates positive emotion pathways, which we touched on in Chapter 8 for stress management. But in the context of antifragility, gratitude offers something more powerful than just stress reduction.

Unlike affirmations, which often create cognitive dissonance when they don't match your current reality, gratitude works with what already exists. When you repeat phrases like "I am successful" but don't feel that way, your brain flags the discrepancy. Gratitude, however, acknowledges real experiences your brain can verify, eliminating this dissonance.

What makes gratitude particularly powerful is how it leverages the Theory of Mutual Exclusivity—a fundamental principle in positive psychology that explains why certain emotional states cannot coexist. Your brain cannot simultaneously maintain contradictory emotional states due to the way neural pathways operate. When you genuinely experience positive emotions like gratitude, joy, or curiosity, you physically cannot maintain high levels of anxiety, anger, or fear at the same time. This isn't just a psychological phenomenon but a neurobiological reality.

By deliberately activating gratitude circuits, you're not just "thinking positive" but strategically suppressing stress responses at the neural level, creating the biochemical conditions for clearer thinking and better decision-making.

Pride reinforces the accomplishment dimension by acknowledging your efforts and progress. This isn't about ego or arrogance; it's about consciously registering what you did well. For high achievers who constantly focus on what's next, this deliberate pause to recognize capabilities builds self-efficacy—your belief in your ability to create desired outcomes.

Success recognition connects daily actions to meaningful progress. It counteracts what researchers call the "arrival fallacy"—perpetually moving the goalposts so that no achievement ever feels "enough." By identifying small wins, you train your brain to register progress rather than constantly scanning for what's still incomplete.

A simple example of a GPSx3 reflection at the end of the day might look like this:

Gratitude:
1. A great conversation with a mentor
2. The opportunity to work on meaningful projects
3. Support from a colleague

Pride:
1. Handling a difficult conversation with confidence
2. Pushing through resistance on a challenging task
3. Staying consistent with a new habit

Success:
1. Completing an overdue report
2. Making measurable progress on a goal
3. Following through on an important commitment

The beauty of this method lies in its simplicity. Five minutes at day's end creates a powerful reset that prevents stress accumulation while building the psychological resources that make you more antifragile over time. Think of it as maintenance for your mental machinery – the regular tune-up that keeps your performance engine running smoothly.

SELF-COMPASSION

If I asked you to name qualities of elite performers, self-compassion probably wouldn't make your top ten list. We tend to associate high achievement with relentless self-criticism, exacting standards, and pushing through pain.

Yet research consistently shows something counterintuitive: self-compassion—treating yourself with the same kindness you'd offer a good friend—actually enhances performance rather than undermining it.

Educational psychologist Dr. Kristin Neff supports that self-compassionate individuals don't lower their standards. Instead, they recover from setbacks faster, maintain motivation longer, and take more strategic risks than those who rely on self-criticism as their primary motivator.

The explanation lies in how self-compassion affects our neurophysiology. Self-criticism triggers threat responses in the brain, activating the amygdala and releasing stress hormones that narrow cognitive function. Self-compassion activates soothing systems, allowing the prefrontal cortex to remain online for better decision-making.

The performance difference becomes more obvious when we look at how people process failure.

Self-critical performers internalize failure as identity ("I am a failure"), avoid similar challenges to protect their self-image, and ruminate on mistakes without extracting valuable lessons. The result? Longer recovery periods and diminished learning.

Self-compassionate performers externalize failure as an event ("That attempt failed"), view setbacks as learning opportunities, and extract lessons without emotional interference. This allows them to return to action more quickly with improved strategies.

At its core, self-compassion for high performers comes down to three key elements, each building on skills we've already developed:

First, recognize that failure is feedback, not a verdict on your worth. This applies the language principles we explored in identity engineering. By separating events from identity—using "That approach failed" instead of "I am a failure"—you create the psychological space needed for objective analysis.

Second, understand that struggle is universal. When setbacks happen, it's easy to believe they are unique personal failures, when in reality, they are part of every ambitious journey. This perspective shift draws on the same reframing techniques we used in our stress mastery work to transform threats into challenges.

Third, develop the ability to observe your emotions without being controlled by them. This builds directly on the interoceptive awareness we cultivated in Chapter 8. By recognizing emotions as temporary signals rather than fixed truths, you can process them without overreaction and maintain cognitive clarity even during setbacks.

Think of it as the difference between two equally dedicated athletes recovering from injury. One berates themselves, creating additional psychological stress that impairs healing. The other acknowledges the setback without judgment, focusing all their energy on optimal recovery. The second athlete returns to peak performance significantly faster, not because they care less, but because their recovery system works better.

Self-compassion isn't a luxury but a necessity for the antifragile performer. Without it, the constant growth from adversity becomes an exhausting grind rather than sustainable evolution. By integrating this approach with the other tools we've developed, you create the neurological conditions where setbacks genuinely strengthen you rather than slowly wearing you down.

Stoicism's Hidden Presence

You've probably noticed the recent explosion of Stoicism in productivity circles—from bestselling books to Silicon Valley CEOs citing Marcus Aurelius. What's interesting is that we've actually been incorporating Stoic principles throughout this book without explicitly naming them.

Stoicism isn't about suppressing emotions (despite the modern misuse of "stoic" to mean emotionless). It's a practical philosophy focused on distinguishing between what you can and cannot control—a principle we've encountered repeatedly in our journey through antifragility.

The Stoic approach can be distilled into three steps:

1. Discern: What aspects of this situation can I directly control?

2. Focus: Direct all energy toward those controllable elements

3. Accept: Let go of attachment to specific outcomes

Sound familiar? When we discussed contingency planning, we emphasized focusing on process rather than outcomes. When exploring stress mastery, we worked on accepting biological responses while controlling our reactions. Our antifragility training centered on directing energy toward areas where effort creates leverage.

The Stoics understood something timeless about human performance: peace of mind comes not from controlling the world but from mastering our responses to it. This perspective creates a natural complement to the positive psychology approaches we've just explored—combining internal resource-building with strategic focus on what truly matters.

YOUR COMPLETE MINDSET BLUEPRINT

What transforms an ordinary performer into an extraordinary one?

After acing time management, exploring the biological foundations of performance, mastering flow mechanics, and building unbreakable grit, we've discovered something profound: the ultimate performance edge lies in your mental architecture. The mindset we've constructed throughout this chapter doesn't just complement your other capabilities; it amplifies them exponentially.

Consider what happens in your brain when you encounter a significant obstacle. With a fixed mindset, that obstacle triggers a threat response. Shift to a growth mindset, and that same obstacle registers as a learning opportunity.

This neurological shift creates dramatically different outcomes. Where one person sees a career-ending failure, another discovers the insight that launches their next breakthrough. Where one sees overwhelming volatility, another finds hidden patterns to leverage. Where one breaks under pressure, another transforms into their most capable self.

Throughout this chapter, we've been systematically building this antifragile mental architecture. We started by understanding how identity literally shapes perception—how the neural networks formed through your experiences, self-talk, and language patterns determine what you even notice about your circumstances. We've seen how self-sabotage operates as a sophisticated thermostat, unconsciously maintaining what feels "normal" even when that normal limits your potential.

We then developed specific protocols to transform these limitations. The barbell strategy showed you how to balance stability with strategic volatility. Psychological optionality gave you the flexibility to shift perspectives when challenges arise. Voluntary hardship trained your capacity to find opportunity in discomfort.

Yet we recognized that toughness alone creates a brittle foundation. By integrating positive psychology practices—from the GPSx3 framework to self-compassion—we've created a complete system that balances resilience with recovery, challenge with support, and growth with fulfillment.

This integrated mindset serves as the control center that directs and amplifies every capability in your performance arsenal. The time management systems from Chapter 4 become exponentially more effective when your mindset supports deep engagement rather than scattered attention. The biological optimization from Chapter 7 creates physical capacity that your mindset deploys with strategic precision. The flow states from Chapter 10 become accessible not by chance but by psychological design.

The true magic of this approach lies in its compound effect. Each individual practice—identity engineering, antifragility training, positive psychology—creates value on its own. However, when integrated into a cohesive psychological system, they create something far greater than the sum of their parts.

This transformation isn't instantaneous. It unfolds through consistent application over time. Small shifts in how you process challenges, interpret setbacks, and maintain motivation gradually rewire your neural architecture. These seemingly minor changes accumulate, creating a mind that naturally sees opportunity where others see obstacles, recovers from setbacks while others remain stuck, and sustains drive when others burn out.

You now possess a mental framework that doesn't just help you perform better occasionally—it fundamentally changes who you become permanently. And that transformation is the ultimate performance advantage.

RESEARCH & RESOURCES

Please visit the Holistic Performance Resource Hub to access the research and additional materials mentioned in this chapter.

To do so, go to hplink.org/resourcehub or scan the QR code below.

CHAPTER 13

PERFORMANCE SYSTEMS

"Losers have goals. Winners have systems."

– Scott Adams

The ultimate test of any performance methodology isn't how well it works when conditions are perfect, but how reliably it functions when they aren't. Even the most disciplined individuals experience fluctuations in motivation, energy, and focus. The difference between sustained excellence and occasional brilliance often boils down to one factor: the systems surrounding the performer.

Throughout our journey together, you've steadily constructed various performance elements: habit loops that automate key behaviors in Chapter 6, physiological optimization systems in Chapter 7, stress management protocols in Chapters 8 and 9, frameworks for reliable flow states in Chapter 10, and psychological resilience systems in Chapters 11 and 12.

What remains unexplored are the systems that exist beyond the individual—frameworks and structures that allow your performance to scale beyond personal limitations, maintain momentum through challenging periods, and evolve alongside your changing goals and circumstances.

Think of it this way: the systems we've built so far optimize you as an individual performer, much like cultivating a champion athlete's mind and body. But even Olympic gold medalists don't achieve greatness in isolation. They rely on coaches, training partners, advanced equipment, and periodization programs that extend beyond daily practice. Similarly, your personal performance requires support systems that transcend individual capabilities.

This chapter introduces four essential system categories that complete your holistic performance architecture:

- Group Performance Systems that extend your capabilities through others.
- Applied Flow Systems that transform your relationship with time and output.
- Technology Enhancement Systems that multiply your effectiveness through strategic tool use.
- Maintenance Systems that ensure your performance ecosystem evolves rather than degrades.

Unlike earlier chapters that built sequentially on each other, these systems function more like specialized tools in your performance toolkit—powerful enhancers you can implement based on your specific needs and circumstances.

Let's begin with perhaps the most powerful multiplier of personal performance: effectively leveraging the capabilities of others through group performance systems.

GROUP PERFORMANCE SYSTEMS

We've spent much of this book focusing on individual optimization—fine-tuning your biology, psychology, and personal systems. Yet even the most disciplined high performers eventually encounter a fundamental limitation: there are only 24 hours in a day, and your personal energy remains finite regardless of optimization.

This is where extraordinary performers diverge from the merely disciplined. While average achievers focus solely on maximizing personal output, remarkable performers build systems that leverage the capabilities, time, and energy of others.

The Accountability Trifecta

Most performance breakdowns occur not from lack of knowledge or ability, but from inconsistent execution. As James Clear notes, "You do not rise to the level of your goals. You fall to the level of your systems." The Accountability Trifecta ensures that your minimum level of performance remains high even during inevitable motivation dips by creating multiple reinforcing layers of support.

The system consists of three distinct but complementary layers:

Layer 1: Social Accountability

Our brains evolved in tribal environments where social standing meant survival. This evolutionary heritage gives social accountability remarkable power in our modern context. When you commit to peers you respect, your brain's reward prediction system links potential failure with social consequences, triggering a protective response that increases follow-through.

Research from the American Society of Training and Development found that making a commitment to someone else increases success rates by 65%, while having a specific accountability appointment with that person raises success rates to 95%.

Andrew, a client who struggled with early morning workouts, finally made them consistent after joining a 6 AM training group. "When I was accountable only to myself, there were always convincing reasons to skip. But knowing others were waiting for me made 'not showing up' feel like the harder option."

For maximum effectiveness, select accountability partners whose standards match or exceed your aspirations. As performance psychologist Jim Loehr observed, "You're the average of the five people you spend the most time with." When those five people consistently perform at a high level, your brain recalibrates its perception of "normal," making excellence your default rather than a constant struggle.

Layer 2: Public Accountability

Public accountability extends social accountability by adding visibility to your commitments. When you publicly announce a goal, your brain's anterior cingulate cortex becomes more sensitive to potential disconnects between your declared intentions and actions, creating an internal error detection system that flags potential failures before they occur.

Ana, a writer who had struggled for years to complete her manuscript, finally finished after announcing her completion date on social media and scheduling a celebration event. "Having a public timeline changed everything," she explained. The social consequences of missing her deadline created momentum that private commitment hadn't.

Effective public accountability includes explicit, measurable declarations of intent; visible tracking mechanisms; and predefined consequences for both success and failure. This creates what psychologists call "pre-commitment"— a decision-making strategy that deliberately limits future choices to overcome potential weaknesses in self-control.

Layer 3: Professional Accountability

The final and often most potent layer involves bringing in specialized expertise in the form of coaches, mentors, or structured programs.

Professional accountability combines financial investment with expert guidance. When you've paid for accountability, your brain's loss aversion circuits—which research shows are twice as powerful as reward-seeking circuits—create a powerful incentive to follow through. Simultaneously, the expert's ability to identify blind spots and refine techniques addresses fundamental limitations of self-guided improvement.

I spent years gathering knowledge and trying to figure things out on my own. Despite all that information, substantial progress in my consulting business only happened when I hired someone to guide me. The financial commitment changed the equation—I wasn't just consuming knowledge; I was invested in execution. More importantly, having someone with experience helped me see patterns I'd been blind to and break through barriers that had kept me stuck far longer than I realized.

Creating Your Integrated Accountability System

The power of the Accountability Trifecta comes from strategic integration rather than the implementation of any single layer. This creates redundancy, ensuring that if one layer falters, others maintain your performance baseline.

Consider how this works for a book writing project requiring sustained effort over months:

At the social layer, you might join a weekly writers' group to share progress. For public accountability, you announce your project timeline with monthly milestone updates on social platforms. At the professional level, you hire a writing coach who reviews chapters and maintains deadlines.

With this system in place, temporary motivation drops don't derail progress. If your internal drive wanes, your group's expectation of new pages keeps you working. If you consider skipping a session, your public commitment maintains momentum. And if both falter, your coach provides the structured accountability ensuring forward motion.

Your specific implementation will vary based on your goals and resources. The essential principle is creating multiple layers of external accountability that complement rather than duplicate each other.

This system isn't about surrendering autonomy—it's about acknowledging the biological reality that internal motivation fluctuates, and creating structures that maintain execution during those natural valleys. When properly implemented, the Accountability Trifecta doesn't feel restrictive but liberating, removing the constant drain of willpower-based execution and replacing it with a system that makes high performance almost automatic.

The Delegation Mastery System

As we discussed in Chapter 5, delegation is critical for effective prioritization. We explored how offloading tasks that don't require your unique talents creates space for high-impact work. But knowing you should delegate is one thing—implementing a systematic approach that actually works is another challenge entirely.

I learned this lesson the hard way. As clinical director overseeing nearly 100 clinicians across a territory of about 5,067 square miles (roughly the size of Montenegro), I found myself drowning in responsibilities. Every day brought new fires to extinguish, reports to compile, and decisions that seemingly only I could make.

I remember sitting in my office at 9 PM one Friday, surrounded by half-eaten takeout and unfinished paperwork, thinking: "I must be surrounded by idiots. Why can't anyone handle these basic tasks without my intervention?"

When I finally attempted to delegate, the results were often disappointing. I'd hand off a task only to find it completed incorrectly, forcing me to redo it with even less time than before. This reinforced my growing conviction that delegation was simply inefficient. "If you want something done right, do it yourself" became my unspoken mantra—a philosophy that nearly led to complete burnout.

What I didn't understand then was that my delegation failures weren't evidence of others' incompetence but the predictable result of a flawed system. I was treating delegation as a binary switch: either I handled something entirely, or I handed it off completely. This all-or-nothing approach ignored the reality that effective delegation exists on a spectrum, with each level appropriate for different situations and team members.

Consider this biologically. Even if you've optimized your sleep, nutrition, and focus to perform at 100% of your potential, you're still constrained by the fundamental limits of human capacity. When you effectively delegate, you're expanding your productive capability beyond what's biologically possible for any single person.

The turning point in my delegation journey came from recognizing a simple economic reality: when I spent time on tasks that someone else could handle at a fraction of my compensation rate, I wasn't being dedicated—I was being wasteful. This isn't just about economics but neurological optimization. The prefrontal cortex has limited capacity for executive function; every decision depletes this resource. By offloading decisions that don't require your unique expertise, you preserve cognitive resources for truly high-value work.

The Five Levels of Delegation: A Progressive System

Effective delegation requires a structured approach that ensures the right level of oversight for each task. Not everything should be handed off the same way, which is why delegation works best as a progression rather than a single-step process.

Level 1: Direct Execution ("Do Exactly As I Say")

At this basic level, you're asking someone to follow precise instructions without deviation. This approach works for simple, standardized tasks with little room for interpretation; training situations where you're establishing baseline procedures; and high-risk scenarios where precision is critical.

The neurological benefit is primarily time recapture, though even this basic level frees up mental bandwidth by removing execution from your plate while maintaining control over the process.

Level 2: Information Gathering ("Research and Report Back")

Here, you delegate the discovery phase while retaining decision-making authority. The delegate researches options and presents findings, but you make the final call.

This works particularly well for decisions requiring specialized information you don't have time to gather, situations where you want to develop someone's research abilities, and complex choices where you need options but want to maintain control.

This level creates more significant cognitive offloading, as the information gathering and initial synthesis—often the most time-consuming parts of decision-making—happen outside your brain.

Level 3: Solution Suggestion ("Propose and Justify Your Recommendation")

At this level, you're asking the delegate not just to gather information but to analyze it and recommend a course of action while explaining their reasoning.

This approach is ideal for developing analytical skills in your team members, situations where you want perspective but need to understand the thought process, and decisions where you're trying to train someone's judgment.

The cognitive benefit is substantial—the delegate handles not just information gathering but also the initial analysis, presenting you with a synthesized recommendation rather than raw data.

Level 4: Decision and Action ("Decide and Update Me")

The delegate now makes the decision and takes action independently, then reports the outcome. You're no longer involved in the decision itself, only in reviewing the results.

This works well for team members who have demonstrated good judgment, lower-stakes decisions where learning opportunities outweigh risks, and situations where speed matters more than perfect execution.

The neurological offloading here is nearly complete—you're freed from both the information-gathering and decision-making processes, only maintaining awareness of outcomes.

Level 5: Full Autonomy ("It's Completely In Your Hands")

The highest delegation level involves transferring complete ownership of an area where the delegate operates independently without regular reporting. This represents the ultimate cognitive offloading, where entire domains of responsibility are managed outside your attention.

This level is appropriate for trusted team members with proven track records, areas outside your core expertise or interests, and functions that benefit from undivided ownership.

José, a marketing agency owner, initially struggled with micromanagement until he implemented this delegation system. "What made the difference was realizing delegation isn't all-or-nothing," he explained. "With new team members, I'd start at Level 2 or 3, then gradually increase their autonomy as they proved themselves. Within six months, I had three key team members operating at Level 5 in their respective areas. My overwhelm dropped dramatically, and our company's output tripled."

Building Your Delegation Mastery System

To create an effective delegation system, begin with a thorough task analysis. Track your activities for a week, documenting everything you do, then classify each task according to:

- *Zone of Genius*: Tasks where your unique talents create exceptional value.
- *Zone of Excellence*: Tasks you do well but others could be trained to handle.
- *Zone of Competence*: Tasks you're adequate at but don't require your specialized skills.
- *Zone of Incompetence*: Tasks others could do better than you.

Your delegation candidates lie primarily in the Zones of Competence and Incompetence, along with many tasks in your Zone of Excellence.

For each task you've identified for delegation, determine who has the capability (or could develop it) to handle it, what level of delegation is appropriate based on task complexity and the person's experience, and what training or resources they'll need to succeed.

Before delegating, document the process for each task. This serves as a training tool for the delegate, a reference for future questions, and a system that can be replicated as your team grows. The most effective documentation combines written procedures with video demonstrations.

For each delegate, implement a structured progression through the delegation levels. Begin at an appropriate level based on task complexity and their experience, establish clear metrics for successful execution, schedule regular review points to assess performance, and incrementally increase autonomy as confidence grows. This progression should be explicit, with the delegate understanding exactly what successful performance looks like at each level and what they need to demonstrate to advance.

Create a system for regular feedback that acknowledges successful execution, identifies areas for improvement, refines the process documentation based on real-world implementation, and adjusts delegation levels based on performance.

Remember that delegation is not abdication—it's a dynamic system requiring ongoing attention, especially in the early stages. The time investment up front pays enormous dividends in cognitive bandwidth and scalable performance over time.

When properly implemented, the Delegation Mastery System creates "performance leverage"—where your impact extends far beyond your personal capacity. This is how extraordinary performers achieve results that seem almost superhuman; they're not doing everything themselves, but orchestrating a system where multiple people execute simultaneously toward a unified vision.

Think of it as biological amplification. Your brain can only control your two hands, but through effective delegation, you can coordinate dozens of hands working in concert. This isn't just about getting more done; it's about exponentially expanding your impact while preserving your most precious resources: time, energy, and cognitive capacity.

APPLIED FLOW SYSTEMS

Have you ever noticed how some days seem to fly by with little to show for them, while on others, you accomplish what feels like a week's worth of work? This phenomenon isn't just a subjective experience but a scientific reality we can harness through "time bending."

In today's world, most of us face time famine—that persistent feeling of having more tasks than time. While the flow states we explored in Chapter 10 help us work more efficiently within our time constraints, time bending takes this optimization to an entirely new level.

Time bending isn't about cramming more work into each hour through sheer effort. It's about fundamentally reimagining our relationship with time itself—creating conditions where your perception shifts and productivity multiplies naturally.

The Dual Nature of Time

The way we conceptualize time profoundly impacts how we experience it. Most of us instinctively operate from what philosophers call "Presentism"— the belief that time flows linearly forward, with each moment unique and fleeting.

But there's another perspective called "Eternalism" that views "now" more like a location in space. In this framework, all points in time exist simultaneously, and our perception of time's flow is partly an illusion. While this might sound abstract, modern physics leans toward this view, suggesting that time is far less linear than our intuition tells us.

If time isn't as rigid as we assume, perhaps our productivity doesn't have to be constrained by conventional time limits either.

Think about how differently we experience time throughout our lives. As children, summer vacations seemed to stretch forever. As adults, years can blur together. Our daily activities similarly warp our perception—an hour with good friends feels like a moment, while a few minutes in discomfort can feel eternal. This malleability is the key to time bending.

Breaking Linear Assumptions

Most productivity frameworks operate on a linear assumption: more hours equal more output. But this relationship often breaks down in practice. I've seen entrepreneurs work 80-hour weeks with less to show for it than colleagues working focused 30-hour weeks.

Parkinson's Law captures this perfectly. Give yourself a week for a project, and it takes a week. Give yourself a day, and surprisingly, you might complete it in a day.

The "Bannister Effect" also illustrates how breaking through perceived limitations can reshape what we believe is possible. When Roger Bannister broke the four-minute mile in 1954, it was considered physiologically impossible. Yet within just 46 days of his achievement, someone else broke it too. Within three years, 16 runners had accomplished this "impossible" feat.

The same phenomenon applies to productivity. Once you experience completing a major project in a fraction of the expected time, your perception of what's possible fundamentally changes.

Strategies for Time Bending

Several scientifically-grounded approaches can alter your experience of time:

Activity Selection & Flow: Deep engagement in challenging, meaningful work can make hours feel like minutes while simultaneously producing exceptional output.

Mindfulness: Full presence paradoxically expands our sense of time. When you're completely engaged with what you're doing, time takes on a different quality. Research shows mindfulness practices physically alter brain regions involved in time perception.

Experience Density: Rich, varied experiences make time feel fuller. This is why travel and novel experiences seem to expand time—your brain creates more memory anchors. Apply this to work by varying your environment or approach to important tasks.

Novelty and Pattern Interrupts: New experiences and unexpected changes in your routine keep your mind alert and engaged, making time seem to slow down as you process new information.

Strategic Variety: Switching between different types of activities can prevent the monotony that makes time blur together, making days feel longer and more productive.

The key insight: you can change your experience of time by changing the content of your experience.

Reality vs. Hype: The One-Day Month

You may have heard of frameworks like the "One Day Month," which claim you can compress a month's worth of work into a single day. The premise is that the average worker only has about 1 hour of "real productivity" per day. In a month, that's roughly 22 hours of actual productive work.

In theory, if you could fit 11 hours of deep work into one day and double your output through flow, you'd get the equivalent of a month's productivity. While I appreciate the concept's boldness, this is significantly exaggerated.

A more realistic but still remarkable possibility: compressing what might take a week into a single, intensely focused day. That's still an extraordinary 5x productivity multiplier without resorting to marketing hype.

Time Bending Is Not Rushing

A critical distinction: time bending is fundamentally different from rushing. Constant hurrying—what cardiologists Meyer Friedman and Ray Rosenman termed "hurry sickness"—is actually time bending's opposite.

This chronic rushing state manifests as speaking rapidly and interrupting others, constant multitasking, always checking the time, persistent anxiety about deadlines, and mentally rehearsing future tasks while completing current ones.

Richard Jolly from London Business School found that 95% of executives exhibit signs of hurry sickness, with entrepreneurs particularly susceptible due to the unique pressures of building a business.

The paradox is that rushing actually makes time seem to pass faster while reducing what you accomplish. The more you rush, the less you achieve, and the more quickly the day disappears. This creates a vicious cycle where you feel increasingly time-poor, leading to more rushing and less actual productivity.

The alternative? Slowing down to speed up. By taking time to be intentional about what truly matters, you make better decisions about where to invest your time and energy. This deliberate approach often accomplishes more in less time than frantic activity ever could.

Creating Your Quantum Productivity Day

Want to experience time bending firsthand? Here's how to structure a quantum productivity day that could compress a week's worth of work into a single focused session:

Preparing for Extraordinary Output

Success begins the day before your quantum productivity session. Just as elite athletes prepare meticulously before a competition, you need to create optimal conditions for cognitive performance:

Ensure you're fully rested. Entering with sleep debt is like trying to run a marathon after an all-night party. Your brain simply won't have the resources needed for sustained focus.

Prepare your physical environment by gathering all materials, resources, and references you might need, organizing them for frictionless access. Every moment spent searching for information during your productivity day is a moment pulled from deep focus.

Clear your schedule entirely and communicate your unavailability. Quantum productivity requires not just physical isolation but psychological separation from pending obligations. When your brain knows nothing else demands attention, it can fully commit to the task at hand.

Set crystal-clear objectives for what you'll accomplish. Vague intentions like "work on the project" won't suffice. Your brain needs specific targets to maintain direction during extended focus.

Plan your sustenance strategy in advance. Decide what you'll eat and when you'll take breaks, eliminating decisions that deplete cognitive resources. Think of this as setting up a cognitive supply line that will fuel your brain throughout the extended campaign ahead.

Execution Day Structure:

For early birds and even larks:

- 5:00-8:00 AM: First Deep Work Block (3 hours)
- 8:00-9:00 AM: Recovery (mindfulness, walk, breathwork)
- 9:00 AM-12:00 PM: Second Deep Work Block (3 hours)
- 12:00-1:00 PM: Recovery (nap, light meal, movement)
- 1:00-3:00 PM: Third Deep Work Block (2 hours)
- 3:00-5:00 PM: Extended Recovery (exercise, meditation)
- 5:00-8:00 PM: Final Deep Work Block (3 hours)

Night owls might start around 9 or even 10 AM and extend deeper into the evening when their cognitive faculties naturally peak. The specific hours matter less than honoring your body's intrinsic rhythms.

Throughout your quantum productivity day, maintain several of the non-negotiable principles we already discussed:

Commit to absolute single-tasking. Your brain isn't designed to focus on multiple complex tasks simultaneously; attempts at multitasking create neurological switching costs that destroy the state you're trying to cultivate.

Eliminate all digital distractions by physically removing them from your environment. Your smartphone should be in another room, not just face-down beside you.

Incorporate strategic recovery periods that involve physical movement. These are deliberate biological resets that clear metabolic waste from the brain and replenish neurochemicals depleted during intense focus.

Fuel your brain appropriately with nutrition that supports sustained cognitive function. Healthy fats or complex carbohydrates provide steady energy, quality proteins support neurotransmitter production, and adequate hydration maintains optimal neural transmission.

Create an environment completely free from interruptions. This might mean working from a location other than your usual space, using noise-canceling headphones, or simply putting a "Do Not Disturb" sign on your door.

This approach yields 11 hours of deep, focused work—far more than most people accomplish in a typical week. But it's not sustainable daily, which brings us to implementation frequency.

Implementation Frequency

The intensity of quantum productivity days means they should be deployed strategically:

- *Acceleration Mode*: Once per month for steady, meaningful progress on important projects.
- *Turbo Mode*: Weekly sessions during intense phases or deadline periods (limited duration).
- *Lightspeed Mode*: Five days per week, but only for extremely short periods (maximum 8 weeks) during extraordinary circumstances like launching a company or completing a make-or-break project.

Remember, the goal isn't pushing yourself to exhaustion. It's creating the optimal conditions where flow becomes probable across extended periods.

Time Bending in Practice: Field Applications

The beauty of quantum productivity isn't just theoretical—it creates tangible results across virtually every professional domain.

Direct Applications:

For many professions, quantum productivity days align perfectly with their work. Entrepreneurs can dedicate entire days to scaling strategies or pivotal business model pivots. Executives might immerse themselves in strategic planning or leadership development. Consultants thrive when crafting comprehensive strategy decks that require both deep analysis and creative synthesis.

Similarly, Software Engineers can tackle complex feature development that demands understanding entire system architectures. Graphic Designers find that creating cohesive visual identities benefits tremendously from the creative evolution that happens during extended immersion. Marketing Specialists can develop launch strategies that require both research depth and creative integration. Writers often experience their most productive sessions when they can maintain narrative flow without interruption.

One founder I worked with used this approach to completely reimagine his company's service offering—work that had lingered on his to-do list for months. The uninterrupted clarity made connections possible that never emerged during his typical fragmented workdays.

Indirect Applications:

Even roles that seem less conducive to day-long deep work sessions have high-leverage projects that benefit from quantum productivity.

Sales Staff might not dedicate entire days to client interactions, but they can transform their effectiveness by using focused days to refine sales scripts based on customer feedback. Real Estate Agents typically spend their days showing properties, but strategic days focused on developing innovative marketing campaigns for unique properties can set them apart in competitive markets.

Teachers can use quantum productivity days during breaks to yield interactive, digital curriculum innovations that would otherwise take weeks to complete in fragmented planning sessions. HR Professionals can revolutionize their impact by creating automated, personalized onboarding systems that improve employee integration for years to come.

Even medical professionals find valuable applications. Physicians can dedicate occasional days to developing new diagnostic techniques or treatment protocols. Therapists might use focused sessions to streamline assessment processes or create client education materials that improve outcomes for hundreds of patients.

The key insight is that quantum productivity isn't about your day-to-day responsibilities—it's about identifying those high-impact projects that remain perpetually on the back burner because they don't fit neatly into fragmented time blocks. Every profession has these opportunities, though they may arise monthly rather than weekly for some roles.

As you consider applications in your own field, look for projects that would create disproportionate value if completed, have resisted completion during standard work patterns, require complex thinking or creative development, would benefit from uninterrupted cognitive momentum, and could establish systems or frameworks that improve all future work.

The Ripple Effect Beyond Productivity

Perhaps the most beautiful aspect of time bending is that it isn't just about getting more done—it fundamentally expands how much life you experience. By mastering your relationship with time, you create space for what truly matters.

This is the ultimate promise of quantum productivity: not just accomplishing more but experiencing more of what makes life meaningful.

When you can achieve a week's work in a day, you gain days to invest in relationships, health, creative pursuits, or whatever brings you joy.

In a world increasingly characterized by time poverty, the ability to bend time might be the most valuable skill you can develop. Not to fill every moment with more work, but to create the freedom to choose how you spend the precious currency of your life.

TECHNOLOGY ENHANCEMENT SYSTEMS

Remember when science fiction promised us robot butlers and flying cars, but instead, we got endless notifications and digital distractions? The irony of our technological revolution is impossible to miss. The very tools designed to make us more productive often end up fragmenting our attention and hijacking our focus.

Yet technology itself isn't the villain in our performance story. Used strategically, it functions as a powerful force multiplier for everything we've built throughout this book. The critical difference between tech as a distraction versus tech as an enhancement comes down to intentionality.

Think of technology like fire—one of humanity's earliest transformative tools. Fire can warm your home or burn it down, depending entirely on how you use it. Our digital tools follow the same principle. When implemented with clear purpose and strategic boundaries, they can expand your capabilities far beyond what's humanly possible alone.

The Four Categories of Performance Technology

When we strip away the endless bells and whistles of the latest apps and gadgets, truly impactful technology falls into four fundamental categories:

1. Automation Systems

The highest leverage use of technology isn't doing things faster—it's eliminating the need to do them at all. Automation systems take repeatable processes off your plate entirely, freeing your cognitive resources for work that actually requires human creativity and judgment.

This goes far beyond basic email filters or calendar reminders. Modern automation tools can handle sophisticated tasks from data collection and analysis to complex decision trees based on predefined criteria. Services like Zapier, Make, or Pabbly connect different applications and create workflows that previously required human intervention.

One of my clients, a marketing consultant, automated her entire client onboarding process—from initial contact form to contract generation, scheduling the first call, and personalizing welcome materials based on the client's specific needs. What once took 3-4 hours of administrative work now happens automatically, allowing her to focus exclusively on high-value strategy.

Sometimes, the highest ROI comes from simplifying everyday annoyances. Consider how much mental bandwidth is consumed when you repeatedly type the same responses to common questions, manually track data you need regularly, convert information between formats, or search for misplaced files. Each of these seemingly minor tasks creates cognitive friction that compounds over time. By identifying and automating these small but repetitive processes, you effectively plug the energy leaks in your day.

2. Augmentation Tools

While automation eliminates tasks, augmentation tools enhance your ability to perform complex work that remains inherently human. These technologies don't replace your thinking—they extend it, allowing you to accomplish more than would be possible through natural abilities alone.

AI writing assistants can help generate first drafts or refine your existing work. Research tools can synthesize information from thousands of sources in seconds. Project management systems can maintain complex organizational structures that would overwhelm the human brain's working memory capacity.

Consider what happens neurologically when you offload organizational functions to appropriate tools. Your prefrontal cortex has severely limited capacity. When you try to maintain complex organizational systems in your head, you're essentially running your brain's most sophisticated region at maximum capacity, leaving little bandwidth for actually solving problems.

By contrast, effective augmentation tools create what psychologists call "extended cognition"—expanding your mental capabilities beyond your biological limitations. Your brain forms a partnership with these tools, focusing its remarkable abilities on what it does best while delegating supportive functions to technology.

3. Integration Systems

While automation eliminates tasks entirely, integration systems solve a different problem—they create seamless connections between your various tools. Think of automation as hiring a robot assistant to handle specific tasks, whereas integration is more like building hallways between previously separate buildings.

Most professionals today use multiple applications: a writing tool, a task manager, a calendar, communication platforms, and specialized tools for their industry. Without proper integration, these tools become digital silos, forcing you to constantly switch contexts. You manually copy information from one app to another, navigate between different interfaces, and mentally reconnect what should be unified workflows.

Here's how this fragmentation typically plays out: You receive project requirements in an email, manually copy them to your notes app, create related tasks in your task manager, schedule time blocks in your calendar, then store reference materials in yet another location. Each transition requires you to shift attention, remember where information belongs, and rebuild context—a process that drains your prefrontal cortex's limited resources.

Integration systems eliminate these transitions by creating automated connections between different tools. For example:

- When you receive a client email, it automatically creates a project in your project management system.
- When you add a task with a due date, it automatically creates a calendar entry.
- When you save a reference document, it automatically links to the relevant project.
- When you complete a task, it automatically notifies team members or triggers the next workflow step.

The practical value of integration comes from what psychologists call "cognitive chunking"—your brain's ability to treat connected processes as a single unit rather than separate tasks. With proper integration, "onboard a new client" becomes one cognitive chunk instead of a dozen separate operations across multiple platforms. This dramatically reduces mental load and preserves your cognitive resources for the work that truly matters.

Unlike automation, which might require learning entirely new systems, effective integration often starts with linking tools you already use through connection platforms like Zapier, IFTTT, or native integrations. The goal isn't adding more technology but eliminating the cognitive gaps between your existing tools.

4. Biohacking Technology

While the previous categories focus on extending your capabilities externally, biohacking technologies work directly with your biological systems to enhance performance from within. These tools help optimize your physiology, creating the internal conditions where peak cognitive function becomes more likely.

The spectrum here ranges from sophisticated to surprisingly simple:

Red light therapy devices emit specific wavelengths that enhance cellular energy production and reduce inflammation—potentially improving cognitive function and recovery. Full-body devices or smaller portable options provide targeted exposure that can regulate your circadian rhythm and boost mitochondrial function.

Neurostimulation tools like the Apollo or Sensate use specific vibration patterns to modulate your nervous system, potentially reducing stress and enhancing recovery. These devices essentially "speak" to your vagal nerve, encouraging parasympathetic activation when needed.

Sleep optimization technology—from the sophisticated trackers we've mentioned before to PEMF sleep-inducing devices—helps ensure your brain completes the essential cleanup and consolidation processes that happen during quality rest. Given that sleep quality fundamentally determines cognitive function the following day, these tools create the foundation for all other performance elements.

Even strategic protection from electromagnetic fields (EMFs) can potentially reduce the background stress on your nervous system. While the research here remains evolving, many high performers report noticeable improvements in focus and energy when implementing targeted EMF protection.

I'll admit, I was deeply skeptical of biohacking tech when I first encountered it. It seemed like the kind of shiny distraction that technology often creates—more focused on novelty than results. However, after systematically testing various approaches with clients (and myself), the performance differences became impossible to ignore. When used selectively and strategically, these tools can create measurable shifts in cognitive capability and recovery quality.

The Minimal Effective Dose

Here's where we need to be careful. The tech world loves to promise revolution through one more app, one more device, one more system. But the most sophisticated technology users understand a counterintuitive truth: less is often more.

Rather than accumulating every promising new tool, focus on creating a minimalist technology ecosystem that addresses your specific performance barriers with the fewest possible components. This approach reduces cognitive overhead while maximizing impact.

Start by identifying your primary performance bottlenecks—the specific aspects of your work where limitations consistently emerge. Is it information management? Task organization? Deep work capacity? Recovery quality? By targeting your most significant constraints first, you create a foundation that supports all other performance elements.

For most people, an effective technology ecosystem might include:

- A comprehensive note-taking and knowledge management system (like Notion or Obsidian).
- A streamlined task management approach (from simple apps like Todoist to more complex systems like Asana).
- Strategic automation for repetitive processes (using Zapier or similar integration tools).
- Basic biohacking tools focused on sleep quality and stress management.

Notice what's missing from this list—the endless parade of "productivity" apps promising revolutionary changes through marginally different approaches to the same problems. The goal isn't collecting tools; it's solving problems with minimal cognitive overhead.

When Tech Becomes the Problem

Sometimes, the most potent technology strategy isn't adding new tools but removing the ones that create more problems than they solve. Digital minimalism isn't about rejecting technology; it's about being exceptionally selective about which technologies earn a place in your life.

The research is clear: our brains simply weren't designed for the constant barrage of notifications, information, and stimuli that modern devices deliver. The average smartphone user checks their device 96 times daily—about once every 10 minutes of waking life. Each check creates a dopamine hit, reinforcing a cycle that fragments attention and makes sustained focus increasingly tricky.

Rather than accepting this fragmentation as inevitable, you can implement strategic boundaries that transform your relationship with technology:

Device Boundaries: involve physically separating yourself from potential distractions during deep work periods. This might mean working in a different room from your phone or using apps that temporarily block distracting websites and services.

Schedule Boundaries: create specific times for checking messages and engaging with social platforms, rather than allowing these activities to interrupt your day continuously. The key is batching these interactions into defined periods, preserving the remainder of your day for focused work.

Design Boundaries: reconfigure your devices to reduce their addictive properties. Switching to grayscale mode significantly reduces a smartphone's ability to capture attention. Disabling notifications for all but essential services prevents constant interruption. Rearranging apps so that productivity tools are prominent while potential distractions require additional steps creates subtle friction that supports better choices.

Social Boundaries: involve explicitly communicating your availability to others, setting expectations about response times, and creating agreements that respect periods of uninterrupted focus. These aren't just personal preferences—they're structural elements of an effective performance system.

While these approaches might seem like minor adjustments, their cumulative impact on cognitive function can be profound. By implementing strategic boundaries, you're not just changing habits—you're literally expanding your brain's available resources for meaningful work.

Creating Your Technology System

The true power of technology enhancement comes not from any single tool but from how you integrate various elements into a cohesive system that supports your specific performance needs. This isn't about following a single template; it's about thoughtfully crafting an ecosystem that addresses your unique challenges and amplifies your particular strengths.

Start by conducting a technology audit, evaluating each tool against three criteria:

1. Does it solve a genuine problem or create genuine value?
2. Does it integrate smoothly with your existing systems?
3. Does the value it provides outweigh the cognitive cost of learning and maintaining it?

For tools that pass this evaluation, create explicit protocols for how and when you'll use them. The goal isn't just accumulating useful technology but developing a coherent system where each element serves a specific purpose within your broader performance ecosystem.

Remember that the most powerful technology isn't necessarily the most sophisticated or expensive. Often, the highest return comes from simple tools used consistently and intentionally rather than complex systems implemented sporadically or halfheartedly.

By approaching technology as a carefully curated enhancement system rather than a collection of disjointed tools, you transform it from a potential source of distraction into a powerful amplifier of everything we've built throughout this book.

MAINTENANCE SYSTEMS

Ever notice how even the most sophisticated machines require regular maintenance? Your car needs oil changes. Your smartphone needs updates. Your home needs repairs. Yet somehow, we expect our performance systems to run indefinitely without similar attention.

This might be the most overlooked aspect of sustained excellence: the need for deliberate maintenance of your performance ecosystem. Without it, even the most brilliantly designed systems gradually degrade, leaving you wondering why approaches that once worked flawlessly now seem to falter.

Think of your performance system like a garden rather than a machine. It's a living ecosystem that requires regular tending, not a static structure you build once and forget. Without proper care, weeds creep in, soil becomes depleted, and once-thriving plants begin to wither. The same principle applies to the performance systems we've built throughout this book.

The Audit System

Just as doctors recommend regular physical examinations even when you feel fine, your performance systems benefit from scheduled check-ins that identify potential issues before they become problems. I call this process the Performance Audit.

Unlike reactive troubleshooting, which happens when something breaks down, the Performance Audit is preventative. It's designed to catch small deviations before they cascade into significant problems. It's the difference between changing your oil regularly versus waiting until your engine seizes.

The most effective audit examines four key dimensions:

Behavioral Consistency: Are you still implementing the core habits and routines you've established? Have any critical practices gradually slipped away? Often, the first sign of system breakdown isn't complete abandonment but subtle inconsistency—skipping your morning routine occasionally, letting recovery practices slide during busy periods, or allowing exceptions to become the rule.

Effectiveness Evaluation: Are your systems still producing the results they once did? Sometimes, practices that worked brilliantly in one life phase become less effective as circumstances change. Maybe your nutrition approach was perfect when you were single but needs adjustment with family responsibilities. Perhaps your focus strategies worked in one role but require refinement in a new position with different demands.

Environmental Assessment: Has your environment shifted in ways that undermine your systems? New relationships, changing work conditions, or different living situations can introduce friction that wasn't present when you established your routines. Even subtle changes in your physical or social environment can significantly impact system effectiveness.

Engagement Check: Do your practices still feel engaging and meaningful, or have they become empty rituals? Systems that once energized you, can gradually become mechanical obligations if you lose connection with their purpose. This dimension examines not just what you're doing but how it feels—recognizing that sustainable practices need to remain internally rewarding.

Conducting this audit doesn't require extraordinary time or effort—just honest reflection and willingness to acknowledge when adjustments are needed. I recommend scheduling a comprehensive review quarterly, with briefer weekly check-ins to catch issues early.

Peter, a finance executive I worked with, discovered through his quarterly audit that his once-effective morning routine had gradually eroded as his children's schedules changed. Rather than maintaining the pretense that the original system was still working, he redesigned his approach to fit his current reality—preserving the core elements while adapting the structure to new constraints.

The Calibration System

Once your audit identifies areas needing attention, the next step is calibration—making precise adjustments that restore system effectiveness without overreacting or unnecessary overhauls.

Think of calibration like tuning a piano. You don't replace the entire instrument when it sounds slightly off—you make subtle adjustments to restore harmony. Similarly, performance calibration focuses on minimal viable changes that address specific issues while preserving what's working well.

Effective calibration follows three principles:

First, start with the smallest possible change that could address the issue. This approach minimizes disruption to functioning elements while providing precise data on what works. If morning workouts have become inconsistent, perhaps the initial adjustment isn't changing the entire routine but simply preparing workout clothes the night before or shifting exercise time by 30 minutes.

Second, calibrate one element at a time rather than making multiple simultaneous changes. This provides clearer feedback about what's working and prevents the overwhelm that often comes with excessive change. Master one adjustment before introducing the next, allowing each modification to stabilize before adding complexity.

Third, ensure each adjustment directly addresses a specific issue identified in your audit. Random changes based on the latest trends or temporary enthusiasm rarely yield sustainable improvements. Every calibration should connect clearly to a particular goal or observed breakdown in your existing system.

This measured approach to system maintenance prevents what I call "productivity whiplash"—the disorienting cycle of complete system overhauls that never fully establish before the next reinvention. By focusing on precise calibration rather than constant revolution, you build cumulative improvements that compound over time.

The Adaptation System

While calibration addresses issues within existing systems, adaptation tackles a different challenge: how to evolve your performance ecosystem when life circumstances significantly change. Career transitions, relationship shifts, health developments, and major life events all require thoughtful adaptation of your performance practices.

The key distinction here is between temporary adjustments and fundamental adaptations. When you travel for a week, you make temporary adjustments to maintain core practices in different conditions. But when you change careers, have a child, or move across the country, you need deeper adaptations that acknowledge the new reality you're operating in.

The Adaptation Protocol provides a structured approach to these transitions:

Assessment of New Constraints and Opportunities

Begin by clearly identifying how your circumstances have changed—both the new limitations you face and the fresh possibilities available. This assessment should cover practical considerations along with energy patterns, responsibility structures, and priority shifts.

When Kevin transitioned from corporate employment to entrepreneurship, his initial instinct was to maintain his existing routines with minor tweaks. But a proper assessment revealed fundamental changes: completely different energy demands, no external structure, new performance priorities, and expanded freedom in scheduling. Recognizing these shifts was essential to developing systems that would work in his new reality.

Core Practice Preservation

Identify the essential practices that contribute most significantly to your performance, regardless of circumstances. These "non-negotiables" form the foundation around which you'll build new supporting systems.

For most people, these core elements include some form of morning routine (even if timing and specific practices change), regular recovery practices (though the specific modalities may shift), consistent sleep patterns (even if scheduling adjusts), nutritional fundamentals (though specific approaches may evolve), and focus protection mechanisms (adapted to new environmental realities).

By preserving these foundations while allowing flexibility in implementation, you maintain performance continuity through life transitions.

Experimentation and Integration

With core practices secured, systematically experiment with new supporting systems designed specifically for your changed circumstances. This isn't random trial-and-error but structured exploration with clear parameters and evaluation criteria.

The key is approaching this phase with genuine curiosity rather than rigid expectations. Instead of forcing old systems to work in new environments, ask: "What approach would work best if I were designing my system from scratch for these specific conditions?"

This experimental mindset preserves what research psychologists call a "growth orientation"—the perspective that systems can evolve through deliberate learning rather than remaining fixed or deteriorating when circumstances change.

The Evolution System

The final maintenance system addresses not just preserving or adapting existing practices but deliberately evolving your approach as you develop mastery. This is perhaps the most sophisticated element of performance maintenance—the difference between maintaining competence and developing true excellence over time.

The natural tendency for any habitual practice is to plateau—reaching a point where familiar approaches yield consistent but no longer improving results. This homeostasis is efficient but ultimately limiting if your goal is continued growth rather than mere maintenance.

The Evolution System deliberately disrupts this homeostasis through structured challenges that expand your capabilities. Unlike the reactive adjustments of calibration or the circumstance-driven changes of adaptation, evolution is proactive—intentionally introducing new elements that stretch your performance capacity.

This might include systematically developing adjacent capabilities that complement your core strengths, incorporating new approaches that enhance existing systems rather than replacing them, or periodically increasing the difficulty of your performance standards once current levels become comfortable.

The key principle here is progressive overload—the same concept that drives physical development in training programs. Just as muscles grow stronger when consistently challenged slightly beyond their current capacity, your performance systems develop through strategic stretching rather than comfortable repetition.

Think of evolution as deliberate discomfort. Not the harmful stress of overwhelm but the productive tension that drives development. Without this element, even well-maintained systems eventually become limitations rather than assets, defining what's possible rather than expanding it.

Your Maintenance Schedule

These four maintenance systems—Audit, Calibration, Adaptation, and Evolution—work together to ensure your performance ecosystem remains vibrant and effective through changing circumstances and growing ambitions. However, like any maintenance approach, their effectiveness depends on consistent implementation rather than sporadic attention.

I recommend establishing a structured maintenance schedule that includes weekly mini-reviews (brief check-ins focused on behavioral consistency and effectiveness), monthly calibrations to make precise adjustments based on insights from weekly assessments, quarterly deep audits examining all four dimensions, and annual evolution planning dedicated to deliberately advancing your systems based on developing mastery and changing circumstances.

This rhythm creates what systems theorists call "nested feedback loops"—interconnected cycles of evaluation and adjustment operating at different timescales. The shorter loops provide immediate course correction, while longer loops enable more substantial evolution and adaptation.

The beauty of this maintenance approach is that it transforms what could be seen as system "failures" into valuable data points that drive improvement. When something stops working, it's not a collapse but an opportunity to refine your approach based on real-world feedback—exactly what any living system needs to thrive.

By implementing these maintenance systems, you ensure that the performance ecosystem we've built throughout this book doesn't merely survive but continues to evolve, creating sustained excellence that adapts to your changing circumstances and expanding capabilities.

MEASURING YOUR PERFORMANCE EVOLUTION

As we close this chapter on performance systems, there's one final element that completes our framework: measurement. Remember how we began this journey in Chapter 3 by establishing your performance baseline through the CEP Framework? That initial assessment provided the coordinates from which we've navigated throughout this book.

Now it's time to check our current location.

Just as a doctor doesn't just prescribe treatment but also conducts follow-up tests to measure progress, your performance evolution requires periodic reassessment. This isn't about judgment or scoring yourself—it's about gathering data that guides your next steps.

Take a moment now to revisit the three assessments we conducted at the beginning:

FUNCTIONAL COGNITIVE SCORE

hplink.org/fcs

FUNCTIONAL ENERGY SCORE

hplink.org/fes

FUNCTIONAL PRODUCTIVITY SCORE

hplink.org/fps

Compare your current scores with the baseline you recorded in your notebook from Chapter 3. What's changed? Where have you seen the most significant improvements? Which areas still present opportunities for growth?

If you also tracked the optional metrics we suggested in Chapter 3, now is the perfect time to revisit those as well. Many readers who measured their Heart Rate Variability (HRV), sleep quality scores, stress levels, and recovery indicators find these biological markers show even more dramatic improvements than their subjective assessments. The body often registers positive change before the conscious mind fully appreciates it.

Similarly, if you documented your digital activity—total screen time, most-used apps, and usage patterns—compare how those have evolved. Has your relationship with technology transformed? Are you spending less time on distracting apps and more on tools that enhance your capabilities? These patterns often reveal subtle shifts in focus and attention that have profound impacts on overall performance.

Beyond the numbers, take a moment to reflect subjectively on how you feel. Many readers report qualitative changes that no metric can capture—a sense of greater control, more consistent energy throughout the day, clearer thinking, or a deeper sense of engagement with what matters most. These subjective experiences are just as valuable as any quantitative measurement.

This comparison isn't just about celebrating progress (though that's certainly worth doing). It's about applying the maintenance systems we just explored. Your reassessment provides precise data for your Performance Audit, highlighting which systems have improved and which might require calibration or adaptation.

Pay particular attention to unexpected results. Perhaps your Energy score improved more dramatically than anticipated, or maybe your Cognitive score hasn't shifted as much as you'd hoped despite implementing several techniques. These patterns aren't failures—they're valuable feedback that helps you refine your approach.

For most readers, this reassessment reveals something remarkable: areas that once felt like permanent limitations have become significantly more flexible. Cognitive fog has cleared. Energy deficits have transformed into surpluses. Productivity drags have evolved into smooth systems.

But the most valuable insight often comes from correlations between the three dimensions. If your Energy score has improved dramatically while your Productivity score has only moderately increased, perhaps the next phase of your journey involves translating that additional energy into more effective output systems. If your Cognitive score has soared while your Energy management hasn't kept pace, your next opportunity might be balancing these systems for sustainable performance.

This measurement completes the cycle we've been building throughout the book: assess, implement, maintain, and reassess. It's not a final destination but a checkpoint in an ongoing journey of optimization.

As you look at your results, remember that this isn't about reaching some arbitrary "perfect" number. It's about creating a personalized performance ecosystem that supports the life you want to live. The goal isn't maximizing every metric—it's optimizing the system to serve your unique definition of success.

With this reassessment complete, you now have everything you need to continue evolving your performance systems long after you finish this book. You understand your current coordinates, you have a comprehensive toolkit of techniques, and you've built maintenance systems that ensure continued growth.

RESEARCH & RESOURCES

As we conclude this book, here is the last reminder to visit the Holistic Performance Resource Hub in order to access the research and additional materials mentioned in this, as well as all other chapters.

To do so, go to hplink.org/resourcehub or scan the QR code below.

THE JOURNEY TO HOLISTIC PERFORMANCE

"It is not the strongest of the species that survive, nor the most intelligent, but the one most responsive to change."

– Charles Darwin

If you've made it this far, congratulations! You've completed a comprehensive exploration of what makes extraordinary performance possible. Not just the highlight reel version that fills most books, but the authentic, science-backed reality of how human excellence actually works.

We started with a fundamental premise: sustainable high performance doesn't come from pushing harder against your limitations, but from systematically removing the barriers that prevent your natural excellence from emerging. Throughout this journey, we've built a framework that transforms performance from a constant struggle into something that feels almost effortless—not because it requires no effort, but because the effort aligns with your biology, psychology, and natural capabilities.

Look at how far we've come together. We began by challenging conventional hustle culture, revealing how most productivity advice actually undermines sustainable performance by working against our natural systems. Then, we explored the AOD3 Framework—reclaiming significant time through strategic elimination, prioritization, and optimization. We built solid physiological foundations through nutrition, sleep, exercise, and stress mastery. We mastered flow states—those remarkable periods where performance feels effortless and time seems to bend. We developed psychological antifragility and mental frameworks that turn obstacles into stepping stones. And finally, we integrated everything into cohesive systems that automate excellence beyond what any individual could achieve alone.

This hasn't been a collection of random "life hacks" or quick fixes. It's been a systematic rebuilding of your entire approach to performance from the ground up. The 4Ps framework—Prioritization, Physiology, Psychology, and Performance Systems—provides an integrated architecture where each element reinforces and amplifies the others.

THE REAL BEGINNING

But here's the truth most authors won't tell you: reaching the end of this book isn't the end of your journey—it's actually the beginning of the real transformation.

If you've been following along actively, you've likely already implemented some changes and seen initial results. That's fantastic! However, the full power of this framework emerges when you approach it as an integrated system rather than a collection of isolated techniques.

Think of this book as your roadmap—one that guides you through a specific sequence designed to build on itself. Start where we began together— with prioritization and time recapture. These foundational elements create the space you'll need to implement everything else. Without this crucial first step, you'll find yourself trying to wedge optimization practices into an already overcrowded life.

Once you've created that essential breathing room, turn your attention to physiology. Identify your most significant physiological bottleneck—whether it's sleep quality, energy management, or stress regulation—and focus there first. When that foundation stabilizes, you can expand to the next area.

Only after establishing these biological fundamentals should you turn your full attention to the psychological dimensions we explored. Mindset work builds upon physiological optimization. Trying to think your way to peak performance while your biological systems remain compromised is like installing advanced software on a computer with faulty hardware.

Throughout this progression, continually refine the performance systems that ensure consistency. As we explored in Chapter 13, sustainable achievement doesn't come from heroic effort but from intelligent structures that make excellence inevitable.

The beauty of this approach is that you're not trying to revolutionize your entire life overnight. You're strategically targeting key leverage points in the correct sequence, allowing each improvement to create momentum for the next. Return to the relevant chapters as needed, using them as implementation guides rather than theoretical reading.

Some changes will take root quickly; others will require multiple attempts and adjustments. Trust the process and remember that sustainable transformation unfolds through consistent application, not overnight reinvention.

THE CHOICE AHEAD

As we reach the conclusion of our time together, you face a fundamental choice that will determine whether this book becomes a transformative tool or just another intellectual exercise.

I've seen this pattern countless times with driven, ambitious people. They consume personal development book after book, podcast after podcast, constantly seeking the next breakthrough insight. They experience that brief dopamine hit of "aha!" moments, only to quickly chase the next information fix without fully implementing what they've learned. It's the modern equivalent of hoarding treasure maps without ever digging for the gold.

Let me be direct: You don't need another performance book after this one. At least not yet.

What separates those who transform their lives from those who merely collect knowledge isn't intelligence or discipline. It's the willingness to pause the endless input stream and focus on output—on actually doing the work. As the saying goes, you can't read about swimming and expect not to drown. You have to get in the water.

The difference lies not just in results but in how performance feels. On one path, achievement remains a constant struggle against biological resistance. On the other, extraordinary results emerge naturally from systems aligned with your innate capabilities. The highest achievers aren't those with superhuman willpower; they're those who've made excellence inevitable through strategic alignment rather than constant struggle.

My hope is that you'll take these principles, make them your own, and discover what becomes possible when performance emerges from alignment rather than effort—when you stop fighting against your biology and start unleashing your full, authentic potential.

The journey continues. And it's just getting interesting.

GOING DEEPER: THE HOLISTIC PERFORMANCE ACADEMY

For many readers, the frameworks and strategies in this book provide everything needed to create transformative change. But if you find yourself wanting deeper exploration or a more personalized application, I've created several resources to support your continued journey.

The Holistic Performance Academy offers a structured pathway to mastering these concepts through guided implementation and expert coaching. Unlike most programs that focus on isolated techniques, the Academy integrates all four pillars of performance into a comprehensive approach tailored to your specific circumstances and goals.

For those who prefer a self-directed approach with additional guidance, our foundational course provides video training, implementation guides, and structured exercises that expand on the book's frameworks. This option includes the core transformation process while allowing you to progress at your own pace. As a reader, you can access this course at a **50% discount** by using the coupon code **HPREADER** at checkout.

For those seeking the highest level of support, I work directly with a limited number of clients through our premium coaching program. This combines personalized strategy development with the professional accountability we discussed in Chapter 13—creating the external structure that ensures consistent execution even when motivation naturally fluctuates.

You can start wherever feels most appropriate for your current situation. Many clients begin with the self-directed course and later upgrade to more personalized support as they advance in their implementation journey.

Learn more by scanning the QR code below.

MAKING THE DIFFERENCE

Now that we've reached the end of our journey together, I'd love to hear what you thought of it.

As an independent author, I don't have the marketing budgets or distribution networks that come with major publishers. What I do have is something more valuable—readers like you. For independent works like this one, reviews are the lifeblood that allow the book to reach others who might benefit from these ideas.

Your feedback is incredibly valuable to me. If there's something you think could be improved or a concept that didn't fully connect, please drop me a line at hello@holisticperformance.co. Your insights help make future editions and resources even better.

If you found value in these pages, please consider taking 60 seconds to leave a review where you purchased this book. Honest reviews not only help this work compete in a marketplace dominated by big publishers, but they also give me a glimpse into your performance journey. Those stories of transformation are what fuel my work.

For an extra touch that makes my day, consider posting a photo with your review showing the book in your workspace or performance environment. It's amazing to see these ideas taking root in different settings around the world. Thank you for being part of this journey. The best is yet to come!

hplink.org/review

ABOUT THE AUTHOR

Kevin Aventura believes one powerful truth: we've only glimpsed the outer edges of our capabilities. His work has helped clients achieve breakthroughs in both health optimization and performance enhancement that many once considered impossible.

His journey began from necessity, not theory. Growing up with health challenges that limited his energy and focus, Kevin found conventional approaches inadequate. This sparked a relentless quest for better solutions, leading him to study physical therapy before pursuing additional education in naturopathy and high-performance coaching.

Kevin's path started with health optimization—addressing the biological foundations that either constrain or unleash human potential. His first book, The Neo Diet, emerged from this journey, establishing the physical foundation for a vibrant life. Yet he quickly realized health was just the beginning. The natural question followed: once you feel your best, what do you do with that energy? This dual focus continues to define his work today, as he guides clients through both health transformation and productivity enhancement.

This holistic perspective shapes how Kevin works with people from all walks of life. While he collaborates with entrepreneurs, executives, and organizations, his approach resonates just as deeply with athletes, students, creatives, and stay-at-home parents. The common thread isn't profession or background—it's simply people who refuse to settle for "good enough" when extraordinary is possible.

When he's not researching the latest breakthroughs in health and performance science, Kevin can be found traveling, chasing adrenaline-rich experiences, and spending quality time with family and friends—practicing the balanced life he advocates for others.

To connect with Kevin and explore how his holistic approach might help unlock your potential in health and performance, visit holisticperformance.co

ACKNOWLEDGEMENTS

They say writing a second book is supposed to be easier than the first. *Whoever "they" are, they lied.* Creating this book has been both exhilarating and humbling, and I couldn't have done it without several key people in my life.

First and foremost, my endless gratitude goes to Andreia. You've been my rock through every late night, every moment of self-doubt, and every small victory. Thank you for believing in me, especially during those times when I couldn't believe in myself. Your support made this book possible, and your perspective made it better. I love you.

To my Inkonas group—you've been daily reminders of all the things high-performance professionals need to fix. *Watching you guys struggle with basic time management and energy regulation has been the best research lab I could ask for.* Joking aside, your friendship and support mean the world to me. Thank you for always being present whenever I needed it.

A special thanks to Miguel for holding me accountable every single week. Those check-ins weren't always comfortable, but they were always necessary. You helped me practice what I preach about the power of accountability systems.

I'm also deeply grateful to the coaches and thought leaders who generously shared their wisdom with me. While this book represents my own framework, it stands on the shoulders of many brilliant minds who helped me refine my thinking and challenge my assumptions.

Most importantly, I want to thank my clients who trusted me with their performance journeys and allowed me to share their stories in these pages. Some appear with their real names, others with aliases to protect their privacy, but all have contributed something invaluable—real-world proof that these concepts work. You've been my greatest teachers, and this book exists because of what we discovered together.

Finally, thank you—the reader who's made it all the way to this page. My sincere hope is that the ideas we've explored together become more than just interesting concepts but transformative tools in your life.

The journey continues!

www.ingramcontent.com/pod-product-compliance
Lightning Source LLC
Chambersburg PA
CBHW071704120626
46550CB00001B/104